RAMTANU LAHIRI

BRAHMAN AND REFORMER

RAMTANU LAHIRI

BRAHMAN AND REFORMER

A HISTORY OF THE RENAISSANCE IN BENGAL

FROM THE BENGALI OF

PANDIT SIVANATH SHASTRI, M.A.

EDITED BY

SIR ROPER LETHBRIDGE, K.C.I.E.

GYAN

Published by

GYAN

Gyan Publishing House
5, Ansari Road
Daryaganj, New Delhi-110002
Phone: 011-47034999, 9811692060
E-mail: books@gyanbooks.com

Distribution Network
gyanbooks.com
India, USA, Canada, UK, Australia

ISBN: 978-93-6208-501-6 (HB)
First Published, 1907

2nd Impression 2024

Printed at: Gyan Press, Delhi.

RAMTANU LAHIRI BRAHMAN AND REFORMER
Author: PANDIT SIVANATH SHASTRI

RAMTANU LAHIRI

BRAHMAN AND REFORMER

RAM TANU LAHIRI.

[*Frontispiece.*

RAMTANU LAHIRI

BRAHMAN AND REFORMER

A HISTORY OF THE RENAISSANCE IN BENGAL

FROM THE BENGALI OF

PANDIT SIVANÁTH SÁSTRI, M.A.

EDITED BY

SIR ROPER LETHBRIDGE, K.C.I.E.

Late Scholar of Exeter College, Oxford
Formerly Principal of Krishnagar College, Bengal; and Fellow of the Calcutta University

WITH TWENTY-NINE ILLUSTRATIONS

LONDON

SWAN SONNENSCHEIN & CO. LIMITED

CALCUTTA: S. K. LAHIRI & CO.

1907

EDITOR'S PREFACE

UNTIL the close of the first quarter of the nineteenth century the vernacular literature of Bengal existed only in a more or less debased form. In its earlier phases of development it had struggled to revert to its original Sanskrit elements; in later days, under the influence of the Muhammadan conquest, it had become largely Persianised. The lifetime of Ramtanu Lahiri was synchronous with the renaissance of Bengali literature—the period of awakening in Bengal that saw also the birth and early growth of English education in the country, and of the various schools of reform in religion and morals that have so mightily changed the whole aspect of Bengali life and thought. It was, therefore, fitting that one of the most important of the works that have as yet appeared in pure Bengali should have been a "Life" of this great educationist and reformer, from the pen of Pandit Sivanáth Sástri, M.A., himself one of the most distinguished writers of modern Bengal.

It was also reasonable to expect that the biography of Ramtanu, covering such an eventful period in the social, moral, and religious history of Bengal, would introduce to the reader a large number of interesting and varied characters and scenes grouped around the central personage. The Pandit's work is quite the most scholarly book of its kind, as well as the most serious and sustained effort to combine, in a biographical work, Oriental and Western modes of thought, that has yet appeared in Bengali.

Viewing this most interesting and characteristic treatise from the point here indicated, I have not deemed it necessary, or even advisable, to make any very rigorous use of the editorial pruning-knife in adapting the Pandit's biography to the taste of the English reader. The translation, into more or less literal English, is due to the filial piety of my friend, Mr S. K. Lahiri, one of the most eminent of Calcutta publishers, and son of the illustrious subject of this memoir; and in dealing with that translation, as with the general scope of Pandit Sivanáth Sástri's work, I have judged it best to present it to the English reader very largely in its original state. I think that excessive alteration might degenerate into mutilation, might often obscure the sense of the original, and would certainly detract from the presentment of transparent sincerity, and of deep love for the subject of the Memoir, that constitutes one of the greatest charms of the Pandit's style in the original Bengali "Life." I have therefore contented myself with a careful verification of the literal accuracy of the English rendering, together with such minor alterations or deletions as seemed to be absolutely required by the occasional divergence of Eastern and Western thought.

ROPER LETHBRIDGE.

Sir Roper Lethbridge, K.C.I.E.

CONTENTS

LIST OF ILLUSTRATIONS

INTRODUCTION BY THE EDITOR

When I came out to India in 1868, as a young Professor in the Bengal Education Service straight from Oxford, one of the earliest friendships I formed on joining the Krishnagar College was that of the revered Ramtanu Lahiri, a gentleman of high Kulin Brahman birth, whose saintly life and lofty patriotism had already marked him out as a leader of men in the cultured Bengali society of Calcutta and Krishnagar. From that date until his lamented death thirty years later in 1898, I had the privilege of retaining his warm and sincere friendship—a friendship reciprocated on my part with the deep reverence which was felt for him by every one who knew him well. Outside Bengal, he was never so well known as his predecessor, the Raja Rammohan Roy, nor as his successor, Keshava Chandra Sen (Kishub Chander Sen); for though his character and his teaching had very much in common with those two great men, his gentle, unassuming temperament always prevented him from taking so prominent a part in public affairs as they were able rightfully to assume. But I am inclined to think that his influence, in bringing out all that was best in the minds and hearts of the young Bengal of his day was not inferior to theirs. And, however that may be, I am confident that a very large number of Bengali scholars and thinkers of the elder generation would gladly acknowledge that they drew from his teaching and example many of the best lessons of their lives. That example and that teaching seemed to me to possess this especial value, that while he stood up for everything that is good and true in national life as valiantly as any of the roughest and rudest of Radical reformers, his conception of "the gentle life," the same for Bengalis as for Englishmen, was full of "the milk of human kindness," and led him to take the truly Conservative line of reform without wanton destruction, and of criticism without rudeness or vulgarity.

It is, therefore, with great pleasure that I have received the warmly appreciative biography of this modest-minded but truly great man, that has been written by his friend and distinguished follower, the Pandit Sivanáth Sástri, M.A.,—and published in excellent form by the filial piety and love of the reformer's son, Mr S. K. Lahiri. And I have been so greatly interested by the perusal of Mr Sástri's admirable work in its Bengali form that, with the efficient collaboration of Mr Lahiri, I now venture to submit to the judgment of the Western world, and of that large class of Indian-born readers who are more familiar with English than with Bengali, an English translation of this remarkable biography.

The learned Pandit writes evidently from a heart full of affection for the subject of his Memoir; for his grandfather had been the "Guru" (a spiritual pastor) of Ramtanu in early youth, and the Pandit himself had been his friend and associate up to the end of his long life, not only in Krishnagar, but also in Calcutta and in Uttarpara.

Lahiri Mahashai, as he was always reverentially called in his later years, was by birth a Brahman of the Brahmans, a Kulin of very high descent. His ancestors for generations occupied important positions as Dewans or some other responsible position, closely associated with the princely family of the Maharajas of Nadia near Krishnagar. His father, Ramkrishna Lahiri, was the Dewan of two of the younger scions of the Nadia family; and was married to Srimati Jagaddhatri Devi, the only daughter of another great Kulin family, that of Radhakanta Rai. Ramtanu was the fifth son; and, as the circumstances of the Dewan were by no means commensurate with his high birth, the early education of the eager young Brahman was a matter of difficulty for his father. Up to the age of eleven Ramtanu attended the village *patshala*. Then his eldest brother, Kesava Chandra Lahiri, took him away to Calcutta, and himself taught him something of English, Persian, and Arabic; and ultimately, by the kind patronage of the famous David Hare, he obtained a free scholarship in the Society's School, whence in 1828 he obtained promotion to the old Hindu College. Here he came under the influence of Derozio, one of the most remarkable of the giants of the pre-

University era in Bengal educational history. Of Mr Derozio, Mr Thomas Edwards writes:

"Neither before nor since his day has any teacher within the walls of any native educational establishment in India ever exercised such an influence over his pupils. It was not alone in the class-rooms and during the hours of teaching that the genial manner, the buoyant spirit, the ready humour, the wide reading, the readiness to impart knowledge, and the patience and courtesy of Derozio won the hearts and the high reverence of his pupils. In the intervals of teaching he was ever ready in conversation to aid his pupils in their studies, to draw them out to give free and full expression to their opinions on topics naturally arising from the course of their work. . . . Mr Derozio acquired such an ascendancy over the minds of his pupils that they would not move even in their private concerns without his counsel. Such was the force of his instructions that the conduct of the students out of the College was most exemplary . . . and their reverence for truth was proverbial."

The extraordinary influence of this remarkable man remained with Ramtanu, and to a great extent determined the character of his active life. He became a reformer after the school of Raja Rammohan Roy, and a leader in New Bengal; but he was never a violent or extreme man—and except on the subject of his own Brahmanical caste, which he threw off as his own personal sacrifice to a great cause, and one or two other points of a like nature, he was never willing to exacerbate the differences between himself and his more orthodox relations and friends.

In 1833 he became a teacher in the Hindu College, and soon became widely known as the friend of the friendless and the deserving. Many pleasant stories are told of his benevolence and philanthropy—one must here suffice. One of his students had the misfortune, in the midst of his preparation for examination, to lose for a time the use of his eyes—Lahiri Mahashai himself read and re-read to him the whole course with all the necessary commentary, and actually enabled him in this way to pass the examination. This quiet useful life went on for thirteen years, and many interesting incidents of it are recorded by the Pandit Sivanáth. His opportunity came in 1846. On New

Year's day in that year the Krishnagar College (of which I was subsequently a Professor, and ultimately Principal) was opened with great ceremony. It was built and endowed partly by Government, partly by private subscriptions—and among the latter, the munificence of the then Maharaja of Nadia, the Maharaja Siris Chandra Rai Bahadur, was conspicuous. The Maharaja was himself an active member of the College Committee, and set the good example of sending his two sons to be educated with the other boys of less distinguished rank and caste. And the strength of the school department attached to this College at its foundation will be appreciated by those who know anything of the early history of education in Bengal, when I mention that the second master was Ramtanu Lahiri, and the head master the famous D. L. Richardson, at one time editor of *The Englishman*, almost the father of English education in Bengal.

Krishnagar was always Ramtanu's home—though he held appointments at various times at Burdwan and also at Uttarpara, and he lived also a long time in Calcutta. At all these centres of educational life he was looked upon as "the Arnold of Bengal," which was the honourable title by which he was commonly known. While at Uttarpara and Calcutta he was the intimate friend of all the most eminent Bengali gentlemen of the time—notably the Pandit Iswara Chandra Vidyasagara, the Maharaja Satis Chandra Rai of Nadia, Raja Radhakanta Deb, K. M. Banerji, Ram Gopal Ghosh, Siva Chandra Deb, Peari Chand Mitra, Tarachand Chakravartti, Devendranath Tagore, Rajendra Datta, Michael Madhusudan Dutt, Kesava Chandra Sen, Bankim Chandra Chatterjee, Dinabandhu Mitra, Raja Peary Mohan Mukerji, Manomohan Ghosh, Professor Peary Charan Sarkar, Mahendra Lal Sarkar, and many others whose association with Lahiri Mahashai is commemorated by his biographer. With some of the younger members of this brilliant circle I had the pleasure of being on terms of personal friendship at a somewhat later period. For instance, with Professor Peary Charan Sarkar, who was first introduced to me, I think by Ramtanu Lahiri, I subsequently worked for some years in a sort of literary partnership, in the task of preparing English text-books for young Bengali boys; and I am therefore entitled, by some personal knowledge, to speak of the influence that had been exercised by Lahiri Mahashai, in guiding the thoughts and aspirations of these representative Bengali gentlemen, and of their disciples in Bengali society. That influence was altogether a wholesome one. It taught men to become, not merely reformers in the ordinary sense of the term—not merely teachers of a destructive creed that is only critical without being sympathetic—but also better citizens and better men, with earnest longings for intellectual and moral progress, yet not without full appreciation of all that was best in the past, and a Conservative desire to retain and improve it.

ROPER LETHBRIDGE.

THE LATE MAHARAJA OF NADIA (MAHARAJA SATIS CHANDRA RAI, BAHADUR) AND RAMTANU LAHIRI.

CHAPTER I

THE HOME OF THE LAHIRI FAMILY AT KRISHNAGAR

THE Hindu biographer usually introduces his hero with a description of his ancestry, the place or places chiefly associated with the history of his family, and the persons who more or less influenced his life and character. We shall follow this plan, and propose at the outset to say something about Krishnagar, hallowed by its associations with Ramtanu and his venerable ancestors, and about its illustrious Rajas. The Rajas of Nadia and the Lahiris have lived together amid the same surroundings from generation to generation, their connection dating back far in the past. It was under the auspices of the Rajas and their Dewans, that the Lahiri family made Krishnagar their home; and we shall see that some of them rendered distinguished service to their patrons. The venerable Ramtanu himself was very intimate with the Rajas contemporaneous with him, Siris Chandra, Satis Chandra, and Khitis Chandra.

When in 1845, Mr Lahiri, on his return to Krishnagar, began to preach his liberal doctrines, he had a cordial and honourable reception from Raja Siris Chandra, who openly encouraged him in his noble work. The next Raja, Satis Chandra, looked up to him as his guardian and guide. When, having renounced the Brahmanical thread, he was spurned by his relations, and had not where to lay his head, the Raja received him with open arms, saying, "Sir, do not be anxious in the least, make my house yours," and from that time regarded him as one of his own family. Whenever Mr Lahiri came to Krishnagar, he was invited to the palace, and shown great attentions. And finally, Raja Khitis Chandra's regard for him was equally great. For some time they stood in the relation of guardian and ward; the Raja would afterwards often say, "When there was nobody to befriend me, it was Lahiri Mahashay alone that helped me."

In the eighteenth century, Krishnagar was the capital of south Bengal. It is still one of the first-class towns, next to Calcutta in prosperity and civilisation, and having many interests in common with Calcutta.

The Rajas of Krishnagar, or of Nadia, are of long-standing celebrity. The whole of the district is indebted to them in many ways for its prosperity. The author remembers, in his boyhood, to have seen on the title-page of the old Bengali almanac, the name of Raja Satis Chandra, under whose auspices it had been got up, and, on inquiring who he was, to have been told that he was the then Raja of Krishnagar, descended from ancestry noted as the leaders of Hindu society, the guardians of Kulinism, and the encouragers of merit. When the country was under the Muhammadan rule, these Rajas, in defiance of the risk of incurring the displeasure of their rulers, defended the cause of Hindu religion and learning. At the time of which we are speaking, the Hindu Rajas were to some extent free from Imperial interference. As long as they punctually paid the revenue, they might do much as they liked in their own territories. They had armies, courts, and ministers of their own; and men of merit flocked to their palaces for rewards and distinctions.

Raja Krishna Chandra of Nadia created for himself an

imperishable name as a great patron of literature and learning. The great poet Bharat Chandra flourished under his patronage, and left to posterity his Annada Mangal, a work that has placed him on a high pedestal of fame.

On the 23rd of December 1686, Job Charnock, of the East India Company, owing to a misunderstanding between himself and the Subadár of Bengal, removed from Hughli to Sutanati, which again he was soon obliged to leave, though for a short time. He returned and built a factory here on 10th August 1690. Modern Calcutta stands on the site of Sutanati. In those days Krishnagar was the chief city in Bengal; and the principal seat of learning and civilisation, owing to the power and public spirit of its Rajas. So I proceed to give a short history of this Raj family. Tradition says that in 1077, Adisur, the King of Bengal, invited five pure Brahmans of the highest class, from Kanauj, to offer sacrifices to the gods on his behalf. Bhattanarayana was one of these Brahmans. His descendant, named Kasi, who had grown into a wealthy landholder, was in Akbar's reign driven from his native place, Vikrampur, by the Nawab. When seeking shelter in some other part of Bengal, he was waylaid and killed by the Nawab's men; and his widow, then about to become a mother, took shelter in the house of Hara Krishna Sammadar, a Zemindar in the Bogwon Pargana. She gave birth to a male child, who in time was adopted by the childless Sammadar and invested with his title. The name of this adopted son was Ram Chandra; who in course of time became the father of four sons, of whom Bhabananda afterwards gained great distinction. It was he who rendered great service to Raja Mansing in quelling the insurrection headed by Pratapaditya of Jessore; and he was rewarded by Jehangir with the Zemindaries of Nadia and some other parganas, and the title of Mazumdar.

This Bhabananda was the founder of the Krishnagar Raj family.

Bhabananda and his son lived at a place named Matihari; but his grandson, Raghab, removed to a small village then called Raooi, but subsequently, Krishnagar, after the God Krishna, who was worshipped here. Since then the Raj family have always occupied this place as their chief seat.

It is true that, pressed by the Mahratta incursions in his time, Krishna Chandra had to leave, for some time, the house of his ancestors, and to live in Shibnibash, a town founded by him, and named after his son, Shib Chandra. But that did not cause permanent separation between Krishnagar and its Rajas; for Krishna Chandra's grandson, Ishwar Chandra, returned to the old home of the family.

Krishna Chandra had eighty-four parganas as his Zemindari; and he was the most powerful and illustrious of his family. He was born in 1710; and it was in his time that Bengal passed from the hands of the Muhammadans into those of the English. He inherited the estate in 1728 when he was only eighteen years old; but even at this early age, he gave ample proofs of his intelligence, and cleverness in achieving his ends. Rumour says, that his father, Raghu Ram, had for some hidden cause disinherited him and had nominated his (Raghu Ram's) brother, Ramgopal, as his successor; and that the latter had on the demise of Raghu Ram applied to the Nawab, to have his nomination confirmed; but that the diplomatic Krishna Chandra by a certain wonderful trick balked his uncle.

In 1740 bands of Mahrattas commenced pillaging and ravaging Bengal; and great were the sufferings of the people. At first those living on the right bank of the Hughli had to bear the brunt of the attack; and to save their lives and property they fled to the other side of the river. But here too the plunderers came; and fearing to face them, Krishna Chandra, as said above, left Krishnagar for Shibnibash. On the south of this town he organised a village of cowherds who now are known as the "Gorhos of Krishnapur"; and two miles to the north-west of it, a mart called Krishnaganj. Near to the mart is a village of the same name. The Eastern Bengal State Railway runs through it, and has named a station after it.

Krishna Chandra was the most important personage of this part of Bengal in his time. So some historians say that the conspirators against Sirajuddaula must have sought, and gained, his accession to the plot and that it was with his advice that they made overtures to the English; while there are others who do not make him a party to the conspiracy. But the weight of evidence is in favour of the former story; for the writer of the "Memoirs of Khitish Chandra and his Ancestry" says, that it is a common belief in the Raj family of Krishnagar that Clive after the battle of Plassey presented Krishna Chandra with five cannon, in token of his services to the British power; and that these five cannon are still in the palace at Krishnagar.

Krishna Chandra had to suffer much from the hands of Meer Kasim when he was the Nawab. Quarrelling with the English, Meer Kasim transferred his capital to Monghyr; and while there cruelly persecuted all those whom he suspected to be friendly disposed towards them. Krishna Chandra and Shib Chandra were among the sufferers. They were both for some time kept in close confinement in the Monghyr fort; and they would have had to pay the penalty of death, had not the tyrant been compelled to quit the city for fear of the English.

After the English Governor's appointment as Dewan of Bengal, Behar, and Orissa, he divided the province into many parganas, and made new fiscal arrangements with the Zemindars; and Krishna Chandra managed to make a settlement with the authorities in the name of his eldest son, Shib Chandra, to whom he transferred by a written deed all his estates. This happened in 1780; and after this he retired to a beautiful house built on the River Alakananda, situated two miles from Krishnagar. Here he passed his days in preparation for death, which visited him in 1782 at the age of seventy-three.

Krishna Chandra had two wives. The first bore him five sons, whose names were Shib Chandra, Bhairab Chandra, Hara Chandra, Mahesh Chandra and Ishan Chandra; and the second, one son, Sambhu Chandra. This young man had by his disobedience incurred the displeasure of his father; and on Shib Chandra's succeeding to the ancestral Zemindari, left the palace with his mother and settled at a place called Haradhan, where his descendants still live.

Krishna Chandra was able, persevering, and of firm resolution. His life was full of trouble, and dangers beset him on every side; but he was never daunted. Besides, having great presence of mind, he was equal to every occasion, however trying; and his misfortunes, however great, never prevented his enjoying the company of his favourite counsellors and friends. He was a Vikramaditya in appreciating and rewarding merit. His court was crowded with men of learning, poets, musicians, and great wits, who always found favour with him. The Raja made a regular allowance to them, and they often received from him free grants of land. The jewel of his court was Bharat Chandra, the model poet. This man was born in 1712 at a village in the Burdwan district; and after receiving a liberal education in Sanskrit and Persian, he travelled in many parts of India, and afterwards came to Chandernagore where Indra Narayana Chaudhri, the Dewan of the French, gave him a horse. It was here that he made his first acquaintance with Krishna Chandra, when the latter was on a visit to Indra Narayana. The Raja, pleased with his accomplishments, took him to his home. The last though not the least brilliant ornament of the Krishnagar court was Gopal Bharh, whose witty sayings are still in the mouth of almost every Bengali. I think it will not be too much to say that the intelligence, learning and wit for which India is still noted, were nurtured and developed under the auspices of Krishna Chandra.

But in spite of his claims to the gratitude of his country in other respects, he was indifferent to social and religious matters. He attempted no reforms. It is said that Raja Rajballabh, feeling keenly for the sorrows of his young widowed daughter, thought of her remarriage, and that he would have accomplished his purpose, had not Krishna Chandra opposed him. The Krishnagar court, instead of alleviating the burden of priestly rule laid on the people, made it heavier. It is said, that it debarred the Piralis, or excommunicated Brahmans of Jessore, and the Baidyas, from the privilege of wearing the sacred thread. How far the rumour is correct we do not know.

Shib Chandra filled the *gadi* from 1782 to 1788. He was very pious, candid and friendly to his people. His successor Ishwar Chandra's career lasted till 1802. He was very extravagant, and loose in his morals. He is said to have spent more than a lakh of rupees on the marriage of a pet monkey. He was so remiss in punctually paying the Government revenue, that to realise it portions of his Zemindari were sold by public auction.

He was succeeded by Giris Chandra. He too neglected his affairs. He spent large sums of money in works of devotion. The eighty-four parganas comprised in the Zemindari of Krishna Chandra, now dwindled into five or six parganas and a few villages free of rent. Giris Chandra, having no issue, adopted a son, to whom he gave the name of Siris Chandra, and who when only a minor succeeded him in 1841. This Raja, like some of his predecessors, encouraged learning and the fine arts. Famous musicians from Delhi were entertained by him.

Siris Chandra on attaining his majority devoted his attention to the affairs of the Raj. At first he tried to recover the lost parganas. Then he organised a philanthropic society, of which he was the president, the chief object of which was to move Government to restore to their former owners those rent-free lands which it had deprived them of. He did not stop here in his good work. He tried every means to ameliorate the social condition of the people of lower Bengal. Having read the Hindu Shastras with learned Brahmans, he tried to glean from them passages sanctioning the remarriage of widows. He would have succeeded in this noble work, but for the strong opposition of the Nadia Pandits.

Siris Chandra appreciated and encouraged the spread of English education in this country. In 1845 the Krishnagar College was founded, and the Raja, unlike his predecessors, sent his son there, and enrolled himself as a member of the managing committee. He established a Brahmo Samaj in 1844; and Babu Debendra Nath Tagore sent a Brahmo preacher, Hazarilal, to permanently lead in the worship. It is said that finding Hazarilal not to be a Vediç Brahman, the Rajah was much grieved, and ordered that the Samaj should no longer meet in his house.

A little after this, an agitation was set on foot against the Christian missionaries at Krishnagar; and to counteract

THE MAHARAJA OF NADIA (MAHARAJA KHITIS CHANDRA RAI, BAHADUR).

their efforts to evangelise the people Siris Chandra started a free English School.

But such a valuable life had a very lamentable end. We here quote the words of the writer of "Khitis Chandra and his Family."

Raja Siris Chandra was till the thirty-fifth year of his age devoted to the service of his country, and to his own good. After this he came in contact with some plausible wealthy men of Calcutta, whose company effected a revolution in his principles and conduct. After this he ceased to attend to his own affairs, and shut his ears against the advice and warning of friends. He became intemperate in every way, and spent days and nights in Bacchanalian revelries. Two years of incessant debauchery told on his body and mind; and at last, on the 21st of the month of Augraham, 1857, he left this world at the age of thirty-eight.

His successor, Satis Chandra, ascended the *gadi* at the age of twenty. Few noteworthy events happened in his time. He neglected his responsibilities, and spent much of his time abroad with bad companions. He was careless alike of his income and his expenditure. He died on the 25th of October 1870 at Masuri, of a disease brought on by too much drinking.

Satis Chandra was a great admirer of English customs. He ate publicly with his European guests. On his death, Mr Lobb, the then Principal of the Krishnagar College, praised him in the following terms:—"The Maharaja was the link of sympathy between the Europeans and the natives, and in his death that link has been broken, and there is no hope for another to take his place."

Satis's widow adopted a son, and named him Khitis Chandra. He is the present Raja of Nadia, and is honoured by all for his learning, intelligence, and good character.

When, in the beginning of the last century, the Rajas were declining in power, and the British rule was being firmly established in this country, a few families in Krishnagar rose to eminence; and of these the Lahiris were the foremost. In a short time, their fame spread far and wide, and great was their influence on the society of the district.

We cannot definitely say when, and under what circumstances, they settled here. But this much is certain, that originally they dwelt in some part of Rajshahi; and that one of them married into the family of the Dewan Chakravarttis, or, as they were latterly called, Rajas of Krishnagar, and as was the custom then of Brahmans of his class, left his own home for that of his father-in-law. Dewan Kartik Chandra Rai, author of the "Memoir of Khitish Chandra and his Family," writes thus of two of his ancestors: "It appears that my great grandfather, Shostidas Chakravartti, and after him, his son, Ramram, were Dewans in the Krishnagar Court from the time of Raja Rudra, the great grandson of Bhohanunda to that of Raghuram, the grandson of Rudra, and in our genealogical records, their names never occur but with the title of their office appended to them." From this it is clear that the Chakravarttis or Rais have held the Diwani for several generations. It was their custom to marry their daughters to Kulins of high caste belonging to Varendrabhumi, or the land of the Varendras, a sect of Brahmans, and then to find homes for them in Krishnagar, or in its neighbourhood. And it is supposed, that this is the reason why there are so many families of Lahiris, Khans, Sandels, etc., to be found in this part of Bengal.

We cannot say who it was among the ancestors of

Jadu Nath Rai, Rai Bahadur.

Babu Ramtanu Lahiri that first married into the Dewan family and settled in Krishnagar. We have been told, however, that some of them lived at Matiari, along with the Chakravarttis; and from thence they came here. Mr Lahiri's great grandfather, Ramhori, permanently made Krishnagar his home. He had two sons, Ramkinkar and Ramgovinda, of whom the former was appointed Munshi in the court. He was childless, and so adopted a son, while his brother had five sons. Under the joint family system, Ramkinkar, as the only breadwinner, was called upon to support Ramgovinda with his wife and children. He submitted to the requisition at first; but soon finding it burdensome, proposed to his brother a division of the family possessions and liabilities, so that they might shift each for himself. Ramgovinda could not say nay to this; and the day of partition having arrived, the wily Kinkar divided the whole property, movable and immovable, into two lots, one consisting of things of high value, the other only of the family Shalgram Shila and some Debuttar land, and gave his brother the first choice. Ramgovinda, being of a pious turn of mind, gladly seized the second lot, willing rather to starve than part with his tutelary god. This step afterwards entailed upon him great poverty, with all its concomitant discomforts, but he had the consciousness of having done right. He had the reputation of being a religious man, and Bharat Chandra in the Annadamangal, alludes to his virtue and high worth.

Of the five sons of Govinda, Kasikanta was the second. He worked for some time under the Raja of Dinajpur. People speak of him as a man of commanding presence, inspiring awe in the minds of all who approached him. The apprehension of his displeasure deterred the children of his house from their juvenile follies. Once his grandson, Kesava Chandra Lahiri, the eldest brother of Ramtanu, received a kick from him for being inattentive to his lessons; and the receiver of the kick would afterwards often refer to it as a successful corrective. Kesava Kanta had two wives and two sons; the elder of whom, Thakurdas, served for some time as the chief agent of Raja Giris Chandra, and was known as Lahiri Dewan. He passed most of his time in Calcutta, and would go to the Governor-General's levees as his Raja's representative.

Ramkrishna, the younger, was of a very pious nature. He devoted the latter part of his life chiefly to religious exercises. He cooked his own food as long as he had strength to do so. Towards the close of his days on earth, he made it a rule to give a quarter-rupee to any Brahman, whom he met on quitting his bed; and after the customary ablutions of the morning he passed several hours in meditation and prayer. He then attended to only such domestic matters as were very urgent, and to the feeding of guests. He took his first meal of the day at four o'clock. In his last days, when almost helpless, he was attended upon, and assisted in his works of piety, by his widowed daughter, Bhola Sundari.

He had eight sons and two daughters. Kesava, his eldest son, having received a good education in English and Persian, was at first appointed by Government as a clerk in Alipur, and then promoted to the head clerkship or Sheristadarship, in the Judge's Court in Jessore. It would not be saying too much in his favour, if one were to speak of him as a model Hindu, doing his duty to all having kinship with him. He employed all his honest earnings in contributing to the comfort of his old parents, and to the bringing up of his brothers and sisters. The subject of this biography would often talk of the un-

Dr Kalicharan Lahiri.

common filial veneration of his eldest brother. On receiving a letter from his father, he used first to reverentially place it on his head, and then to take it down, and read its contents. Besides this, as his descendants still say, he rendered divine homage to his mother during his stay at home. Installing her on the wooden seat of the gods, and placing her feet on the copper vessel sacred to them, he worshipped her as a goddess. Great were the lady's fears at this. Trembling in every limb, she used to say, "Kesava, what are you about? I am afraid to receive such honours as are due to the gods alone." Kesava's reply to this was, "Holy mother, you are my adorable deity."

Ramtanu Babu was the fifth son and seventh child of his parents. Kesava died when young. He had three brothers younger than he, and their names were Radhabilash, Sriprasad and Kali Charan. The first having finished his collegiate education went to work in Jessore as Kesava's assistant. Here both the brothers died of malarious fever. Kali Charan Babu, having studied medicine and surgery in the Calcutta Medical College, set up as a doctor in Krishnagar, where he practised till a few years ago. Dewan Kartik Chandra Rai, in his "Memoir," says of his childhood; "The boy Kali Charan was extremely fond of me. He brought me books from Calcutta; and when at home, would help me a great deal in my studies. Kali Charan was very nice in his selection of dress. With the scholarship he got in the Medical College, he bought very fine dhutis, chadars, and shoes. On coming home, he would force some of them on me, saying, 'Cousin, you would look much better with these on than I.'"

Kali Charan always through life displayed the same warmth of heart as in boyhood. When, in after years, he stood very high in his profession, he won the esteem and love of all, by his affability, kind behaviour, and sympathy for the afflicted and poor. He visited them gratis; and often supplied them with medicines from his own dispensary without charging them anything. There are many anecdotes illustrating his liberality, one of them being as follows. Once a prescription written by him was brought to his dispensary to be made up. It ended with the words "a cartload of straw." He meant that with the medicine the straw should be supplied. The public at first made it a matter of wondering what the patient would do with straw. At length they asked Kali Charan to explain himself, and he said, "On going to his house, I found that the thatch had given way, and that it should be instantly repaired, otherwise, in spite of all the medicines he might take, he would die of exposure, and so I thought of sending him, along with the medicine, a cartload of straw." What wonder that the man who gave so much thought to the wants of the needy, would be loved by all? Whenever he stepped into a house, the children in it welcomed him with a shout of joy. We here give a translation of what the poet, Dinabandhu Mitra, said about this good man's sympathy with the youth of his time:

"Sweet was his nature, and like honey were his words. The young regarded him as their own, and to them he gave his heart. He and they mixed as milk and water."

Radhabilash and Sriprasad, like Ramtanu, were educated in Mr David Hare's school in Calcutta. Sriprasad, having gained scholastic distinctions himself, undertook the noble work of spreading the light of knowledge among the rising generation in his own city. He opened a school for them in his house, and himself imparted to them instruction. About this, Dewan Kartik Chandra Rai says,

"In 1243 or 1244 of the Bengali era, the lover of his country, Sriprasad Lahiri, established a free English School in his own house. He threw himself, heart and soul, into the work of teaching, and supplied the poor among his pupils with books, paper, and pens. In a short time the Institution attained a very flourishing condition, and sent out numbers to fill important positions in Society."

Sriprasad's philanthropic spirit found a full development in after years. To relieve the poor, and thus to help them to forget their afflictions, was his chief end in life. From the salary of eighty rupees a month, which he got as Sheristadar of the Court of Krishnagar, he would help the poverty-stricken to the best of his ability. The Durga Puja season is to the Hindus what Christmas is to the Christians. The poorest of the poor even are at this time accustomed to appear in their best costume. There were many families known to Sriprasad who could not afford holiday attire; but they had a friend in this kind man to help them in their difficulty. He made presents of money and clothes to them. Besides this, he held his purse open to relieve the needy whenever he came across them. He distributed his charities in an admirable way, never letting his left hand know what his right hand gave. He is said once to have given half his monthly salary to a friend in distress, with the strict instruction that he would not say a word of this to anybody.

Sriprasad was deeply learned in Sanskrit, Persian and English; and his abilities were of a very high order. He filled the Sheristadarship with so much credit, that he was soon appointed as a Deputy Collector; but the hand of death snatched him away, and thus prevented him from enjoying his promotion.

One word more about this great man. He could have

amassed a fortune if he had only compromised a little his strict principles, and availed himself of the questionable means which Government servants of his position then had of enriching themselves. In those days the influence of the amlas was very great; and in most cases the judges and the magistrates saw with the eyes, and spoke through the mouths, of their head clerks or Sheristadars, thus giving them frequent opportunities for taking bribes. Sriprasad might have, if he had liked, used such opportunities to his advantage; but to swerve even an inch from the honest path was against his noble nature. Through his whole career he evinced that sense of justice, that integrity of purpose, and that horror of sin, which had made his ancestors conspicuous, and for which the present representatives of his family are still noted.

We have hitherto dwelt on the merits of the descendants of only Kasikant, the second son of Ramgovinda Lahiri. Let us now say something of his other sons. The eldest, Krishnakanta, married in Mymensing and settled there. His branch is yet to be found in that place; while those that are descendants of the third and the fifth sons, Gaurikanta and Shambhukanta, are known as the Lahiris of Doulia and Baganbatti, villages adjacent to Krishnagar. They are so called to distinguish them from Kasikant's descendants in the city, the Lahiris of Kadamtolla. And in many of them was reflected the noble and pious character of Ramgovinda. Not finding it necessary to bring them all before the reader, we pass them over, save one in whom the religious temperament, so characteristic of the Lahiris, found a new presentment. His name was Dwarkanath Lahiri; and here is a brief account of his life: He was the grandson of Shambhu Chandra; and was born in 1827 at Baganbatti. Having lost his father at a very early age, he passed his boyhood with his mother, in her brother's house. While here he attended Babu Sriprasad Lahiri's school, and gained some knowledge of English and Bengali. When he was fifteen years old, something happened to cause his mother great trouble; and thinking that poverty was at the root of this he quitted his uncle's house, with the resolution of trying his fortune in the wide world, and seeing if he could, with his earnings, make her independent and happy. He resolved, too, that should he fail in his endeavour, he would end his days in obscurity far from home. Starting with a few pieces of copper in his pocket, he tramped continually for two or three months, till he arrived in Agra, and found shelter in the house of a Bengali gentleman, who not only supplied him with the necessaries of life, but bore the expense of his education. Dwarkanath in a few years distinguished himself as an English scholar, and secured a lucrative position in the city. On getting his salary for the first month, he wrote to his mother asking her to come to him, and sent her the fare for her journey. It is not difficult to imagine the joy the mother felt in realising that her only son whom she had given up as lost was still alive, and in affluent circumstances! Tears of gladness rolled down her cheeks, when she raised her thankful heart to the Great Disposer of all events. After a short preparation she undertook the journey, and reached Agra, to meet her son, whom she found unremitting in his attentions to her. In course of time Dwarkanath married, and was blessed with two daughters.

In a short time an important, perhaps the most important, event happened in Dwarkanath's life. Being naturally of a religious turn of mind, he would often study works on religion, and think of such momentous questions as had reference to man's destiny here, and in the next world, and to sin, and salvation from it. At length, coming in contact with an official superior, an Englishman and a disciple of Christ, he was led to inquire into the claims of Christianity. His candid inquiry was followed by conviction, and Dwarkanath accepted Christ as his Saviour by baptism. This step poisoned his cup of domestic bliss; and great was the persecution he had to receive from the hands of his mother, his love and respect for her adding to its bitterness. It was the time of sore trial indeed. There was a hard contest within him between the heart and conscience, in which the latter however came off victorious. His younger daughter thus speaks of his sufferings at the time:

"My grandmother, under the groundless belief, that should the Christian Scriptures, or works on theology, be destroyed or placed beyond the reach of her son, his faith in Christianity would be shaken, burnt them wholesale. Innumerable were the occasions on which she would disturb father in his devotions. She would hide the Bible, and try mischievous tricks of the kind, so that her son might not worship the object of her hatred. There hardly passed a day without father's smarting under the cruel treatment of his mother. Till the last day of her life, she was in the habit of saying, 'Can I bear the thought that this jewel of a son is a traitor to his own religion?' But father was too tough for even this. He did not for a moment waver in his duty; his faith was not disturbed in the least; and he was never found disrespectful to his mother. He never lost the placidity of his countenance; nor did he lose his patience in the midst of his sufferings. Filial reverence like this is very rare. The mother seemed to be wanting in common-sense, but yet all the son's earnings were placed at her disposal. Self-denial in the service of Christ, unrivalled patience which is the gift of Heaven, and a forgiving spirit, were gloriously displayed in his conduct; and it seemed that he had followed his Divine Master, to illustrate in himself the working of His Spirit. Instances of such self-consecration are rarely found in this world. We in his Christian life clearly saw, and strongly felt, the sacred solemnity of the Lord's Day. We ate very little on that day, and spent our time chiefly in prayer, solitary meditation, and the reading of the Book of God, and my grandmother as before, expecting to reclaim her son by means of persecution, would take unusual pains to wound his feelings, by doing everything in her power to interrupt him. But he patiently bore all this, and with a sad smile on his face, was heard to say, 'Mother, you would never do this, if you knew what my Bible contains.' My father's patience was a wonder for all who observed it. They would say among themselves, 'Whence has he got the patience, to put up with such ill-treatment from his mother?'"

Blessed are those children who have such a father enshrined in their memory. It is no wonder that a family in which a mother has once been worshipped as a goddess had a scion like Dwarkanath, so respectful to his mother in spite of the flame of persecution she kindled. It was for this excellent trait in his character, that during the Sepoy Mutiny of 1857, when the Christians in Agra—European and Indian—were foully massacred, Dwarkanath was screened from the fury of the fanatics by the Hindu residents of the city. It was of him, that the Rev. Mr Evans, the well-known advocate of temperance, who was his fellow-prisoner in the Agra Fort, thus speaks eulogistically, "He was meek as a lamb, humble as a baby, and true as steel." Ramtanu greatly appreciated the excellence of his character, and was once heard to say, "My cousin was younger than I, but in the force and beauty of his character, he ought to be ranked with my venerable ancestors."

It is a matter to be regretted that Dwarkanath passed away prematurely. He died in October 1874.

We see from what has preceded that many of the Lahiri family were kind, benevolent, truthful, generous and pious. It is not at all a matter of wonder, that the subject of this biography, who belonged to this family, should possess such moral power as to challenge the veneration of all. The saintly character of Ramgovinda, displayed in its full glory in Ram Krishna, was a precious legacy to their children. Even now the Lahiris enjoy in Krishnagar the first place in people's estimation. Their claims to honour and esteem are indisputable. Business has taken many of them far from their place of their birth; but wherever they have gone, they have, with few exceptions, been honoured and revered by their neighbours.

The Maharaja Sir Jotindra Mohan Tagore, Bahadur, K.C.S.I.

CHAPTER II

RAMTANU'S BIRTH AND CHILDHOOD IN KRISHNAGAR

RAMTANU LAHIRI was, like all his brothers and sisters, save the eldest, Kesava Chandra, and the youngest Kalicharan, born in his maternal uncle's house at a village named Baruihuda. Kesava's birthplace was Sivnibash, and Kalicharan's Krishnagar. Their mother, Jagaddhatri, was the daughter of Dewan Radhakanta Rai.

We have mentioned before, that the Rais or Dewan Chakravarttis, made themselves famous for their devotion to their masters the Rajas. We have also said something of their ancestor Shashtidas, who is known as a great patron of the Kulins, and one of the first Dewans of Krishnagar. The Rais or Dewan Chakravarttis were men of high principle. Though their influence on the Raj was so great that they could have, like the Mahratta Peshwas, grown rich and powerful at the expense of their masters, yet they never took advantage of the trust reposed in them. They were so mindful of the interests of their masters, that no consideration of their own convenience would slacken their zeal in rendering them full service. Many of the landed properties of the Raj, sold by auction for the realisation of the Government rent, were bought "benami" by the Rais, for the benefit of those whose salt they ate. We read in Babu Kartik Chandra Rai's autobiography that, not only did his ancestors scrupulously avoid enriching themselves by questionable means, but they sometimes, for the sake of duty, voluntarily drained their own purses, so as to straiten themselves considerably. Besides this, they spent almost all their earnings in such works of public utility as the excavation of tanks, and the building of temples, and in feeding and making gifts to the Brahmans, and the poor in general; and many of them possessed such noble traits of character as to command our admiration. One of these was Babu Tarakanta Rai; and Dewan Kartik Rai, his nephew, writes of him:

"My uncle, the elder brother of my father, was matchless in the excellence of his character. His language was full of sweetness; and never did he talk disrespectfully to anybody. He was so bountiful, that all applying to him for help were listened to and relieved to the full extent of his power. He was the master of his passions: and equally kind to friend or foe. Some of his spiteful relations had done him great harm, and had caused him great trouble; but never was he wanting in kindness to them. He helped them in distress, watched by their beds of sickness, had them carried to the banks of the Ganges to ensure them a peaceful death, and, when they were no longer on this earth, saw to the decent performance of their Sraddhs. For the benefit of my sons, I give here two incidents displaying the largeness of his mind. Once he got a young Kayasta, living in great poverty near our house, employed in the palace. In a short time, the Kayasta became the Raja's pet Khansama, and grew into a man of substance. He no longer remembered what the Dewan had done for him, and, in his cupidity, tried to deprive us of a few bighas of land. On this my eldest brother with his friends went to chastise him, and he in fear sought the protection of my uncle, who strictly commanded my brother not to molest the man. But the ungrateful wretch in a short time forgot this act of kindness, and sought, through the Civil Court, to dispossess us of a part of our landed property. When the suit was going on, it happened that one night a gang of *dakaits* broke into his house. This he tried to turn into a weapon against us, by deposing before the Magistrate that the Dewan Babu and his brothers had instigated the *dakaits*, and that some of the Chowkidars of our house had been found in their gang. Uncle Tarakanta with his brother, to avoid being arrested by the police, sought protection in the Rajbatti. They enjoyed the sympathy of their neighbours; and these, much annoyed with the Khansama, said to the investigating Daroga that they knew of no *dakaiti* having been committed in the neighbourhood; and he on their evidence reported to the authorities, that the whole affair had been got up by the plaintiff. The Peshkar in the Magistrate's Court sent word to our guardians that they could at little cost and trouble send the bringer of this false accusation against them to jail. All our friends and relations wished to make an example of him; but Uncle Tarakanta without heeding their wishes said: 'It is enough that we are ourselves out of trouble. It is no use proceeding against a fool like the Khansama.' Such a forgiving spirit is rare indeed. One night in winter, having returned from the Rajbatti, Uncle Tarakanta found his bed occupied by his cook, whose custom had always been to attend on his master at his evening meal, and then to retire. He thought that the poor Brahman was not well; and so, instead of disturbing him, he laid himself down on two pieces of *Kushachon* (a small mat formed by the texture of *Kush*, a species of grass, seated on which Brahmans say their prayers, and do other devotional duties), and, wrapping himself in only a piece of shawl, resigned himself to sleep. Knowing that the Raja was fond of news, someone who had seen the Dewan in this plight, hastened to him the next morning with the intelligence. On this the Raja, anxious to know how his favourite Tarakanta fared, went to his lodgings, and found him snoring away the morning hours. The little excitement caused by the presence of the august guest awoke the sleeper, who got on his legs in surprise. On being asked by his master the cause of his strange proceedings during the past night, he said in reply, 'I thought he was unwell, and so instead of disturbing him, I shifted for myself in the best way I could. I was not, however, put out in the least.' This act of generosity on the part of my uncle, seemed a wonder to the Raja; and he said, 'If there be virtue in this world, it is in my Dewan, Tarakanta.' One could never recount all the noble qualities of my uncle. His self-control was uncommon. He lost six or seven sons; but no one ever saw the least sign of grief in his countenance. At the time when each passed away, he not only maintained his equanimity, but also tried to console his afflicted family. It is a mystery, that he, who would weep for his bitterest enemies in distress, could remain so unmoved by the death of his children, dearer to him than life."

How unusually great was the nobility of this man's character! The history of his life is really edifying. We should here say that Dewan Kartik Chandra Rai, too, from whose autobiography we have made these extracts, was himself one of the foremost among men noted for their excellent natural qualities. There are very few who are so scrupulous, dutiful, truthful and benevolent as he was. Many of his uncle's good qualities were seen in him. He felt an intuitive impulse to attend to the wants of his fellow-creatures, to encourage by every means in his power men of real worth, to honour the honest and the just, and to relieve the distressed. It was these qualities for which such great and patriotic characters as Iswar Chandra Vidyasagar, and Akshaykumar Datta,

Raja Pyari Mohan Mukerji, Bahadur, C.S.I.

admired and respected him so much. We feel a pleasure in speaking of a man like him and our character is exalted in studying his exemplary nature.

Ramtanu's mother, Jagaddhatri Debi, was born in this great family, and inherited its virtues. She was undoubtedly rich in intellectual and moral gifts. She was the only daughter of her parents, she presided over her father's house as the goddess of good-luck. In her childhood, she was loved by Raja Shib Chandra as his own daughter; and, mounted on an elephant by his side, she often accompanied him in his excursions. We can easily conceive how much this girl was loved by her parents. It is no exaggeration to say that her father occupied, next to the Rajas, the most honoured position in Krishnagar, and she could have, had she liked, always lived with him. Her husband, Ramkrishna, too, in accordance with the custom of the Kulins, might have lived permanently in his father-in-law's house. But Jagaddhatri did not like it. She valued her husband's self-respect so much, that some time after her marriage, she gladly left her parental roof, for that of her husband at Kadamtala; and passed her days happily there in spite of her straitened circumstances. Gladly she cleaned the floor, carried water, and husked paddy for the consumption of the family; and in addition to these onerous domestic duties, she had to bring up her children. If any of her neighbours or friends would pity her for her having so much to do, she would scorn their pity. On one occasion an old servant from her father's came to see her, and finding her husking paddy, expressed her sympathy; but Jagaddhatri said to her, "I am very happy here. Tell my mother there is nothing to make me sad. I am very fond of work." People were so taken with her amiability, and her excellent qualities, that wherever she passed them, they said, "She is the Goddess Lakshmi incarnate."

One circumstance is noteworthy. While Jagaddhatri passed her days happily amid all kinds of domestic privations, her brothers were very kind to her. Almost daily, when returning home from their indigo factory, they called on her, and offered her such help as she needed.

At the time of Ramtanu's birth, his father, with the small income of the landed property he had inherited, and with the salary he got as manager of the estates of the then wealthy Lala Babus, could hardly meet his own wants and those of his family. The Lala Babus were the two grandsons of Raja Shib Chandra through his daughter. Their names were Hariprasanna and Nandaprasanna; but they were called by the people of the time the elder and the younger Lala Babus.

There are many anecdotes about them illustrating their truthfulness and generosity; and of these we quote one from Kartik Babu's autobiography.

Nobody ever saw or heard anything against the rectitude of the Lala Babus. Everyone talked of their good and noble qualities, and many interesting anecdotes are told to illustrate their virtues.

The younger Lala Babu was once, in course of conversation, informed by a neighbour of his mother's death. Apparently no notice was then taken of it by the Babu; but when, after two or three months, the man turned up again, he presented him with ten rupees, saying, "When you told me of your mother's death, I had no money in hand, and so I could not help you then; but yesterday I received some money from my *taluk*, and that reminded me of my debt to you." We have heard of many such instances in the lives of the two brothers.

Ramkrishna took great pleasure in working under such

a virtuous master. Though his salary was small, he never grumbled, nor did he use doubtful means to increase his income. In managing his family affairs, he had great difficulties to cope with, till Kesava, his eldest son, could help him with his earnings.

Ramkrishna took great care to keep his children from bad company. Every evening he used to take with him Kesava Chandra and afterwards Ramtanu, to the house of a neighbour named Debiprasad Chaudhuri, who was *Mahafez* in one of the courts of Krishnagar, and had the reputation of being religious. He strictly observed the Hindu festivals, and had the Shastras regularly read and expounded in his house. His influence was great, and every evening a pious group met in his parlour. Ramkrishna was one of the group, and Nashiram Datta another. There was a young man in Debiprasad's house who knew English, and under whose eyes the young folk learned their lessons, while their guardians, relieved of their presence, enjoyed a devotional *tête-à-tête* with Nashiram Datta, just mentioned as one of Debi Babu's guests. Ramtanu in after years wrote thus in his diary: "Alas, I shall never more see him in this life." We find the following instance of his integrity in Babu Kartik Chandra Rai's writings:—"The son of Nashiram Datta, being in the central part of Krishnagar, built a hall for the worship of God, and, to add beauty to its position, it was found necessary that the plot of ground in front of it should be included within its court. But the land belonged to another party who was unwilling to part with it, and so Nashiram's son had recourse to force in order to make it his own. The aggrieved party sought the protection of the court, and, when the judge came to make a local investigation, said that his chief witness was the defendant Nashiram himself; and that if he affirmed before the judge that the disputed land was his, he, the plaintiff, would give up his claim to it. Nashiram's son, who knew his father's probity, had kept him concealed in the house; but at last, when the judge insisted on his appearing, he was produced before him. When questioned on the matter Nashiram in great anger uttered these words: "I strictly forbade my son to take possession of that piece of land, but the wretch did not listen to me. I have not the least right to it."

The children of Ramkrishna, as they grew older, followed the noble example of their parents. Kesava in his very boyhood learned to give respect where it was due, and to be obedient to his parents.

Once, when he was between boyhood and youth, he came home from Goari with a maund of rice on his shoulders. This he did because he had been ordered to do so by his father, or someone else equally worthy of obedience. On another occasion, happening to find that the solitary step leading into his grandmother's sleeping-room had given way, he called in one or two lads of his acquaintance, collected bricks and other materials for building, on the sly, and repaired the steps in the dead of the night when his grandmother was fast asleep. On coming out of the room early next morning, and finding that the steps had been thoroughly repaired, she delightedly exclaimed, "This is Kesava's doing, and no one else's." So well she knew her Kesava.

We have no means of knowing minutely the occurrences in the life of Kesava. But from the deep respect in which the venerable Ramtanu Lahiri held his brother, it seems that Kesava's high character was chiefly instrumental in the formation of his own. We have numerous proofs of Kesava's probity. When clerk in the Judge's Court at Alipur, he used, after the duties of his post, to look after the lawsuits of many, both Bengalis and foreigners, and act as *Mukhtiar*, and thereby used to earn something extra. In those days, people connected with courts of law had a chance of soon making themselves rich, by taking bribes, giving false evidence, and practising some kind of deception or other. But Kesava was above these practices. His gains were honest, and therefore small, too small for him to meet his own wants, to remit money to his father, and, at the same time, to bear the expenses of his brother's education in Calcutta; and for this he had to look for help from others. The child Ramtanu was ushered into the world amidst circumstances favourable to his being received by his people as a special gift of heaven. He was a male child seventh in the order of birth, and some of his brothers and sisters that had preceded him were no more. His birth therefore was a cause of great rejoicings in the family and an event of interest to the people of Baruihuda and Krishnagar, where his maternal grandfather was greatly loved and revered. The little village of his nativity expressed great joy at the occurrence. Matrons crowded to the Dewan's house, and in honour of the auspicious event blew conch shells, the sounds of which sent a thrill through the whole neighbourhood. Bands of musicians came, in the hope of *bakshis*, to greet the new-comer; and played on their drums and pipes to their hearts' content. Ladies at the bathing *ghat* talked of the incident, and prayed that the new-born child might enjoy a long life. Then followed the many religious rites prescribed by Hinduism for an occasion like this: there were the *alkaura*, or the feast for the boys on the eighth day, and the *Shashti puja*, or thanksgiving to Shashti, the guardian goddess of children, on the twenty-first day, the day of the mother's and the child's purification.

The boy Ramtanu began to grow strong and healthy, to the great joy of his parents and brother, Kesava, who often congratulated his mother on the birth of such a beautiful and promising child. When five years old he was initiated into the mysteries of the Bengali alphabet. There was a *patshala* in Babu Debi Chaudhuri's house; and it is probable that the boy was sent there to receive his first education. Here we find it necessary to say a few words about the constitution and management of *patshalas*, as they then existed. It usually happened that some of the Kayastas of the Burdwan District, pinched by poverty, left their homes in quest of bread, and failing to find other employments, established themselves as teachers for the young in different parts of the country. They were called *Gurumahashais*; and the apologies for our modern vernacular schools, which they started, were called *patshalas*. These were generally located in the outer halls in gentlemen's houses, dedicated to the worship of the gods, and therefore called *Poojar dalans* (hall of worship) or chundimondops (houses for Durga). The former was roofed with bricks, and the latter thatched with straw. There were two periods of work in a *patshala* every day, excluding the generally recognised holy days, one of about three hours in the morning, and the other of as many hours in the afternoon. The *Guru* was the sole instructor, but he was assisted by the *Sirdar porohs* or senior students. He sat in the centre with his back against a pillar or a post, and always with a cane in his hand. Dozing during the hours of work was his favourite occupation, and if any of his pupils happened to read, talk, sneeze or cough so as to rouse him from his slumber, the terrible cane, after being for some time

Michael Madhusudan Dutt.
1824–1873.

brandished in the air, mercilessly fell on the poor delinquent's head.

Patshala boys read little but wrote much; seated each on his own mat, they went on writing, on palm or plantain leaves, according to the progress they had made. Paper was used only by the most advanced. Arithmetic and *Subhongkori* were very carefully taught. Letter writing and the drawing out of promissory bonds, *pats*, *Kabolyats*, etc., formed the highest branch of education. There was one subject which the *Gurus* taught with greater efficiency and better results than the pandits or the English schoolmasters of our time — I mean mental arithmetic. Boys in a short time became uncommonly expert in mental calculation. In the twinkling of an eye they could work out a sum which would puzzle many an arithmetician.

The education given in *patshalas* was, in the majority of cases, only preparatory. The sons of the priests left them for Sanskrit *tols;* those intended for Government service, to learn Persian; and only those continued to the last whose aim in after life was either to work in Zemindari *cutcherees*, or to set themselves up as traders. At that time the *Gurus* did not, like the masters and pandits of the present time, receive his salary from any community or society. Each father at the time of putting his boy under the *Guru*, promised to pay him a small fee; and the man's earnings in this way amounted to four or five rupees. But he had other sources of income. Every festival brought some pice into his box. He used very cleverly to cheat his pupils out of money or articles of use. Besides this, to be in his good graces, boys frequently gave him whatever they could by stealth procure from home, a little tobacco even not being too insignificant a gift to him. Those making such presents were always petted in spite of their shortcomings. Those who were naughty and inattentive to their lessons had no punishment to fear, if they could in some way or other satisfy his greed; while on the other hand the best-behaving were sure to be in disgrace, if they brought him no presents.

Now we come to the modes of punishment that prevailed in *patshalas*. The punishments commonly inflicted were barbarous in the extreme. They were *hat-chari*, *laru-gopal*, *tribhanga*, etc. One doomed to the first had to receive as many cuts from the cane on the palm of his hands as the *Guru* was pleased to inflict. In *laru-gopal*, the offender was made to stoop with his knees and one of his hands on the ground, and then to stretch out his other hand, on which a full-sized brick or some other heavy weight was placed. The victim was required to remain in this condition for some prescribed time, and if, his hands being tied, the weight was even slightly displaced, he had to receive a sound caning. In *tribhanga*, the sufferer was made to stand on one leg, placing the other on it so that the two might form something like a prop; then, as in *laru-gopal*, some heavy weight was placed on his stretched-out palm. If in this painful position the poor boy bent a little, changed his attitude in the least, or happened to throw down the weight, then who could count the cuts he received from the cane of the tyrant? There was another mode of punishment which was called *chyangdola*. This was inflicted on boys playing the truant. So-and-so has not come to the *patshalas*, or has run away from it, and the *Guru* deputes half-a-dozen strong lads to capture him. They do their errand in the best way they can. They seize the delinquent, throw him on his back on the ground, and then lift him up in the air, some holding him by the arms and others by the legs, and carry him to the *Guru*, who gives him a severe flogging.

In 1834 Mr Adams was appointed by Lord William Bentinck to report on the system of education then in vogue in this country. He, having inspected the *patshalas*, spoke in his report of fourteen methods of inflicting punishment in these. Some of them were very horrible indeed; and we here mention two. One was to make the offender powerless by tying his hands and legs, and then to apply nettles all over his body. How the young sufferer smarted under this severe infliction! But there was another still more terrible punishment, diabolically ingenious; it was to put the victim in a sack together with a cat, and to roll it about. The cat tore the boy's body with its teeth and claws; and when the boy was brought out, it took some time to revive him.

The very presence of the *Guru* was a great terror to the boys, and it was not at all strange that they would often run away from the *patshala*, and hide themselves in unfrequented parts of the neighbourhood, for fear of being captured, and taken to the merciless pedagogue. Dewan Kartik Chandra Rai refers to a case like this. "Some of our neighbours' boys, of the same age as I, used to attend the *patshala* in Babu Debi Chaudhuri's house. A cousin of mine belonged to it, and was frequently punished for being inattentive to his studies. Sometimes, to avoid being dealt with in this way, he would take refuge in our house, hoping that while there he was outside the jurisdiction of the *Guru*; but often myrmidons of this relentless man would lie in ambush, and would capture my cousin by surprise. One day, finding no other place sufficiently safe, he entered a hut, got on the scaffold on it, and passed there full twenty-four hours without food or drink. On another occasion he spent a cold night in an *abrhur* field. Once he received from the *Guru* such a cut on his cheek as to leave a mark there for years.

Ramtanu writes in his diary that he too had often to run away from the *patshala*, for fear of being beaten; and that this grieved his father very much.

The *Guru* did nothing to improve the moral character of his pupils, but much to spoil it. He countenanced, nay, enjoined, petty thefts when they made him the gainer. The language he used was often vulgar and obscene; and no wonder that the boys under his training contracted this nasty habit from him. The majority of them, especially those enjoying the rank and privileges of senior students, were proud of stealing, lying, and imposing on others, and their examples infected those junior to them. We read in Mr Lahiri's diary, that once a fellow-student induced him to steal. Kesava Chandra somehow or other came to know this, and upbraided him in the strongest terms. Instead of confessing or denying his fault, the young offender took to crying, implying thereby that he was innocent. Ah! he knew not then what a pang the recollection of this would in after years cause him!

As a boy, Ramtanu was very fond of riding; but neither he nor any of his friends had a horse. The desire to ride, however, was too strong for him to resist; and to gratify it he used to lay hold of strayed nags belonging to the hackney men. This sometimes caused him and his companions considerable trouble; for the owners, coming to know of their trick, pursued them with hostile intentions; and then they had to clear off with breakneck speed. At length the band of youngsters got a horse of their own, though by nefarious means. One of them purloined a large sum of money and a nice pony was bought. He was highly applauded by his friends, and Ramtanu was one of them.

Mr Lahiri always loved what was beautiful. Even at the time of which we are speaking he took a pleasure in visiting scenes rich with the charms of nature. There were many attractive gardens within which he spent much of his time, the best being Sriban. It belonged to the Rajas, and in it Raja Iswara had had a beautiful house built. Alas! Sriban is no more an object of attraction; the house is now in a ruined state. But the scenery around it is yet enchanting. The river Anjuna, on which the house stood, has still many of its early charms. On each side of it there is a row of trees for about a mile. One passing in a boat, at any hour of the day or of the night, is sure to enjoy the refreshing influence of the excursion. A few years ago, the great poet, Michael Madhusudan, visited the scene and gave vent to his rapture thus—"O! Anjuna, great is my delight in seeing thee. I will never forgot thee, or refrain from speaking of thy charms."

We can, from the recollection of our experiences of childhood, appreciate the spirit in which the boy Ramtanu and his associates viewed such natural beauties. Then we fully enjoyed the charms that Nature spread around us, but alas! we no longer retain that acute capacity for enjoyment, though the things that once pleased us are still in existence. With our age, we have ceased appreciating those little beauties which charmed us then. The cause of this change is in ourselves. Time has hardened our hearts, and therefore we no longer taste the sweets that Nature holds before us. The world is full of the beautiful and the sublime, and the hearts of those alone are touched with them who are devoutly disposed. The writer of the "Memoir of Khitish Chandra and his Family" in his autobiography thus laments his own shortcomings in this respect: "It seems that all the pleasures of life have vanished with my youth. I fly from those scenes of enjoyment which fascinated me in my boyhood; and even if I eagerly attempt to make them my own, I miserably fail. That *Sriban*, that *Lalbag* [the garden of red flowers] are still there; but no longer do I care to visit them. Their very names I seem to have forgotten."

Our hero's boyhood was also spent in rambling in fields over which Nature had spread a rich verdure. It is known that a large portion of Lower Bengal has been formed by alluvial deposits, that places now teeming with inhabitants were once under the sea, and the cities like Tamluk, now at a considerable distance from it, then stood on its shore. Not only have the limits of the southern parts of the province been enlarged by the uprising of the soil, but its productive power has been much increased. Lower Bengal is called by Europeans the "Garden of the World"; and the banks of Mother Ganges fascinate the eye with their luxuriant vegetation. In the centre of this "Garden of the World" stands Nadia; and young Ramtanu delighted to visit its verdant scenes.

But while he was enjoying these pleasures, his parents were very anxious about his future. The moral atmosphere of Krishnagar at the time was tainted. Pious men like Ramkrishna found the city badly wanting in those virtues that they desired to see displayed in their families. We cannot help weeping, when the fact is forced upon us, that the same Hindu race that the Greek and the Chinese travellers who visited India before the Muhammadan conquest, or even before the Moslem rule had been firmly established, admired as brave, truthful, frank, and hospitable, became so degenerate in a few centuries of foreign rule. The cause of this degeneration is not far to seek. The conquerors established their palaces, here and there, all over the country; and the luxury and immorality that were rampant there exercised their contaminating influence first on the upper and then, through these, on the lower classes, and, indeed, throughout Hindu society.

Another evil attending the Muhammadan supremacy was the aptitude of Hindus to flatter those in authority, and to practise deception for the furtherance of their own ends. Rich Hindus, by these means, ingratiated themselves into favour with the Emperor and the Nawabs under him, and thus they lost the truthfulness for which their ancestors had been famous. The lower classes received their lessons from the upper, and men were not ashamed publicly to violate truth. Again, if after this, there was anything wanting to make the deterioration complete, it was supplied by the policy the English followed in realising the rents due to them, and the spirit of setting truth at naught which their courts showed. It is said that these courts had no regard for actual facts, if they were not borne out by evidence. Truth was not esteemed by them in itself, but only when it was supported by witnesses. So the practice of suborning these soon prevailed. The violation of truth was soon followed by forgery, chicanery, bribery, and what not! It was this state of affairs in Hindu society that brought upon it Macaulay's vituperation. It is not strange then that morality was at a low ebb at Krishnagar.

Ramtanu was born in the time of Raja Giris Chandra. The society of Krishnagar then was divided into three classes: First, the Rajas and their connections, who formed the most important section. Secondly, certain families of independent means, the heads of most of which, having received a good education in Persian, had gone on business to different parts of the country. And thirdly, men who worked as pleaders, mukhtears, or amla in the English courts. Most of these lived at *Goari*, on the right bank of the *Khoresi*.

We have before said something of Raja Giris Chandra. One great fault in him was that he was subject to the influence of men of mean intellect and bad morals. He was surrounded on all sides by the selfish and the mean-minded; and it is easy to imagine what a baneful effect on Krishnagar society these circumstances produced. At this time there was a link of connection between the Raja and the Lahiri family; for the half-brother of Ramkrishna, Babu Thakurdas Lahiri, was, as we have before said, the chief agent of the Raja in Calcutta.

Raja Giris Chandra was succeeded by Shiris Chandra, and a terrible picture is drawn of the corruption of which the palace was full during the time of the latter. The Raja, in spite of his many good qualities, was addicted to some vices which were not then regarded as such. It was a period of gross public immorality such as happily exists no longer, either in Bengal or elsewhere in India; and the Dewan Kartik Chandra in his "Memoirs" has much to say about the immorality of Krishnagar, and of the court of its Rajas at this time, over which we will now draw a veil.

We have alluded to these evils only to show the state of Hindu society at the time of Ramtanu's birth. The loose lives of the men influenced the conduct and the language of the rising generation. Boys were familiar with odious scenes; and that their pet child, Ramtanu, should get spoiled in such company was the constant fear of Ramkrishna and Jagaddhatri; so they were anxious not to let him remain in the contaminating atmosphere of Krishnagar. At length they hit upon an expedient.

Kesava's home was at Chetla near Kalighat; and to him they represented the necessity of his younger brother being taken there. So at the age of twelve the subject of this biography left his native city for Chetla.

CHAPTER III

RAMTANU'S SCHOOLDAYS IN CALCUTTA

KESAVA, as desired by his parents, brought Ramtanu to Chetla in 1826. But anxious as he was to give his brother an English education, he did not find it easy, for his salary of thirty rupees a month, together with what he made by helping people in their lawsuits, barely enabled him to make both ends meet. There being no English school at Chetla or Kalighat, it was necessary that Ramtanu should be lodged somewhere in Calcutta; but who was to take care of him, and whence was the money for his board and education to come? These questions puzzled Kesava. For a time he was compelled to put them aside, and to give his brother as good a home education as he could. Possessing a good knowledge of Persian and Arabic, he taught him these languages. English handwriting too was attended to so well, that in after years, when Ramtanu Babu was praised for his penmanship, he attributed it to the care and skill with which his brother had taught him to write.

But this was an arrangement with which Kesava could not long remain satisfied. He could give very little time to his brother; and besides that he had to spend the greater part of the day in his office, leaving the boy in the companionship of the servants, who were by no means fit to associate with him. The moral atmosphere of places like Kalighat was tainted, and Chetla was not free from the infection. It is a known fact that places of Hindu pilgrimage are full of corruption. Vicious characters of

Statue of David Hare.

every description are to be met there, especially women of ill-fame. Chetla was infested by such characters then as now, and the boy Ramtanu had often to come in contact with them. But, fortunately, he was then too young to understand the nature of their vices, or imitate them.

Kesava felt that to keep his brother long amidst these surroundings was dangerous, so he was anxious as soon as possible to remove him from their influence. At length a favourable opportunity presented itself. One day a gentleman of Nadia, Kali Sankar Chakravartti by name, saw Kesava with the object of getting some employment. The latter promised to help him to obtain a post, on condition that he would influence a relation of his, Gaur Mohan Vidyalankar, a pandit in one of David Hare's schools, to get Ramtanu admitted as a free student into the institution which then passed under the name of "Society's School," but is now called the "Hare School."

We have brought Gaur Mohan before our readers, and we cannot dismiss him without saying something of his uncle, Jai Gopal Tarkalankar, famous for his erudition in Sanskrit. He first came into public notice as Dr Cary's pandit, and as editor of the *Ramayan* in verse. Afterwards, in 1824, on the establishment of the Sanskrit College, he was appointed the Professor of Literature there, and the most distinguished Sanskrit scholars of Bengal, Premchand Tarkabagish, Taranath Tarkabachaspati and Ishwar Chandra Vidyasagar, were his pupils. There are many anecdotes illustrating his excellent mode of teaching. It is said that when reading, with his scholars, Kalidas' *Sakuntala* or Bhababhuti's *Uttararamcharita*, he would be so carried beyond himself, as, even at the age of eighty, suddenly to leave his seat and play the most interesting parts with the gesticulations of a perfect actor.

On the appointed day Ramtanu was taken by Gaur

Mohan to Mr David Hare, who was then living with Mr Grey in his house on the riverside. Mr Hare was every morning and evening visited by a large number of situation-hunters and schoolboys. The latter were so much loved by him that he would never send them away without treating them to sweets of different kinds. There was a confectioner near his house, who had orders to supply the boys with what they wanted. On the day in question, Gaur Mohan, leaving Ramtanu in the sweetmeat shop, went to Mr Hare and asked him to take the boy as a free student. The gentleman was not then in a mood to confer the favour. He had received too many applications of the kind. In fact, he could hardly come out of his house without being pestered by such requests as "Me poor boy, have pity on me and take me into your school"; and the suspicion had taken possession of him that Bengalis were taking advantage of his philanthropy. It was under these circumstances that he flatly refused to comply with Vidyalankar's request, saying that the list of free students was full. But the pandit knew Mr Hare's nature, and he hoped that a little importunity would serve the purpose. So he told Ramtanu for a few days continually to run with the sahib's palanquin, and to repeat in his ears the prayers of being taken in as a free pupil. The boy did accordingly. After an early breakfast, sometimes without it, he would walk from Hatibagan, where Vidyalankar lived, to Mr Grey's gate, there watch the coming out of Mr Hare's palanquin and then trot by its side. One evening, alighting from his conveyance, the sahib noticed how pale and tired the boy looked, and, rightly conjecturing that he had had no food during the day, asked him if he would eat anything. Ramtanu, fearing to lose his caste, denied having fasted the whole day; but when he was told that the food would be supplied not from Mr Hare's house but from the confectioner's shop, he burst into tears, and said that he was suffering from extreme hunger. On this he was served by the shopkeeper with a good meal of sweetmeats. This was not the only instance of his being thus regaled. There followed many an evening, when, at Mr Hare's orders, the confectioner held before the half-famished boy his basket full of sweets.

Two months passed in this way, Ramtanu being the pursuer, and David Hare the pursued, after which the latter, being convinced that the boy was really anxious to learn English, and that it was cruel to put him off any longer, promised him a free education. But now a new obstacle presented itself. Mr Hare wanted his boys to be neat and clean, and so particular was he in this respect that it was almost his daily practice to stand at the school gate with a towel in hand, and rub them clean both on their entrance in the morning, and on their exit in the afternoon. He had also made it a rule that the guardian of each free boy should, at the time of his admission, bind himself by a written agreement to be liable to a fine whenever his ward came to school untidy, and the existence of this rule for some time stood in Ramtanu's way, for Kesava objected to sign the bond, inasmuch as his brother, on his admission into school, would live in Calcutta, and not with him at Chetla, and it would be impossible for him to see to the boy's cleanliness. He was not the man to enter into an agreement which he knew he could not act up to, and as Mr Hare was not disposed to make allowance for such scruples, Ramtanu's admission into any of his schools was for the time out of the question. But there was an influence at work, to which Kesava had soon to yield. Gaur Mohan showed him that he was making too much of the difficulty, and he at last consented to sign the bond.

The impediment removed, Ramtanu got his admission into the school, now known as the "Hare School."

A few words about Mr Hare seem necessary here.

He was born in Scotland in 1775, and he came to India as a watchmaker in 1800. In course of time he became familiar with many Hindu gentlemen of rank and education, and Rammohan Roy was one of them. Mr Hare, though not highly educated himself, felt that for the real intellectual development of the natives of this country, it was absolutely necessary that they should have a liberal English education. He boldly set forth his views, not minding at all to what taunts and jeers he might be exposed. He sought out opportunities for promulgating his ideas. One day he attended of his own accord a meeting held by Rammohan Roy and his people, and had a talk with this great man, about giving the youth of this country a good education in English. The opinions of the others there present were taken; and it was at length decided that an English School for native students should be established in the centre of Calcutta. The then Chief Judge of the Supreme Court was informed of the project, and it was under his auspices that the Hindu College was founded. The Hindu School thus rose into existence. A committee was formed for its management; and Mr Hare belonged to it. He, with Dr H. H. Wilson to guide him, exerted himself greatly to give the institution the desired prestige.

The Hindu College was opened on 20th January 1817. In that year, too, the School Book Society was started by Hare's exertions and under the patronage of some of the leading European and Indian gentlemen of the time. The Society undertook to prepare and publish good school books; and Rammohan Roy, with the assistance of his friend, Mr Hare, compiled suitable English and Bengali selections for the students of this country. Two of his chief works were a Grammar and a Geography in Bengali. Other men of education contributed their quota to the formation of a school library. On the 1st of September the next year another Society was formed, the object of which was to found schools, English and Vernacular, in different parts of Calcutta. Mr Hare and Radhakant Deb were its joint-secretaries. The former might be said to be its very life. He laboured hard in its cause; so much so, that he hardly found time to attend to his business of watchmaking. That he might work uninterruptedly in this new field he disposed of his business to one Mr Grey; and with the proceeds of the sale he bought a piece of ground the produce of which supported him, and helped him to devote himself entirely to the training of the young. Schools were soon established at Thunthania, Kalitolla, Arpuli, and other localities in Calcutta; and it was Hare's favourite practice every morning after breakfast to take his rounds in a palanquin, inspecting his own schools and *patshalas*, visiting such poor boys in their homes as were ill, and providing them with whatever they might want. Last of all, he went to the Hindu College and there watched the boys collectively and individually doing their work. The work of the day being finished, he returned home in the evening, there to enjoy the consciousness of having done something for the good of the people among whom he lived. We have heard from some of the men of his time that the boys that knew him and their guardians regarded him as their great benefactor; and his name was sacred in almost every home. He was a father to his pupils, and he tried his best to amuse and to instruct them. He was especially kind to his free boys; and Ramtanu, being one of them, had always a son's place in his affection.

We give here an incident that happened at the time when Ramtanu presented himself for admission into the Hare School. Mr Hare, at the time of enrolling him, asked him his age, and he said it was thirteen years. Mr Hare said it was twelve. The boy contradicted him, and maintained that he was thirteen years old; but Mr Hare did not believe it, and so put down twelve years as the boy's age in the admission-book. This occurrence shows how well acquainted the English gentleman was with Bengali customs. He knew that here in India, a boy entering the thirteenth year of his life was said to be thirteen years old, and not twelve, as he really was. Even now the illiterate of this country in this way increase their age by one year in each case.

At the time of which we are speaking a sufficient number of teachers was not available, and so instruction was in the lower classes given by monitors. When our hero belonged to the seventh class his monitors were two boys of the first class, Jadava and Aditya by name. The recollection that he in after years had of these two young men was not at all creditable to them. The one he remembered not only as a great thrasher, but also as a glutton, threatening or cajoling the well-to-do among the boys into presenting him with edibles; the other as the man who had cheated Dakhinaranjan Mookerjee of 700 rupees under the pretext of starting a school.

Ramtanu got on well at the school, but this in no way lessened Kesava's anxiety for him, but rather increased it. Gaur Vidyalankar's lodging, where he resided, was not a fit place for him. Vidyaratna was himself profligate; and his co-lodgers, almost all of whom held him in great respect, imitated him in his favourite vices. Sometimes they surpassed him in profligacy. They were all foppish in their modes of living, and idle in the extreme. Not one of them would stir even when required to cook a meal. Men working in Calcutta then never brought with them their families; but lived in the houses of their wealthy relations, if they could find any, or in common messes. It was a custom then, that if anyone from the Mufasal secured a good position in the city, the men of his village, or of the Mauza to which he belonged, flocked to his lodging in search of employment, and there attached themselves to him entirely as long as they could not find work, and partially when better luck attended them. Not to entertain such guests brought upon one great censure. But the new-comers were often asked to cook if the master of the house they came to could not afford to keep professional cooks; and greatly amusing the scene was when they tried each to shift from his shoulders the cares of cookery. Seniority in age was most made of on an occasion like this, and the youngest had to bear the burden. The moral depravity of these men was as great as their indolence. The use of wine was not then prevalent; but there were many that indulged in hemp-smoking and bhang.

How great then was the danger of boys living in lodgings full of such men. Their juvenile tastes, conversation, and amusements, were tainted by wicked examples. They grew very precocious, and frequented the streets like so many dandies, in thin black-bordered dhutis and English shoes, with teeth dyed black and hair parted. Their predilection for intoxicating drugs sometimes grew strong, and in other respects their conduct was immoral.

In Gaur Vidyalankar's lodging Ramtanu was subject to such evil influences. Besides that, he was made to cook for the host of idlers there, a circumstance that interfered greatly with his studies. Kesava, on learning this, removed his brother to the house of Ram Kanta Khan, a cousin of his father. This was at Shampukur, where

Khan Babu lived with his family. The mistress of the house, the Babu's wife, was very kind to Ramtanu, who received every attention from her. Kesava had to pay only for his tiffin and milk; while the kind lady supplied him with everything else. He fared as one of the children of the family. He had another advantage here. Digambar Mitter (the future Raja Digambar), who had been admitted into the Hare School on the same day as our hero, and belonged to the same class as he did, lived close by in his maternal uncle's house. Here would young Lahiri often go to see his friend, and in a short time he so ingratiated himself with the latter's mother, that she looked upon him as her own child, and was lavish in her presents to him. The lady's kind treatment was ever remembered by him, and years afterwards he would talk of it with a grateful heart.

Fellow-students then loved one another with a love which is rare now. Boys who, leaving the joys of home, came to Calcutta to prosecute their studies, received so much kindness from the mothers, aunts, and other female relations of their classmates, as to be able to bear without repining their separation from home and its dear associations. These ladies shed a benign influence around them, and with their advice and instruction they saved many a lad, far from home, from pit-falls of temptation and danger. Frequently it happened that a boy, transplanted from his native soil, found in the houses of his friends an atmosphere congenial to his spiritual growth, though he had no claims of consanguinity.

The mothers and sisters of his friends regarded him as their son or brother. We have some experience in this matter. The comfort these ladies administered to the heart smarting under the pangs of separation from its kith and kin, the moral strength that was given by them in the

KARTIKEYA CHANDRA RAI.

hour of temptation, are still vivid in our memory. The houses presided over by them were seats of virtue and happiness; and most of those that afterwards distinguished themselves for their philanthropy received their first lessons in universal sympathy in these happy abodes. Pandit Iswara Chandra Vidyasagar, in speaking of one of these (the mother of the friend of his boyhood, Gopal Chandra Ghosh) says: "There is no doubt that Raimani's love for her son was very great, and I believe that her love for me was no less. In fact, in the whole range of my experience, I have never found one equally loving, kind, courteous and amiable. Her divine image is still enthroned in my heart, and the bare mention of her name awakens the most pleasant recollections. People say I am prepossessed in women's favour, and I believe they are correct; for he who has personally come under the benign influence of a woman like Raimani cannot help adoring the sex to which she belonged."

Now a few words about the sanitary condition of Calcutta at the time. The inhabitants of modern Calcutta, with its hygiene and sanitary arrangements, can hardly conceive what a hot-bed of disease it then was. Bad drinking water, with the miasma generated in the filthy sewers, killed its residents in numbers. Besides such acute diseases as cholera and typhoid fever, diarrhœa did its slow but sure work of undermining the vigour of life and making it a burden. Many a robust youth from the Mufasal, on spending a few months here, lost his health, and had to return home to recruit it. The description of the unhealthy condition of Calcutta given by Kartik Chandra Rai, who came to the city some time after Ramtanu, and lodged with him, is as follows:—

"Almost everyone coming to Calcutta for the first time was sure to have his digestive powers greatly injured.

Diarrhœa was the first complaint, then followed fever. Recovery was doubtful, unless the sufferer hurried home, and placed himself under a regular course of treatment. I came here quite healthy, but within a short time my digestive powers were so injured that I was compelled to be very careful about my diet. I lived on very simple food; but yet, far from being better, I rather grew worse, lost all appetite, and my constitution became a wreck of what it had previously been. At length, my guardian took me home, and I commenced feeling better the day following my arrival there."

Calcutta spread a moral infection also. Men did not hesitate to feather their nests by telling lies, cheating, taking bribes, and committing forgeries and similar crimes, and, instead of being looked down upon, they were praised for their cleverness. The rich vied with one another in extravagance; and they were not ashamed to indulge in open immorality. The more nautches a Babu gave, the more was he extolled as a man of taste and fashion. Next in importance to the rich ranked another class of Bengali Babus, who knew Persian and had only a smattering of English, and, backed by this knowledge, held in contempt the religion of their country. Without any higher end in view, they lived for themselves alone, pleasure being the be-all and end-all of their existence. With faces bearing marks of debauchery, heads covered with a profusion of waving curls, tinged teeth like so many pieces of jet, pieces of thin, black-bordered muslin round their waists, cambric banians so made as to show their figures to the best advantage, neatly folded scarves thrown over their shoulders, and shoes ornamented with broad buckles, they strolled along the streets, humming or whistling a favourite tune. Their chief enjoyments during the day were sleeping, flying kites, watching bul-bul fights, and music; and the night brought other and less reputable amusements. Smoking hemp was a vice very prevalent then. There were in the city of Calcutta houses where hemp-smokers met, and passed hours, and even days, together with no other motive than to inhale the exhilarating fumes of *ganja.*

One house at Bowbazar was the most famous among these. The company that met here were each named after a bird, and so the name given to the association was "Birds' Association." A member on his admission received as a rule the name of a tiny bird, which, with his progress in hemp-smoking, would be changed into that of a larger one, and it was compulsory that he should imitate the sounds and movements of the feathered biped the name of which he bore. There is a funny story about one of these *ganja* smokers, who, having been missed by his father for several days, was at length found in the house at Bowbazar. As soon as he laid hold of his son, and attempted to drag him out, the young man, who was called "Woodpecker," and who held between the teeth an apparatus resembling the beak of his prototype, commenced pecking his father.

We come next to the religious or spiritual attitude of the inhabitants of Calcutta at that time; and to enlighten the reader on this point we can do nothing better than quote the following passage from Babu Nagendranath Chatterjee's "Life of Raja Rammohan Roy":—

"The people of Calcutta did not observe the Vedic rites, or follow the doctrines inculcated by the Upanishads; but they delighted in offering sacrifices to Durga and celebrating the festivals in connection with Krishna's birth and amours. Bathing in the holy Bhagirathi, feeding and making gifts to Brahmans and Vaishnavas, making distant pilgrimages, and observing the fast-days were believed, by almost every Hindu, to be tne means whereby the pardon of sins of the darkest dye could be obtained. They were held also to be the only passports into heaven. A man's position in God's sight depended on what he ate. Fare cooked by oneself, and consisting of boiled rice and peas with a little ghee or melted butter, was regarded in itself as sanctifying. Caste distinctions were very rigidly observed. A Brahman who served under Europeans used, every evening on returning from work, to take a bath in the holy river, supposed to have the power of washing away the pollution he had contracted from a Mlechchha; then to go through the routine of his daily devotion, and at length to take his meal to break his whole day's fast. This austere life made everyone think highly of his virtues.

"There was a class of Brahmans who devoted their lives to the study of the Shastras, and followed the priestly vocation. They were newspapers in flesh and blood. After bathing in the Ganges early, and greeting the sun with words of adoration, they went about gossiping from house to house. The chief subject of their conversation was how So-and-so had performed his father's or his mother's *Shradh* or funeral ceremonies, with what spirit he had fed and given presents to Brahmans, and so forth. And in relating these circumstances, they extolled some for their munificence, and ran down others for their niggardliness, their main object in doing this being to give their hearers an inkling of the praises or censures they themselves would have according as they were liberal or close-fisted, and thus to screw out valuable gifts from them by working on their desire for fame or fear of slander. And the wily priests were always successful. These Brahmans were versed in *Smriti* [theology] or *Naya* [logic or science of reasoning], but they were quite ignorant of the Vedas, so much so that few of them knew the meanings of the Vedic words they used in their prayers."

On the one hand there was this spiritual torpor in Calcutta, on the other there was a good deal of excitement attending the religious innovations introduced by Raja Rammohan Roy. Though the life of this great reformer is well known to the public, still we deem it necessary to say briefly something of him hereafter in the appendix, which will contain a short account of most of the important personages of the time.

CHAPTER IV

THE INTRODUCTION OF ENGLISH EDUCATION INTO BENGAL; AND THE EARLY HISTORY OF THE HINDU COLLEGE

IN 1828 Ramtanu left the Society's School with a scholarship, and was admitted to the Hindu College. Before we describe his college career we propose here to dwell on the points noted at the head of the present chapter.

After the civil administration of the country had come into the hands of the East India Company, every English judge, supposed to be ignorant of the people, their manners, and the spirit of the law which had so long been administered to them, had a Maulvi in his court to assist him in his work. But it was difficult to get a clever Maulvi. To supply this want, and partly to reconcile the Muhammadans to the British rule, Warren Hastings established, in 1781, the Calcutta Madrasah for the education of their children in Arabic and Persian. He took so great an interest in the matter that, without consulting the authorities in England, he gave a large sum for founding the institution. The money was afterwards refunded by the Court of Directors. Besides this the Madrasah had a grant of a landed property producing annually 30,000 rupees.

In 1792, a start was given to a Sanskrit College in Benares by Jonathan Duncan, the British Resident, who was one of those men who had at heart the welfare of the people of this country. For the support of this institution, the Government gave 14,000 rupees during

SIR JOHN PHEAR.

Photo. J. R. Browning, Exeter.

the first year; and the next year it sanctioned 30,000 rupees as the annual expenditure. It was made a rule that the teachers should all be Brahmans, except the Professor of the Science of Medicine, and the students received instruction in the way prescribed by the Shastras.

The attitude of the Government at that time towards the religion of the Hindus and the Muhammadans was very friendly. It did not in the least interfere with their religious institutions and customs, but rather countenanced them. It is said that on the occasion of festivals, guns were fired from English forts in their honour, and British soldiers, and even magistrates, were found at the scenes of these festivals, not only to keep the peace, but to make a respectful recognition of their sacred and solemn character. The East India Company was supposed to be the guardian of the big temples in the country, and made a large income by imposing a tax called "The Pilgrim's Tax." This amounted to a very large sum. In 1840 it was found that the tax had brought three lakhs of rupees annually into the Government's treasury. It was abolished in that year, and we hope it will ever remain a thing only of the past. There was another freak of the Government which should be noticed here, and which, even after so many years, has not lost its interest. The Governor-General, in the event of the Company's success in war, or in any other serious undertaking, made valuable offerings to the gods in their temples through their priests. This was regarded as un-Christian, and Lord Auckland abolished all such taxes and pujas. From the reports which Englishmen at home received of the people of India, most of them believed that these people were deficient in intellect, depraved in morals, and ignorant of their spiritual concerns. The "Gentoo" was, in the estimation of the average Englishman, almost a being of the same class with the Red Indian of America. The opinions of those who had lived in the country, and observed the people, were more flattering. To this class belonged Charles Grant. He was a real friend of India, and he laid its claims before Parliament. He moved "that a thorough education be given to the different races inhabiting the country, that the Gospel be preached to them, and that the conduct of no servant of the East India Company be such as to throw a stumbling-block in their way." He also wrote a pamphlet on the last of these points and placed it in the hands of the Board of Control. Wilberforce, the great philanthropist, promised to support him. The Chairman of the Board at first showed an inclination to support Grant's views, and to see that practical measures be taken to carry them out; but afterwards, influenced by the Court of Directors, he changed his mind; and so Mr Grant's endeavours were fruitless.

When some noble-minded Englishmen had set their hearts on ameliorating the condition of the Indians, the people themselves showed little desire for such pursuits as might raise them in the scale of nations. Education was greatly neglected. When Dr Hamilton, deputed by the Government to go through the country, and to report on certain important matters concerning it, education being one of them, visited the district of Bakarganj, with a population numbering 926,723, he was surprised not to find a single *patshala* or village school there. The condition of Bakarganj was not unique in this respect. Almost the whole of Bengal was very backward in education. There were *tols* for the study of Sanskrit, but the only subjects taught in them were grammar, Hindu theology, and logic. No attention was given to studies tending to the development of the mind. Even the

Pandit Iswara Chandra Vidyasagara.

Vedas, the Vedantas, the Gita, and the Puranas were unknown to the pandits of the time.

However, people, especially the inhabitants of Calcutta, soon felt the necessity of giving their sons some education in English. They were sharp enough to see that familiarity with this language would shortly be the only passport to respectable positions; and the establishment of English schools was eagerly desired by them. But who was to respond to their wishes? Not the Government at first, but the Christian missionaries, Carey, Marshman, and Ward, who, under the auspices of the Danish Governor at Serampur, had there begun their labour of love. They started English schools among the people with whom they came into contact.

We should here allude to the encouragement given by Lord Wellesley to the improvement of Bengali literature. In 1800, with the object of giving to young civilians from Haileybury College a tolerable knowledge of Bengali, so essential to them, he established the College of Fort William. But there were then no good text-books in the language. This he felt, and requested some of the Sanskrit scholars of the day to remove the want; and at his instance Dr Carey wrote his Bengali Grammar, and Mritanjoy Vidyalankar, Ramram Bose, Haraprosad Rai, Rajib Lochan, and Chandi Charan Munshi, several works in Bengali prose. These works were studied from 1800 to 1818. But they were not specimens of chaste Bengali; for, the language not having a copious vocabulary then, there were too many Persian words in them.

The Fort William College is no longer in existence, but it has still a sacred place in our memory, being associated with Iswara Chandra Vidyasagara, who was a teacher there for some time, and who wrote for its use the

"Vetala-panchabinsati," in 1847. This was the first work in pure Bengali.

Along with the impetus that was given in the city to the study of Bengali, English schools were established by several Eurasians, of whom Sherbourne, Martin Bowles, and Arathoon Petras were the chief. Many of those who distinguished themselves in after years received their education in these schools; such as the great Dwarka Nath Tagore in Sherbourne's, Mati Lal Seal in Martin Bowles', and blind Nitya Sen and lame Adaitya Sen in Arathoon's. As soon as the young men of the time got a smattering of English they commonly abandoned their national costume, and substituted for it loose trousers, *chapkans*, and laced shoes. As to their attainments in English, there was neither grammar nor idiom in what they wrote or spoke; but they enjoyed greater credit as masters of the language than any distinguished English scholar of the present day. According to the system then followed, English grammar and composition were totally neglected. The boys were taught only words and their meanings; and one who could learn by heart most of these carried off the palm. It is said that the Serampur missionaries, in giving certificates to men, stated how many English words they knew. It was the custom in the schools we have mentioned to make the pupils learn by heart a certain number of words every day. Committing an English dictionary to memory was the most laudable feat that a student could achieve.

We may be asked how such a poor and imperfect knowledge of English could be of any use. How could people, supplied only with this knowledge, make themselves intelligible to those whose language they had learnt? There are many stories on the point, and we notice one. A *sircar* used to lunch every day on some of the grain kept for his master's horses. It soon came to the notice of the sahib, and on his asking the *sircar* why he had meddled with the grain, the latter tried to justify himself, saying, "Yesh, Shir, my house morning and ebening too, twenty libesh full, litteel litteel pay, how manage?" This oration in correct English means, "Yes, sir, I have to feed the members of my family, twenty in number; the salary I get is too small to enable me to do so; how can I manage to buy my lunch?" It is said that this magnificent speech secured the *sircar* an increase of pay. Englishmen were greatly amused at hearing the Bengalis' ridiculous attempts to speak their language. It supplied them with an inexhaustible fund of mirth at their tables.

The Government, as we have said before, did nothing at first for the spread of English education in the country, because it feared lest by doing so it should incur public disfavour. One of its chief weaknesses, though amiable in motive, was the apprehension that the introduction of anything new, or the least criticism made on anything dear to the people, would be dangerous. As an instance, we may refer to the high-handed proceedings of the Governor-General in 1807, to stop the circulation of a Persian pamphlet written and published by Dr Carey to show the superiority of Christianity over Muhammadism. A letter was at once sent to the Danish Governor at Serampur asking him to take possession of his house in Calcutta; and Carey was deprived of the only means he then had of approaching the followers of Islam with the truths so dear to him. Owing to the same timidity, also, the East India Company strictly enjoined the Governor-General not to take any direct steps towards giving English education to their subjects.

But in 1811, Lord Minto, being impressed with the backward condition of the people under his rule, made the following representation to the authorities in England:—

"It is a common remark that science and literature are in a progressive state of decay among the natives of India. From every inquiry I have been enabled to make on this interesting subject, that remark appears to me but too well founded. The number of the learned is not only diminished, but the circle of learning, even among those who still devote themselves to it, appears to be considerably constricted. The abstract sciences are abandoned, polite literature neglected, and no branch of learning cultivated but what is connected with the peculiar religious doctrines of the people. The immediate consequence of this state of things is the disuse, and even actual loss, of many books; and it is to be apprehended that, unless Government takes action in the matter, the revival of letters may shortly become hopeless, from the want of books or of persons capable of explaining them. I would accordingly recommend that in addition to the college at Benares (to be subjected, of course, to the reform already suggested), colleges be established at Nadia, and at Bhowi in the district of Tirhoot."

The question may here arise, what made Lord Minto take up the matter. His predecessors had slept over the wretched condition of learning among the people of India; and the same lethargy might have kept him inactive, but for a certain new force that was made to act on him. Since the time of Sir William Jones, Englishmen in India had been possessed by a mania for learning Sanskrit; and at the time of which we are speaking every educated Englishman took a pride in knowing, more or less, this classical language. The great Sanskrit scholars, Colebrooke, Dr H. H. Wilson, Messrs James and Thoby Prinsep, Hay, MacNaghten, Sutherland, and Shakespear, originated the movement; and, acting in accordance with their wishes, Lord Minto took this step. These illustrious scholars had come to know the shallowness of the pandits' knowledge of Sanskrit, and, in their anxiety for the revival of its ancient literature, they moved the Governor-General to make the appeal to the home authorities. And his appeal was partially listened to by them, for the next despatch of the Court of Directors contained the instruction, "That a sum, of not less than a lakh of rupees in each year, shall be set apart and applied to the revival and improvement of literature, and to the encouragement of the learned natives of India, and for the introduction and promotion of a knowledge of the sciences in the British territories of India."

The Court of Directors did not of their own accord undertake to spend so large a sum of money for the education of their subjects in India, but they did so under Parliamentary pressure, at the renewal of the Company's charter in 1813. Nothing material was done to carry out the instruction of the directors till the 17th of July 1823, when the Committee of Public Instruction was formed. The annual grant of a lakh of rupees made by the directors was utilised by the Committee in having ancient Arabic and Sanskrit works printed, and in awarding scholarships to distinguished pandits and students desirous of studying those works. We will deal more particularly with this afterwards.

We have already said how, at the commencement of the past century, some of the people of Calcutta felt the necessity of giving an English education to the rising generation of their time. And we have indicated the imperfect attempts that were made to supply the need. We now propose to follow the chain of events that led to the establishment of the Hindu College in Calcutta, and of the Missionary College at Serampur. Schools also were founded at Chinsurah and Benares.

The reader has already been told that the Hindu College was established under the joint exertions of David Hare, Raja Rammohan Roy and Baidyanath Mukerjee, backed by the Chief Justice, Sir Hyde East. After these four gentlemen had come to the conclusion that there should be in Calcutta an English College for the education of Hindus, one of them, Baidyanath Babu, went round collecting the opinions of the public. They gladly embraced the project; and on the 14th of May 1816 a meeting of the chief Hindus of the city was convened in Sir Hyde's house. At this meeting, matters went smoothly for some time; when, someone having mentioned that Raja Rammohan Roy was one of the chief projectors of the college, and suggested that he should be a member of the Managing Board, all the Hindu gentlemen present passionately exclaimed, "Then we will have nothing to do with the proposed college!" —so greatly was the Raja hated for obeying the voice of his conscience rather than man. Sir Hyde did not know what to do. He was in a dilemma. To offend these magnates was to aim a death-blow at the project, while to exclude Rammohan from the Managing Committee would be discourteous in the extreme. At a loss to decide his course, he consulted Mr David Hare, who extricated him from the difficulty, saying, "Sir Hyde, there is no cause for anxiety. Rammohan will, on learning the feelings of these gentlemen, withdraw his name from the Committee." Mr Hare was right in his conjecture; for no sooner had he told his friend what had happened than the latter said, "What, shall I insist on my name being in the Committee and thus jeopardise the noble scheme?" And immediately after this, he wrote to the Chief Justice to strike out his name. Another meeting was held on the 21st of the same month, at which it was finally resolved that the Hindu College should be established; and a new Committee was formed, with ten Englishmen and twenty Hindus. Lieutenant Irving and Babu Baidyanath Mukerjee were its joint-secretaries. The Hindu College began its work on 20th January 1817. Another school was founded at Chinsurah, by Rev. Robert May, of the London Missionary Society, in 1814, with only sixteen boys. But the number soon increased. At length Mr Forbes, Commissioner of Hughli, gave to the school a part of the Dutch fort at Chinsurah. There was soon such a large influx of students that Mr May was compelled to open several branch schools. The total number of pupils in all these institutions was 951, and Mr Forbes, satisfied with their efficiency, secured for them Government aid amounting to 600 rupees a month.

The Serampur College was founded by the Baptist Missionaries in 1815. Besides this they, with the help of Rammohan Rai and Dwarkanath Tagore, opened many schools here and there in other parts of Bengal. The former had a great dread of purely secular education. He knew the wholesome influence of religious training, and that was the reason why he helped the missionaries so much in their educational work. It was for this reason too that Alexander Duff afterwards found a friend and coadjutor in him.

In 1814 a rich Hindu of Benares, Jagatnarain Ghoshal by name, at his death bequeathed to the London Missionary Society 20,000 rupees, with the condition that it should support an English school. The London Missionary Society accepted the trust. The school has now been raised to the status of a college, but it is no longer in the hands of this body, but under the Church Missionary Society.

But amidst all these efforts in the cause of English education, the Governor-General and his Council remained quite inactive in the matter. They thought only of the revival of classic learning. The project of establishing a Sanskrit College in Tirhut was given up, because the distance of the place from the metropolis did not admit of proper inspection or superintendence, and with the funds originally intended for it the Calcutta Sanskrit college was founded.

Finding that the claims of English education were entirely ignored by Government, Rammohan Rai, in a letter to Lord Amherst, urged the necessity of giving young India a thorough knowledge of the Occidental sciences through the medium of English. We quote the last paragraph of the letter, which shows how the writer's master mind was possessed of such broad and exalted ideas as have developed, even in European minds, only in modern times, and such as no Indian intellect, save his, has yet been able to grasp.

The paragraph runs thus:

"If it had been intended to keep the British nation from real knowledge, the Baconian philosophy would not have been allowed to displace the system of the Schoolmen, which was the best calculated to perpetuate ignorance. In the same manner the Sanskrit system of education would be the best calculated to keep this country in darkness, if such had been the policy of British legislature. But as the improvement of the native population is the object of the Government, it will subsequently promote a more liberal and enlightened system of instruction, embracing mathematics, natural philosophy, chemistry, anatomy, with other useful sciences, which may be accomplished with the sums proposed by employing a few gentlemen of talent and learning, educated in Europe, and providing a college furnished with necessary books, instruments, and other apparatus."

Bishop Heber kindly put the letter into the Governor-General's hands; and though it failed to gain its object it did some good in another way. Lord Amherst promised to have a house built for the Hindu College, contiguous to that intended for the new Sanskrit College; and the foundations of the two buildings were laid on the 25th of February 1824.

In this very year circumstances soon happened to bring the Government into a closer relation with the Hindu College. An Italian merchant in Calcutta, named Berretta, to whose keeping the college funds had been committed, became a bankrupt, and involved the college in his ruin. Of the sum of 113,179 rupees which had belonged to the college, there remained only 23,000 rupees. The Committee were thunderstruck when this was discovered; and, having no other alternative, applied for Government aid. The Governor-General and his Council promised the help solicited, on condition that the college should be placed under the inspection of an officer appointed by them. The Committee gladly availed themselves of this arrangement; and Mr H. H. Wilson, secretary to the Committee of Public Instruction, was the first inspector, and 900 rupees was the grant for the first month. In 1830 the grant was raised to 1250 rupees.

The reader has already been informed that Ramtanu was admitted into the college in 1828. It was customary then to send to the Hindu College such boys from the Society's school as had creditably completed their course there. The Society paid the fees of those among them who were poor. Ramtanu was one of these. He and

Digambar Mitra (on whom the title of Raja was afterwards conferred) were admitted on the same day into the fourth class. The well-known Mr Henry Vivian Derozio was the master of this class. This young man was gifted with extraordinary talents, and we intend giving a short history of his career in the Appendix. This much we say now, that he introduced a new epoch in the intellectual and moral history of Bengal, and moulded, when they were boys, the character of men like Ramtanu Lahiri, Krishnamohan Banerji, Ram Krishna Mullick, Dakhinaranjan Mukerji and Ram Gopal Ghosh. Though he taught the fourth class alone, he was friendly with almost all the students of the college.

Every day after school he helped them to get up the next day's lessons, and entertained them with his amusing and instructive conversation. His house again was the favourite resort of many among them, who, when there, received every courteous attention as guests. Ram Gopal Ghosh, Dakhinaranjan Mukerji, Mahes Chandra Ghosh, and a few others who afterwards distinguished themselves as men of deep erudition and great ability, received their early training from him not only while in the college but also when in his own home.

Mr Derozio's house had a great attraction for these young lads. There they learnt much and enjoyed much. Ideas quite novel were so presented before their minds that they could easily grasp them. Not only were their intellects sharpened, but their views with regard to their moral duties too were expanded under his influence. The hitherto impregnable stronghold of prejudice and superstition was adroitly attacked by him; and Hindu lads, brought up from infancy in the belief that the society of a Christian is contaminating, and that the food touched by him or prepared in his house is so defiling as to hurl him

H. L. V. Derozio.
1809–1831.

who ate it to the lowest depths of hell, broke asunder the shackles of caste, and freely ate with their Eurasian friend. Ramtanu was at first backward in taking his rank among the reformed, and he used to narrate the following incidents:—

Once when on a visit to Mr Derozio in company with Dakhinaranjan and Ram Gopal, he was asked by them to drink a cup of tea with them. Request and even urgent solicitation failing, Dakhinaranjan attempted to use force; but Ramtanu's reply was, "I am a Kulin Brahman's son; how can I join you? If you actually use force, I will so cry out as to bring the whole house, nay, the whole neighbourhood, here."

A similar incident happened a few days afterwards; and in it Ramtanu showed less repugnance to the reforming proclivities of his associates. The Rev. Mr Hough of Howrah had an "At Home" one evening for the English-speaking youth of Calcutta and its neighbourhood. Nearly all the advanced students of the Hindu College were there. Dakhinaranjan asked Miss Hough to offer Ramtanu a glass of sherry; and to persuade him to drink it, said in his ear, "It is a custom in English society, never to refuse any food or drink proffered by a lady; so take a sip of it, if you cannot drink it all." And Ramtanu touched the glass with his lips, though very reluctantly.

Such offers of wine were often made to the educated young men of the time; and drinking in parties became a fashion with them. It was regarded as one of the chief indications of the superiority of a young Bengali to old-fashioned Hindu prejudices, and one of the chief characteristics of an enlightened mind. Raja Rammohan Roy recommended the use of wine. It was his daily custom to eat food prepared and cooked in accordance with Hindu prejudices in the morning, and in the evening to regale himself on English dishes and to drink a moderate quantity of liquor. He never took a drop too much. Once a pupil of his tricked him into drinking an extra glass, to see how he could bear it; and it is said that the Raja, coming to know this afterwards, was so annoyed with the man, as to shut him out of his presence for the next six months.

Raja Rammohan Roy did not know that he was leaving an evil example behind him; and that it was not so easy for others to be moderate like himself. Alas! the abuse of wine has been the cause of the untimely death of many promising sons of Bengal, and of the ruin of many families.

Here is an anecdote, showing how innocent moderate drinking was held to be in English-educated Hindu families. Babu Rajaram Bose, afterwards one of the leading members of the Adi Brahmo Samaj, had got into the habit of drinking at the age of fifteen or sixteen years. Once it came to the knowledge of his father Nanda Kisor Bose, a disciple of Rammohan Roy's, that his son had drunk too much and had showed signs of intoxication. The young man being called into his father's presence and asked if the report were correct said it was. On this the father, taking from his almira a full bottle and a glass, poured out a little wine, drank it himself and then offered an equal quantity to his son saying, "Whenever you drink, drink with me in this way." This was one of the many instances showing how drinking was countenanced by men who had come into touch with the English, and it is not a matter of surprise that the pupils of Derozio progressed in it as rapidly as in other matters. Mr Derozio's influence produced a mighty revolution in Hindu society. With his pupils he founded an association, named the "Academic Association," of which he himself was the president. It was something like a debating club, and we shall give a description of its work in the next chapter. It was at this time that some of the senior students of the Hindu College started *The Athenæum*, a journal in which they mercilessly attacked the orthodox institutions of Hinduism. One of the students, Madhab Chandra Mullick, once wrote thus of the religion of his forefathers: "If there is anything that we hate from the bottom of our hearts, it is Hinduism."

This Madhab Chandra Mullick in time became a deputy-collector; and Kartik Chandra Roy thus writes of him in his Memoirs: "Madhab Chandra Mullick, one of the *alumni* of the Hindu College, and friend of Ramtanu Babu, was Deputy-Collector of Nadia. He was, when here, very kind to us, and we respected him much. He did much to improve Sriprasad's school, and to carry out our schemes of social reform."

There is another passage in Kartik Babu's Autobiography which runs thus: "That wine is an abomination, and that drinking it is a great sin, has been the belief of this country, but we cannot but condemn this belief as erroneous. Can the practice, so common among the most intelligent and civilised nations of the world, be anything but highly salutary, and therefore commendable? How shall we Indians be civilised, and how will our country be free from the tyrannical sway of error and superstition, if we abstain from wine? The *alumni* of the Hindu College, who set themselves up as reformers, all drank. When one of them, Babu Madhab Chandra Mullick, was here, we now and then went to his house of an evening and drank each a glass or two of the best liquor."

Ramtanu, as said above, was admitted into the fourth class of the Hindu College. He studied with so much success that he was soon known as one of the cleverest boys. In time he reached the first class; and having read a year in it, applied for a scholarship to Mr David Hare, who recommended him to Mr Wilson, Secretary to the "Committee of Public Instruction." Being examined, and found worthy of encouragement, he was awarded a scholarship of sixteen rupees a month.

Having now means of his own, in addition to what his eldest brother Kesava gave him, he had his younger brothers, Radhabilash and Kalicharan, brought to Calcutta for their education. The three brothers lodged in a house near the college; and having no cook or menial servant of their own they themselves had to work as such. Trouble of another nature soon crossed their path. Unexpected calls on Kesava's purse having drained it, he could no longer send them any money. Ramtanu, therefore, was thrown upon his own resources, and was sometimes so hard pressed as to have to run about in quest of loans.

We cannot conclude this chapter without mentioning two instances showing Mr David Hare's love for the youth of his acquaintance. Once our hero was seized with cholera, and Mr Hare nursed him at great personal risk. On another occasion this noble-minded Englishman, at an advanced hour of the night, escorted a young lad, named Chandra Sikhar Deb, who had called on him at Mr Gray's house in the street now called Hare Street, and had been detained there by a storm, almost to the lad's house at Puttoatola, for fear lest the latter should be molested on the way by some bad character.

CHAPTER V

THE BEGINNING OF THE SOCIAL REVOLUTION IN BENGAL

WE propose in this chapter to illustrate the processes by which a new epoch in the political, social, and educational history of Bengal was introduced during the twenty years following 1825.

It is known to every reader of history that the English had come to this country as merchants, and that as merchants they had conquered it. Even when they had virtually become the masters of India, they were governed and guided by the purely mercenary spirit, the spirit of making money by hook or by crook; and it took some time to obliterate this stain.

In the early history of British India there was a class of officers under the East India Company called factors, whose business it was to superintend the Company's factories, and the purchases and sales made in its name, to keep accounts, and in general promote to its mercantile interests. When, in 1765, the Company was entrusted with the civil administration of the country, these factors became the collectors of revenue; and the chief feature that marked them was their desire to enrich themselves in every way they could. Having no love for the people, they screwed money out of them by fair means or foul; and did nothing for the benefit of the millions over whom it had pleased Providence to place them, because it never entered their minds that they were responsible for the comforts or discomforts of those under them. Their conduct in connection with the great famine that devastated the whole province of Bengal in 1770-1771 may be cited as an illustration. One-third of the inhabitants were carried off, yet the collection of the revenue was made unremittingly, and even with greater rigour than before. To convince the reader of this, let us draw his attention to a portion of Warren Hastings' letter to his masters in England, in regard to this famine:

"It was naturally to be expected that the diminution of the revenue should have kept pace with the other consequences of so great a calamity. That it did not was owing to its being violently kept up to its former standard. To ascertain all the means by which this was effected is not easy. . . . One tax, however, we will endeavour to describe, as it may serve to account for the equality which has been preserved in the past collections, and to which it has principally contributed. It is called Najay, and it is an assessment upon the actual inhabitants of every inferior description of land to make up for the loss sustained in the rents of their neighbours, who are either dead or have fled the country."

The following statement showing the collections made during the year of the famine and the years immediately preceding and following it may interest the reader:—

1768-69 . .	Rs. 15,254,856
1769-70 . .	13,149,148
1770-71 . .	14,006,030
1771-72 . .	15,726,576

We can, from the passage just quoted from Hastings' letter, see that diminution in the revenue on account of the death of so many as one-third of the population of Bengal was made up by enormously increased demands upon the remaining two-thirds. Hastings, in justification of this, said that the method adopted was in accordance with the practice previously in vogue during the civil administration of the Mughuls, and that the English Government had not directly enjoined this mode of procedure. But this is not a sound plea. Government may not directly have told the revenue officers to be so relentless; but it virtually did so when it ordered its subordinates to see that the rents collected did not fall short even by a *kauri*.

The East India Company, and their myrmidons in the country, remained quite indifferent to the interests of their subjects. These, again, did not regard them in any other light than that of foreigners who had come to enrich themselves at their expense. The people also doubted the stability of their rule; for it was a matter of doubt if they could get the better of the mighty opposition received from different sides. There were the Nawabs, the Mahrattas, the Burmese, all arrayed to contend for supremacy with the English. There were bands of rebels, too, in Bishnupur and Birbhum, places close to Calcutta. But this state of things soon passed away; and the English at last became the undisputed masters of the country. The people on this became more mindful of their duties to their new rulers; and the latter, in their turn, came to understand their new responsibilities. There grew up a sympathy between conquerors and the conquered, who now desired to win the good will of each other; and in this state of mind, the important question that the rulers were called upon to decide was whether, in governing the country, they should follow the plan of administration still extant, or introduce a new and reformed system. The ruled also had to work out the problem whether it was expedient for them to remain staunch Conservatives, or to hail the changes the new Government might effect. It took the parties twenty years, the period between 1825 and 1845, to come to a decision on these points; and at last both the English and their subjects arrived at the conclusion that radical reforms were essential.

The local English authorities before this had carefully avoided introducing the least change in the administration of the country. They had first entrusted intelligent Indians with the responsible duty of collecting the revenue. But these men soon betrayed the trust by robbing the ryot right and left; and it was found necessary to abolish the posts they filled. These revenue collectors were called Naibs or Dewans; and two of them, Govinda Ram and Ganga Gobindo Singh, who were respectively the Dewans of Clive and Hastings, are notorious in history as speculators of the first class. There were several others of the same stamp; and Government thought it best to do away with them all. Their conduct had served so much to disgrace the native character, that Lord Cornwallis, on taking into his hands the reins of government, dismissed the Hindus and the Muhammadans from all responsible posts, and appointed Europeans in their stead.

The English Government had at first, as we have already said, a predilection for Oriental learning. It did much for the culture of Sanskrit, Persian, and Arabic, while English was carefully excluded. But circumstances soon made it necessary for the Government to act otherwise, and to give the natives of India means of obtaining some insight into the treasures of literature and science amassed by the Western intellect. And in this way a new epoch in the intellectual history of Bengal, if not in that of all India, was inaugurated—an epoch rendered especially illustrious by its association with such men as Bentinck, Macaulay and Raja Rammohan Roy. The last of these three not only drew Lord Amherst's attention to the expediency of giving English education to the people of India, but also opened the eyes of his countrymen to the benefits of such education. He, as it were, turned their faces from the East towards the West. In spite of his great regard for everything Oriental, he held up the Occidental's love of science, of moral excellence, and his desire to promote the welfare of all, as worthy of imitation. In time he drew many to his side, and a movement was soon organised, the object of which was to cultivate the knowledge of English literature and science, and to introduce such social and moral reforms as were deemed necessary. The end of these reformers was noble, but the means used by them were not always prudent. They had a strong orthodox party to oppose them, and in their contest with it they at times ran to extremes; and the collision between the two classes was, as we will show hereafter, productive of great evil.

Most of those who had received their education in the Hindu College, and the other seminaries in Calcutta, were fired with the desire to do away with everything that was old and embrace everything that was new. "Cast off your prejudices, and be free in your thoughts and actions," was their watchward; and there was at the time a new force at work to foster this independent spirit.

Stirring reports of the French Revolution reached their ears. Some of their English friends expressed sympathy with the movement; and such works in English literature as advocated its course were placed within their reach. No wonder then that they soon became thorough revolutionists, and were resolved to lay the axe at the root of everything that savoured of ignorance and superstition. The orthodox customs of the country were run down wholesale by them; and the cry they raised was: "Break down everything old, and rear in its stead what is new."

It was at this crisis that Lord William Bentinck came to

India as its ruler. His keen preception, sedate judgment, and firm resolution have immortalised him in history. With a strong hand he put down the cruel and barbarous custom of the self-immolation of Hindu widows on the funeral pyres of their husbands, and rid the country of those murderous fiends in human shape, the Thugs. He was no less zealous in the cause of education. The Calcutta Medical College owed its birth to him; and it seemed that he had come to India with the firm resolution of giving it a place among countries noted for intellectual and moral progress. Rammohan Roy felt a new stimulus for work at this time of general excitement. He openly and courageously attacked Puranic Hinduism; neither did he hesitate to use his rationalistic weapons against Christianity. He wrote his "Precepts of Jesus," "Appeals to the Christian Public," and *The Brahmanical Magazine*, and thereby brought upon himself the displeasure of the Serampur missionaries. On their refusal thenceforth to publish his works, he managed to get a press of his own, and named it the "Unitarian Press." He also inaugurated a Unitarian prayer meeting, which was held in the upper storey of the house whence the *Harkaru*, an English journal of the time, was published.

The question of *Sati* had first attracted the attention of Government at the beginning of Lord Amherst's administration. It had from that time to the year 1828 been a "burning" question; and the opinions of those considered as authorities on the subject were collected. A good deal of correspondence on the subject had taken place between the Indian Government and the Court of Directors. Eminent men like Messrs Courtney Smith, Alexander Ross, and H. Rattray, men whose opinions then carried great weight, had advised the Governor-General at once to put down this form of cold-blooded murder committed

TARACHAND CHAKRAVARTTI.

in the name of religion; while others, more wary, recommended that the experiment be first made in the non-regulation provinces. At length, in the early part of 1828, Lord Amherst, fearing to interfere with this custom of the Hindus, enjoined, as he saw, by the Shastras, left the custom to die a natural death, as the following extract from his writings will show:—

"I think there is reason to believe and expect that, except on the occurrence of some general sickness, such as that which prevailed in the lower parts of Bengal in 1825, the progress of general instruction, and the unostentatious exertions of our local officers, will produce the happy effect of a gradual diminution, and at no distant period the final extinction, of the barbarous rite of *sati.*"

When the Governor-General thus shelved this important question the dissatisfaction of Rammohan Roy and his party knew no bounds. They bound themselves by solemn pledges to trace, whenever the cruel rite was performed, all the monstrous circumstances attending it, and then to lay these before Government.

In the month of *Bhadra*, 1828, Rammohan Roy established the Brahmo Samaj in Chitpore Road. Hitherto he had attended for worship the Unitarian prayer meeting where his friend Mr Adam officiated as minister. One Sunday evening, as he was returning home from prayers with his friends, Tarachand Chakravartti and Chandra Sikhar Deb, the latter, in course of conversation, said to him, "Dewanjee, we now go to a house of worship where a foreigner officiates. Should we not have a place where we might meet and worship God in our own way?" This appeal touched the heart of Rammohan, and he hired the parlour of one Kamal Bose, in the Chitpore Road, that he and his friends might assemble there for worship.

They first met in this place on the 6th of Bhadra,

with Babu Tarachand Chakravartti as their secretary. The service was held every Saturday evening, and conducted in a way to show that Rammohan Roy's "Brahmism" was Hinduism in a more refined form, and something quite different from the religion of modern Brahmos. The Vedas and Upanishadas were honoured as revelations of the Divine will, and read with as much reverence as the Bible receives from Christians. But still the new form of religious thought was very much hated by almost all the Hindus of the old school; and Bengal became the scene of a continual warfare between these and the party under Rammohan Roy's leadership.

The general excitement attending the conflict between the old and the new school soon got within the academic portals of the Hindu College. There many young minds, under Mr Derozio's instruction, acquired the inspiration requisite for a successful conflict with whatever might interfere with the cause of reformation. Mr Derozio's connection with the Hindu College lasted only for three years; but in that short period he implanted such noble principles in the minds of his pupils as stood them in good stead all through life. Many of them in after years filled distinguished positions in the world, and stood unrivalled in their many qualifications. We here give an account of one of these, as recited in the story of one of the members of the "Prayer Society" in Bombay, the well-known Mahadevan Paramananda: "In my youth I met in the city of Bombay an ascetic with an assumed name, which I do not now remember, who was well educated in English. In a short time I got acquainted with him. He did not long remain with us, but left for Kathiawar. Shortly after this there appeared in one of the leading journals in Bombay a series of articles in English on the misgovernment of Kathiawar. They were so well written as to create a great sensation. They attracted the notice of the Raja of the Kathiawar State that was referred to, who, after some inquiry, discovered that the writer was a certain *Sanyasi*. The Raja had the *Sanyasi* brought before him, and heard from him that, moved by the ryots' sad account of their grievances, and their entreaties for help, he had taken up their cause in the hope that their Raja would adopt a better and more considerate policy. The tyrant at first threw the *Sanyasi* into prison, where he remained for a year. But the agitation was continued; and the Raja, to follow a conciliatory policy, set him free, and offered him the post of Prime Minister. On this, the answer he gave was, 'I have no such desire, otherwise I should not have taken the vows of asceticism. I can, however, give you the necessary instruction.' That day, virtually, commenced the *Sanyasi's* administration. His first order was, that the existing corrupt body of officials should be dismissed, and that English-speaking men with some knowledge of the principles of British administration should be appointed in their places. To secure the services of such men he himself came to Bombay. We had, in the meantime, heard everything concerning the *Sanyasi's* doings; and great was our surprise when we found that the champion for the oppressed people of Kathiawar was no other than the *Sanyasi* who had previously been with us. He took a body of men with him to serve in the Kathiawar *raj*, and I was one of them. We had worked for about a year when the old officers, whose places we had taken, and who had ever since been plotting against us, at last succeeded in getting us dismissed, at forty-eight hours' notice, and we all returned to Bombay. During our intercourse with the *Sanyasi* he, when asked his past history, among other things, talked highly of the teacher of his youth, Mr Derozio."

We now resume the thread of our narrative. In a year Mr Derozio gained so great an ascendancy over the minds of his pupils that its effects were visible on all their thoughts and actions. Babu Hara Mohan Chatterjee, at that time clerk of the Hindu College, writes on this point, and we quote his very words without altering them in the least:

"The students of the first, second, and third classes had the advantage of attending a conversazione in the school held by Mr Derozio, where readings in poetry, literature, and moral philosophy were carried on. The meetings were held almost daily, before or after school hours. Though they were without the knowledge or sanction of the authorities, yet Mr Derozio's disinterested zeal and devotion in teaching the students these subjects was characterised by a noble philanthropy. The students in return loved him most tenderly, and were ever ready to be guided by his counsels, and imitate him in all their daily actions. In fact, Mr Derozio gained so great an ascendancy over the minds of his pupils, that they would not move even in their private concerns without his counsel and advice. On the other hand he fostered their taste in literature, taught the evil effects of idolatry and superstition, and so far reformed their moral feelings as to place them completely above the antiquated ideas and aspirations of the age. Such was the force of his instruction, that the conduct of the students out of the college was exemplary. It gained them the applause of the world, from the literary and scientific point of view, and also, what was of greater importance, they were all considered men of truth. Indeed, it was a general belief and and saying amongst our countrymen, which those that remember the time must acknowledge, that 'such and such a boy is incapable of falsehood, because he is a Hindu College boy.'"

THE REV. KRISHNA MOHAN BANERJI, C.I.E.
1813–1885.

With such materials did Mr Derozio form his "Academic Association." He was its president, and a young man, Umacharan Bose by name, its first secretary. Krishna Mohan Banerji, Rupi Krishna Mullick, Ram Gopal Ghosh, Radhanath Sirkar, Dakhinaranjan Mukerji, Hara Chandra Ghosh, and other senior students addressed the meetings. Ramtanu Lahiri, with Sibchandra Deb, Peari Chand Mitra, and others formed the audience. The proceedings of the association in time attracted so much public attention that men like David Hare, Colonel Benson, Lord William Bentinck's private secretary, Colonel Beaton, afterwards Adjutant-General, Dr Mills, Principal of Bishop's College, used to attend the meetings and watch the discussions with keen interest and admiration. Moral and social questions were fearlessly discussed there, and the result was that the pupils of Derozio learnt to appreciate freedom of thought and action. The boldness with which they attacked the religious and social institutions of their country was thus set forth by the same Hara Mohan Chatterjee whom we have just quoted:

"The principles and practices of Hindu religion were openly ridiculed and condemned, and angry disputes were held on moral subjects. The sentiments of Hume had been widely diffused and warmly patronised. The most glowing harangues were delivered at debating clubs, which were then numerous. The Hindu religion was denounced as vile and corrupt, and unworthy the regard of rational beings. The degraded state of the Hindus formed the topic of many debates; their ignorance and superstitions were declared to be the causes of such a state, and it was then resolved that nothing but a liberal education could enfranchise the minds of the people. The degradation of the female mind was viewed with indignation. The resolution, at a very large meeting, was carried unanimously that Hindu women should be taught; and we are assured of the fact that the wife of one of the leaders of the movement was a most accomplished lady, who included, amongst the subjects with which she was acquainted, moral philosophy and mathematics."

War was thus declared between the orthodox and the reformers among the students of the Hindu College; and the question of religion was threshed out, not only in the college, but also within their own homes. Old grandmothers were shocked to hear their grandsons vilifying the gods; and fathers were dismayed to find that their sons, expected to offer cakes and balls of overboiled rice to their ancestors' *manes*, had turned traitors to their ancient faith. There are many instances on record in which guardians, failing to gain their wards over by argument or persuasion, had recourse to bitter persecution; and the latter had often to leave their homes and seek shelter elsewhere. In these family dissensions the young Bengali never lost his temper, but had often recourse to tricks showing how sprightly and humorous he was. Peari Chand Mitra, in his "Life of David Hare," refers to the many shifts to which some of the students were put. He says: "Many a Brahman lad who had lost faith in the idols, and refused to worship them, was often thrust into the room of the tutelary god of the family, and left there with the hope that his obstinacy would soon yield to the august and awe-inspiring presence of the deity." But far from that being the case, the young student would utilise the period of his incarceration by reciting selected portions from Homer's *Iliad*. Some there were again whose aversion to the orthodox Hindu was so great, and whose desire to make themselves merry at his expense so strong, that, whenever they met a *Chanshould* Brahman with the sacerdotal mark on his forehead, they danced round him, bawling in his ears, "We eat beef, listen, we eat beef."

There was at this time a Brahman in Calcutta named Brindaban Ghosal, whose favourite practice was, every morning, after a bath in the river, to visit the houses of the rich and carry reports—often exaggerated—of the young men's attacks on Hinduism. He represented them as atheistic in their beliefs, disrespectful to their parents, and capable of committing the most heinous sins; and he abused Derozio as the root of all this. He even went so far as to insinuate that among the educated class the question of marrying one's sister was being mooted, and that Dakhinaranjan's sister was soon to be given in marriage to his Eurasian *Guru*. Rumours like this created immense excitement throughout the city. They at length reached the ears of the College Committee, which directed the headmaster, Mr Anselmnot, to forbid any master engaging in conversation with the boys, either in or out of study hours, on religious subjects—also to forbid their eating any food while in the college.

While Hindu society was in this excited state another circumstance happened, on the 4th of December 1829, to add fuel to the fire. Lord William Bentinck issued his edict against *Sati* in the following terms:—

"It is hereby declared that after the promulgation of this regulation all persons convicted of aiding and abetting in the sacrifice of a Hindu widow by burning or burying her alive, whether the service be voluntary on her part or not, shall be deemed guilty of culpable homicide, and shall be liable to punishment by fine or imprisonment, or both."

A few days after this—*i.e.* on the 11th day of the month *Magh*, 1830—Rammohan Roy's Brahmo Samaj first met in the house newly built for its use. At the time of inauguration the following words from its trust deed were read out:—"Men of all classes, without distinction of caste, colour, or creed, shall have access to this building, only on condition that they worship the one true God alone, and know no god save Him." Both these events maddened the orthodox Hindus of Calcutta. Raja Radhakanta Deb, at that time leader of their society, inaugurated the "Religious Association," a branch of which was established by Mati Lal at Colootola. Bhavani Charan Banerji, editor of the Bengali paper *Chandrika*, went about preaching Hinduism with zeal. Almost all the rich people of Calcutta were admitted into the "Religious Association," and innumerable carriages were to be seen at the gate of the house where it was held on the days of meeting. Its members had a great spite against Rammohan, and it was to crush him, they said, that they had combined. They resolved to excommunicate his party.

But the founder of the Brahmo Samaj remained unmoved. He, with his few adherents, went to the Samaj for worship as if nothing had happened. On many occasions, while returning from there in his carriage, he was waylaid by the mob, instigated by his opponents, abused and pelted, but he bore all with calmness. The regulation against *Sati*, and the establishment of the Brahmo Samaj, had so infuriated the minds of the citizens of Calcutta that Rammohan Roy could get only a very limited number—consisting of his personal friends alone—to sign their name to the letter of thanks to Lord William Bentinck for the humane measure he had taken to stop the self-murder of the widows.

It was a few months after these events that the noted missionary, Dr Duff, came to Calcutta, and with Rammohan Roy's help established an English School with the purpose of educating the native mind so that it might grasp the truths of the Gospel. He began at first with six boys. There was, however, a number of young men who had received, or were receiving, instruction from Derozio, whom he could approach with Christian truths; and it was in the hope of acquiring a closer acquaintance with them that he took his lodgings in a house near the Hindu College, and commenced delivering lectures to them. That Hindu boys, who had already to some extent broken with their religion, should have an opportunity of hearing Christian doctrines, was a cause of great grief to the College Committee, which went so far as to interdict the students of the college from attending the lectures. The Committee did not stop there; it caused the dismissal of Mr Derozio from his post in the college.

Babu Ram Kamal Sen, grandfather of the late Keshub Chandra Sen, acting as their mouthpiece, called a Committee meeting, and moved that Mr Derozio's manners and conduct were such as to injure the morals of the boys in touch with him, and that he should be removed from the staff of masters. David Hare and Dr Wilson took Mr Derozio's side, and the majority of the members did not dare to oppose them. The proposal had to be given up. But the young man's enemies did not give up their hostile intentions. They objected to his being retained in service on the ground that, in the present state of the country, the continuance of his connection with the college would be detrimental to its interests. Here Mr Hare and Dr Wilson were compelled to remain silent. They did not know fully what the state of the country was, and therefore felt themselves unable to give their opinion. Having insured their silence, the majority of the Committee passed the resolution that Mr Derozio be dismissed.

But he was not the man to be thus downtrodden. Having been informed by Dr Wilson of the Committee's resolution, he sent in his resignation, together with a letter refuting the charges against him, and protesting against the unjust treatment he had received. He said he had never preached Atheism, never recommended marriages between brothers and sisters, and never inculcated disobedience to parents. On leaving the college, in April 1831, Mr Derozio started a daily paper, under the name of *The East Indian*, which in a short time obtained a considerable prestige. He became, by dint of his intellectual gifts, the leader of the Eurasian society in Calcutta. But Providence willed that he should soon leave this world of trial. It was only for a few months, after which he was called away to his final rest. On the 17th of December 1831 he was seized with cholera, and died six days after. On his sick-bed he received the kindest attentions from Krishna Mohan Banerji, Dakhinaranjan Mukerji, Ram Gopal Ghosh, and other Indian admirers.

In spite of the dismissal of Derozio from the Hindu College, the current of free thought that had had its rise in his instruction did not die away. It was as impossible for the orthodox party to oppose this current as to obstruct the rush of an avalanche. "Down with idolatry, down with superstition," became the general cry of young Bengalis. On the 23rd of August 1831 his favourite pupils got into a scrape. They used to meet in Krishna Mohan's house; and on the day in question they came there as usual. Having feasted on loaves from a Muhammadan bakery, and on roast meat from the butcher, they threw the refuse of the dishes into the court of an adjoining house, and bawled, "This is beef, nothing but beef." The cry drew a crowd around Krishna Mohan's house; and the offenders

RAMGOPAL GHOSH.

fled. The neighbours in a body then interviewed Krishna Mohan's grandfather, and threatened to excommunicate him if he did not then and there expel his grandson from the house. Poor Krishna, having been absent from home the whole day, was quite ignorant of all this; and was on his return quite thunderstruck to find the forces in array against him. He was forced to leave his maternal roof at once, and having no place to lay his head during the night he sought shelter with his friend Dakhinaranjan.

This incident made him and his friends more unsparing in their criticisms on Hinduism. Since the previous May he had been editing a paper called *The Inquirer*, and now, when an outcast, he assumed a very bitter tone against his persecutors. It was as if the trumpet of war had been sounded; and the phalanx of Bengali reformers now advanced to throw down the castles of error and superstition.

Mr Duff had in the meantime been doing his work as a Christian missionary. He had been busy sowing the seeds of truth; and these at length fell on good soil. Mahes Chandra Ghosh, an old pupil of Mr Derozio, accepted Christ as his Saviour on 28th August 1832; and on the 17th of October the same year Krishna Mohan was admitted into the Christian Church.

After this long digression, we at length come to our hero. Having completed his education in the Hindu College, he became a teacher in it in 1833. We will conclude this chapter by noticing how the door to high offices under Government was thrown open to Indian gentlemen. The efforts of Rammohan, backed by the advice of Lord William Bentinck, succeeded in moving the British Parliament to legislate, at the renewal of the East India Company's charter in 1833, that no native of British India be by reason of his creed or colour excluded from high offices under Government. We quote *verbatim* the 87th Section of the Act:

"And be it enacted that no native of the said territories, nor any natural born subject of his Majesty, resident therein, shall by reason only of his religion, place of birth, descent, colour, or any of them, be disabled from holding any place, office, or employment, under the said Company."

CHAPTER VI

LIFE FROM 1835 TO 1845

We now return to the appointment of Ramtanu Lahiri to the tutorial staff of the Hindu College. The modest salary of thirty rupees a month, which was all that he got at first from this appointment, enabled him not only to support his brothers in Calcutta, but also to receive as his guests several of his acquaintances in difficulty, who worked in the city on a very small salary, or were unemployed.

One of those whom he thus helped was Shama Charan Sirkar, afterwards known as the chief interpreter of the High Court, and a man of great talents. At the time of which we speak he was employed at Kidderpore under Mr Reid, at a salary of only ten rupees a month. In this state of poverty he often sought Ramtanu's lodgings for help, and ultimately he became a permanent guest there, in the following circumstances:—One Manilal Khotta, cashier to Mr Reid, dismissed for certain misconduct, brought a suit against his employer for arrears of salary. The man had been paid his wages, but entered into litigation only to harass his former master. Mr Reid thought of citing Shama Charan as a witness for himself—a circumstance which filled the young man with the fear lest he might unintentionally slip into some falsehood, while giving his evidence, in spite of his determination firmly to stick to the truth. On account of this fear he suddenly left Mr Reid's service. From Kidderpore he came direct to Ramtanu Babu, and told him everything.

Mr Lahiri was very much pleased by his guest's scrupulous regard for truth, and invited him to become an inmate of his house. While here, Shama Charan Sirkar came to know Babu Ram Gopal Ghosh, already a man of influence, who got him appointed as tutor in Hindu to Mr Joseph, the head of the firm of Joseph & Co., and also to Mr Kelsall. But he felt that, in order to get on in the world, he ought to acquire a knowledge of English; and so, at the age of twenty-two, he began taking lessons in the language from Ramtanu Babu.

Another young man was afterwards received as a guest by the hospitable Mr Lahiri, our hero. It was Kartik Chandra Roy, with whose name the reader is familiar. This young man was admitted into the Medical College then recently established, and Ramtanu received him with a hearty welcome.

Though Ramtanu's guests were happy in the enjoyment of one another's company, yet often had they to rough it. They had by turns to cook, shop, draw water and do other household services; and we have been told that, owing to these hardships, Shama Charan Mitra left the house as soon as he could slightly better his condition, while Kartik Chandra's health so gave way that he had to give up his studies and return home.

We need hardly say that Ramtanu was exceedingly kind to his brothers. In after years, Dr Kali Charan Lahiri was often heard to speak of the following incident with great emotion:—A few months before his examination he got some eye disease, and was told not to read. We can easily imagine his position then. On the one hand, his eyes were bad, and he was not to study, on the other hand the examination was pretty close. The poor lad was in a strait, when his loving brother, Ramtanu, solved the question for him. Every day, on returning from his duties in the college, he sat by his younger brother's bed till late at night, and read to him the text-books, without showing any signs of fatigue. Kali Charan was much benefited in this way, and he passed the examination. Was not this a striking incident of love and self-denial?

While Ramtanu was happily passing his time with his brothers and friends, his attention was often drawn to the great public questions of the day. In 1834 Lord William Bentinck, desirous of placing English education within the reach of the natives of this country, entered the lists against the majority in the Committee of Public Instruction, organised in 1823. They were in favour of the exclusive culture of Oriental languages, which they thought would be more desirable for Indians than the study of English literature. He was fortunate to find help in this arduous work from Lord Macaulay, who had arrived in Calcutta as a legal member of his Council, and whom he asked to see if the grant the Court of Directors had made in 1813, for the revival and improvement of literature, could not be utilised in promoting the cause of English education. Macaulay, after a careful examination of the document placed in his hands, gave, on 2nd February 1835, his opinion in writing; and the last paragraph coming from his pen was: "To sum up what I have said, I think it is clear that we are not fettered by any pledge, expressed or implied; that we are free to employ our funds as we choose; that we ought to employ them in teaching what is best to know; that to know English is better than to know Sanskrit or Arabic; that the natives are desirous to be taught English and are not desirous to be taught Sanskrit or Arabic; that neither as the language of law, nor as the language of religion, have the Sanskrit or Arabic any peculiar claim to our encouragement; that it is possible to make natives of this country thoroughly good English scholars; and that to this end our efforts ought to be directed."

With Macaulay to support him, Lord William Bentinck boldly took action. On the 7th of March 1835 he made known, by a formal order, that the annual grant of the *lakh* of rupees, which the directors had sanctioned in 1813 for the education of the natives, and which up to that time had been applied to the encouragement of Oriental learning, should thenceforth be utilised in imparting instruction in European languages and sciences through the medium of English.

This decided step of the Governor-General angered those in the Public Instruction Committee who differed from him in opinion. Dissension on a public question became changed into individual hostility, and Macaulay became the bugbear of the supporters of Oriental learning. But he was never a man to give up his point; or even argue it in a lukewarm way. Whatever appeared right was urged by him with great force and vehemence.

He showed this spirit all through the discussion; and as an example we quote the following passage from the written opinion he had given about expending the Company's yearly grant:—

"I have no knowledge of either Sanskrit or Arabic. But I have done what I could to form a correct estimate of their values. I have read translations of the most celebrated Arabic and Sanskrit works. I have conversed both here and at home with men distinguished by their proficiency in Eastern tongues. I am quite ready to take the Oriental learning at the valuation of the Orientalists themselves. I have never found one among them who could deny that a single shelf of a good European library was worth the whole native literature of India and Arabia."

The last sentence set Macaulay's antagonists in a frenzy. Mr Shakespeare, the president of the Instruction Committee, and Mr Prinsep, its secretary, resigned. The Governor-General put Macaulay into the president's chair, and from that time the latter reigned supreme in the Committee.

Krishna Mohan Banerji and Ramtanu Lahiri, who had at the time drunk deep at the fountain of English literature, and who were anxious to see their views accepted all through the country, hailed Macaulay as the harbinger of light. True these young men showed an extreme partiality to what was English; but one thing must be said in their favour: they were candid and they conscientiously used the light they had received from their late teacher, Mr Derozio, and from Ram Mohan Roy. Lord Macaulay sowed his seeds on the prepared soil, and rich was the harvest reaped. The cry they had long since raised for the demolition of everything Oriental to make room for what was Occidental became louder as he infused into them a fresh spirit of reformation.

One of the foremost among these young Bengalis was Ram Gopal Ghosh. In his house all his former college mates met almost every evening. One notable and noble feature of his character was that he heartily loved them. At the time of which we are speaking he was a man of position and influence; and though he had much to do, in the shape of mercantile business, he, far from regarding the attendance of his friends as an interruption, felt uneasy if they ever failed to give him the usual call. For Ramtanu he had a great affection. He gave him the pet name of Tanu. The party present in Ram Gopal's parlour consisted of the *élite* of Bengal, who made the best use of the time by conversing on useful subjects. Glasses full of sherry and champagne went round, but, far from muddling their brains, these potations enabled them to discuss with keener intellects and greater zest the important questions of the day. The young men were all actuated by an ardent desire for knowledge, and Ram Gopal Ghosh's sitting-room was invariably their reading-room. Nor were they unmindful of the intellectual needs of others. They edited for some time two journals, called the *Gyanumeshum* (Search after knowledge) and *The Bengal Spectator*, which contained columns both in English and Bengali, and established a circulating library and an Epistolary Association. The former consisted of good books bought with the money raised among themselves, and according to the rules of the latter they communicated to one another by letters the gist of what they had read during any particular period.

Not content with these arrangements, they started a club, in 1838, the object of which was the acquisition of knowledge, and the promotion of brotherly feelings among themselves. This club intended to work in a more general and comprehensive way than the "Academic Association," still extant under the presidency of David Hare. We here mention one of its rules which shows how earnest the young men were. It was that a member, nominated as the leading speaker in any future meeting, but failing to keep the appointment, without sufficient cause, should be subject to a fine. The club was named the "Society for the Acquisition of General Knowledge"; and the inaugural meeting was held on the 12th of March, in the Sanskrit College hall, lent by Babu Ram Kamal Sen, then secretary to the college, with Babu Tara Chand Chakravartti in the chair. To give the reader a fair idea of the subjects generally discussed in the association we place before him the following list of the topics at different times handled by some of the leading speakers:—

DINA BANDHU MITRA, RAI BAHADUR.
1829-1873.

	SUBJECTS	LEADING SPEAKERS
1.	Reform, civil and social, among educated natives . . .	K. M. Banerji.
2.	Topographical and statistical survey of Bankura . .	Hara Chandra Ghosh.
3.	Condition of Hindu women .	Mahes Chandra Deb.
4.	Brief outline of the history of Hindustan	Govinda Chandra Sen.
5.	Descriptive notices of Chittagong	Govinda Chandra Baisak.
6.	State of Hindustan under the Hindus	Peari Chand Mitra.
7.	Descriptive notices of Tipperah	Govinda Chandra Baisak.
8.	The physiology of dissection .	Prasanna Kumar Mitra.

When young, we now and then heard our seniors referring to the "Chakravartti faction," but did not understand its meaning. But knowledge increases with years, and we now know the meaning and origin of the designation. Captain D. L. Richardson was present at one of the meetings of "The Society for the Acquisition of General Knowledge," in which Dakhinaranjan was the chief speaker. The Englishman was a Tory to the backbone; and the Liberal sentiments expressed by the speaker offended him much. He went so far as peremptorily to order silence, and then and there to nickname the association as the "Chakravartti faction," or a faction led by

Tara Chand Chakravartti. The young reformers for years afterwards passed under this nickname. Tara Chand was understood by Government to be hostile to it on account of the Liberal views he expressed in a newspaper called *The Quill*. We have omitted to notice certain events of general interest in which this band of educated Bengalis had taken a more or less prominent part; and we will notice them here in chronological order.

First.—In 1834 the leaders of the European and native communities in Calcutta held a meeting in the town hall to consider how to perpetuate the memory of Raja Mohan Roy. Rupi Krishna Mullick, one of the young reformers, took a prominent part in the proceedings of the meeting.

Second.—The establishment of the Calcutta Medical College in June 1835. The want of an institution like this had long been felt by the Europeans residing in the country, as well as by the intelligent portion of the native community. There had been in existence an apology for a medical school in Calcutta, called the Medical Institution to train Native Hospital Assistants. All that these men were required to know was the nature of a few English medicines, their qualities, and their use; and the lectures were delivered in Hindustani. In 1834 Dr Tyler was the superintendent of the institution, and Dr Ross lecturer on chemistry. There is a funny account of the latter's method of teaching. He began and ended every lecture with an enumeration of the qualities of soda; and the students were so worried by his harping on the many uses of this substance that they called him Mr Soda. Young Bengali would often associate his name with the ludicrous; and K. M. Banerji once wrote an article in one of the newspapers of the day headed "Mr Soda."

There was a class for medical students in the Sanskrit and the Madrasah Colleges; but they were taught the

Hindu and the Muhammadan mode of treatment. With the extension of the British dominions, and the greater influx of Europeans into the country, the Government saw the necessity of preparing from among the natives a number of efficient doctors familiar with English medicine and surgery. Lord William Bentinck, in 1834, appointed a commission to report on the existing methods of treatment in the country. The members of the commission submitted their reports, with the opinion that it was full time for Government to establish an institution in Calcutta for giving natives such a knowledge of the medical science, as taught in Europe, as would qualify them to cope with diseases that defy the native physician's skill. The Governor-General no longer hesitated to take the step which prudence and benevolence had suggested, and the Medical College was founded, with Mr Brambley as its principal. The institution had at first to meet with an obstinate opposition from orthodox Hindus, on the ground that students would have to touch and dissect human bodies. A corpse is an abomination to the Hindu, and the more so if it be one of a lower caste. So the opening of the Medical College was dreaded by the bigoted followers of Hinduism as a surreptitious attempt to destroy it, and make the people atheists, or, what was worse, Christians.

Here again the old pupils of Derozio came to the front. They entered into a crusade on behalf of the new college, and went about persuading whomsoever they met to join it.

Third.—An act conferring full liberty on the Press was drawn up in April, 1835, and made known to the public on the 15th of September that very year. New light now dawned on the horizon of India. Not only did new journals come into existence, but the rise of a new independent spirit in the people became evident. Mr Derozio's pupils, who had in the preceding year called a meeting with the purpose of petitioning Government for the privilege, were transported with joy at the new power that the public voice gained, and the new opportunity they thus had for ventilating their political opinions freely was used by them in different directions—viz. introduction of trial by jury, removal of the grievances of coolies working in Mauritius, and the supersession of Persian by English in the pleadings in Mufasal courts.

To show what a valuable acquisition the liberty of the Press was to the people of the country we deem it necessary to dwell on the indignities to which journalists before the passing of the Act had been subjected, and the steady and fruitless contest that Rammohan Roy and Dwarkanath Tagore had carried on against the policy of the Government. The first English newspaper published was *Hickey's Gazette*, started in 1780. Then followed *The Bengal Journal*. The editors criticised each other in the strongest language. On one occasion Mr Dane, editor of *The Bengal Journal*, was so vulgar, that the authorities sent him to England under arrest. Then, when the East India Company became involved in war with Tipu Sultan, and the English in India were divided into factions, Lord Wellesley, to exercise proper control on the journals of the day, made it a law that every article before being published must be approved by the censor, or the officer appointed to sanction or disallow any publication, before its appearance in print. This rule was made still more stringent in 1813. But in 1818 it was in a manner set aside by the Marquis of Hastings; and the result was that several jonrnals made their appearance, of which *The Calcutta Journal*, with Mr Buckingham as editor and Mr Arnot as sub-editor, was one. When, on the departure of the Marquis, Mr John Adam officiated as Governor-General, it was a bad time again for journalists. Buckingham, having wielded his pen against Dr Bryce, a Government official, was ordered by the Governor-General to quit India within two months; and after his embarkation Arnot was shipped off in the next vessel leaving for England. To be sent home then was the punishment inflicted on Anglo-Indians if they conducted any newspapers in a way to offend Government; and the question that puzzled the authorities was, how to deal with Eurasians and English-speaking natives if found guilty of a similar offence. To send them to England at the expense of the East India Company was not to be thought of. Mr Adam met the difficulty by passing the Press Act, and getting it approved by the Supreme Court. Rammohan Roy, backed by Dwarkanath Tagore and some clever barristers, tried to prove that the Act was illegal. But the judges remained firm in their decision. An appeal was then made to the Sovereign, but it was of no effect.

Lord William Bentinck had a desire to give the Press its liberty; but, through ill-health, he had to leave India before conferring on it the boon intended, and it was reserved for his successor, Lord Metcalfe, to repeal, with the assistance of Lord Macaulay, the obnoxious Act that had been passed against the Press by Mr John Adam.

Fourth.—The Calcutta Public Library was established through the joint endeavours of European and native gentlemen. This was a godsend to the young men of the "new school." They went to the library regularly, and read to their hearts' content. One of them, Peari Chand Mitra, got employed there; and his connection with this institution helped him afterwards to higher positions. The library was, on the completion of Metcalfe Hall in 1842, removed there, and Metcalfe

Hall or the Public Library has since meant the same thing.

Let us now return to the point at which we left the young reformers of Bengal in 1838. In spite of the strong opposition they had to meet, they firmly held to the career they had marked out for themselves. They espoused the cause of every beneficial movement, no matter if it had been projected by the party hostile to them. For example, when the Hindu College Committee, most of the members of which were conservative Hindus of the first water, and unfriendly to them, proposed to change the infant class in the Collegiate School into a Vernacular School, they put their shoulders to the wheel, and the project owed its success chiefly to their endeavours. The foundation of the schoolhouse was laid on 14th July 1838.

Their activity was not circumscribed within the bounds of their native country. To enlist in its cause the sympathies of the English public at home they made their voices heard on the banks of the Thames.

Retaining the favourable impressions they had made on him, Mr Adam, the Unitarian friend of late Raja Rammohan Roy, of whom we have already spoken, on his return to England, organised, in July 1839, an association called the "British Indian Association," with the object of making Englishmen familiar with the experiences of the Indians under British rule, and of pointing out to them their duties to the so-called "Gentoos." After two years' useful existence, in 1841, the association commenced publishing a monthly journal, named *The British Indian Advocate*, under the editorship of Mr Adam. Speeches were also delivered by the members of the association in different parts of England. Ram Gopal Ghosh and some of his friends used to send telling articles to *The British*

Indian Advocate, and large sums of money to help their champions in England.

Events have brought us at length to 1842. It was in this year that Babu Dwarkanath Tagore, who ranked among the nobility of the country, and who was one of the foremost in intellectual gifts, embarked for England. He was noted for his munificence. He did not hesitate to make very large donations to such useful projects as the founding of the District Charitable Society and the construction of the Medical College Hospital. There was no distinction of race, creed, or colour in the gifts he made. It is said that he allowed a lifelong maintenance to Sherbourne, the Eurasian whose school he had attended when young. When in England he was as much honoured as in his own country. Our late Empress, her Consort, and the King and Queen of France, were among his friends. The East India Company, too, was not backward in honouring him.

Another important though very sad event happened in this year—the death of David Hare. He died of cholera on the evening of the 1st of June. We shall notice more particularly the circumstances attending his illness and death in the short account of his life we intend giving in the Appendix. We here give only the scene before his burial. The morning after his death, when the sun rose and shone on his dead body, the whole city of Calcutta was in mourning. Voices of lamentation were in almost every house. Old or young, rich or poor, all went in crowds to the house where their friend had died. Even Raja Radhakanta Deb, the leader of the Hindu Society, stood by his coffin. His funeral procession consisted of thousands and thousands of men, women, and children, some following his body in carriages, and others on foot. The street now known as College Street was thronged.

The corpse at length reached the spot fixed on for its interment, in the plot of ground in front of the Hindu College, and Hare's bones lie there, under the monument that still draws everybody's attention. He was buried there because the gates of the cemetery were shut against him, he having lived as a professed non-Christian. To add to the sad awfulness of the scene a terrible storm, attended with a fearful downpour of rain, convulsed Calcutta when his body found its last home.

Language fails to describe Ramtanu's grief at this sad loss of his friend. It was terrible for him to realise that Hare, who had been a father to him, had helped him in hours of affliction, had put him and his brothers in the way of acquiring that knowledge that ever afterwards stood them in good stead, and who had nursed him when ill, was no more. To the last moment of his life the mere mention of his benefactor's name caused tears to roll down his cheeks. And as long as he had strength to do so he called a meeting on the 1st of June every year, at his friend's tomb, to render unto the departed the tribute of love and gratitude.

Ram Gopal Ghosh and other *alumni* of the Hindu College were as much grieved as Ramtanu. In *The Spectator*, which they edited, they put in a circular recommending that something should be done to commemorate their departed friend. Raja Krishna Nath Roy of Kassimbazar called a meeting in the Medical College Hall on the 18th of June, the result of which was the formation of an Executive Committee, of which Ram Gopal Ghosh was a member. Influenced by his zeal and example the other admirers of the late David Hare contributed considerable sums, and the marble statue now in front of Hare's School and Presidency College was erected.

David Hare's death was not the only bereavement which

Ramtanu had to suffer at this time. His brother, Radhabilash, had died about four or five years before, and Kesava, the chief breadwinner of the family, was carried off about the time of which we write. His death took place either in 1841 or 1842. He had been ailing for about four years, and was quite prepared to meet his death. His father, too, met the calamity with admirable fortitude and resignation. Knowing that in a few hours his eldest son, his only prop in old age, was to leave him, he, for the sake of his soul's welfare, had him carried to the banks of the Ganges. Kesava was in full possession of his senses on his way to the river, and asked that the dust of his father's feet might be put on his head. The father, unmoved and calm, walked up to the litter and complied with his son's request. We can easily conceive how the poor old man's heart bled at the thought that the son in whom all his hopes had been centred was soon to quit the world. But Hindus are fatalists, and Ramkrishna Lahiri bowed before the decree of fate without a murmur.

Both Radhabilash and Kesava died of the malarious fever they had caught in Jessore, the former after suffering only a few months, and the latter after a prolonged illness of four or five years. We must here say a few words about the origin and progress of this fell disease as it broke out in the Jessore district. In the cold season of 1835 and 1836 some 300 inmates of the criminal jail in Jessore were employed in the construction of a road from Jessore to Dacca. For about three months the work went on without anything especial happening, but in March fever of a very virulent kind broke out among the coolies, and, in a day, carried off about 150 of them. It spread so great a dread that the labourers and their overseers refused to remain on the spot any longer. The fever raged far and wide, and having almost depopulated Jessore it entered Nadia, and there did its work of havoc.

On Kesava's death Ramtanu's responsibilities greatly increased. On him fell the duty of maintaining the whole family—a duty very onerous to a man of his means; but nevertheless he was fully alive to it, and determined that, to support his old parents and younger brothers, he would himself, if necessary, forgo every comfort.

It was at this time that he married for the third time. His matrimonial connections before this had not proved happy. His first wife, whom he had married when a boy, had died in childbed. His second marriage also had been broken by the hand of death three years after its consummation. This marriage had been the cause of much uneasiness to him, for his father-in-law, having a deep-rooted antipathy against his attitude towards the Hindu religion and its customs, had sedulously prevented all intercourse between the husband and the wife. It was this painful circumstance that Ram Gopal Ghosh thus alluded to in his diary: "4th April 1839. But our conversation did not take on a personal aspect till we touched the subject of women. We spoke of the peculiarities of each other's wives. Poor Ramtanu appeared to be worried about his wife. But I should not indulge myself in writing the secrets of my friends in this book."

Let us after this digression once more draw the reader's attention to matters affecting the native society in Calcutta and its neighbourhood. Dwarkanath Tagore returned from England at the close of 1842. The famous Mr George Thomson came with him. This Mr Thomson was a great orator, and the stirring speeches delivered by him against slavery, both in England and America, have immortalised him.

Young Bengal gave him a hearty welcome. Ram Gopal Ghosh, Tarachand Chakravartti, and others of the new school, became in a short time his admirers. They often called meetings to be addressed by him. At length he delivered a series of lectures in a house in Calcutta, called *Fauzdari Balakhana.* The audience was charmed by his eloquence, the like of which they had never heard before. As a result of these lectures the "Bengal Indian Society" was established, on 20th April 1843, after the "British Indian Society" in England. The educated Bengalis were delighted, and Ramtanu Lahiri was behind them—we say behind, because, though equally fervent with his friends in such matters, he was too modest to come forward. It was through this modesty that he always remained silent unless his opinion were directly asked. We give here what Ram Gopal Ghosh writes in his diary showing his friend's taciturn nature: "20th November 1839. In the evening Tarachand, Kalachand, Peari, Ramtanu, Ramchandra, and Haramohan, were here to make arrangements for conducting *Gyananameshum.* It appeared, from what the two latter said, that it was a losing concern. This they never before gave me to understand, which they should have done before calling the meeting. Everybody spoke freely on the subject with the exception of Tanu, who was silent."

Though Ramtanu was associated in every movement his friends undertook, he loved not to obtrude upon them his individual opinions, unless he was especially called upon to do so. But his sympathies were always enlisted in their favour, and he heartily felt as they felt.

Another incident worthy of notice happened this year. Babu Debendranath Tagore publicly joined the Brahmo

Samaj with about a score of friends—to which movement he afterwards gave new life and new vigour. A few years before this the Samaj had lost much of its former prestige, and the number of its adherents had considerably fallen away; so it may be said to have risen to new life on Debendranath's joining it and taking up its cause. The *Tatwabodhini Patrika* was started, with the object of ventilating theistic Vedic doctrines. Babu Akhai Kumar Dutta was its editor, and Rajendralal Mitra, Ishwar Chandra Vidyasagara, and others equally learned, were its regular contributors. Debendranath established the *Tatwabodhini* school for the purpose of initiating Brahmans into the mysteries of the four Vedas.

The year 1844 is memorable on one account—the sending of four of the students of the Medical College to complete their education in England. These were Bholanath Bose, Kanto Chakravartti, Dwarkanath Bose, and Gopal Lal Seal. Dwarkanath Tagore was the first to suggest the idea to Chakravartti of the Education Council, who selected the young men named above. Before they started it was settled that Mr Tagore would pay all the expenses of the first two and Government of the last two. They sailed in the same ship with him, in this the second voyage he made to England; and availed themselves also of the companionship and tutelage of Dr Goodeve. In this voyage Dwarkanath Tagore left India never to see it again; for when in the midst of strangers death snatched him away, in 1846.

In the midst of these social and political excitements Ramtanu was visited by another domestic affliction. His mother became seriously ill. She was brought to Calcutta for treatment, where her children were assiduous in their attentions to her. No wonder that the lady who had received divine honours from Kesava, whom the neighbours

BANKIM CHANDRA CHATTERJI, C.I.E., RAI BAHADUR.
1838–1894.

respected as the incarnation of the goddess of love and beauty, and who was admired by all for her firm devotion to truth, was loved by all that knew her; and all her acquaintances were deeply anxious for her recovery. But Fate determined otherwise. She was never to leave her sick-bed alive. She died surrounded by her children.

CHAPTER VII

SOME DRAWBACKS IN THE REFORM MOVEMENT

In this world there is often a mixture of good and evil. A drop of honey may hide a sting; a cup of nectar may contain a drop of poison. This may be said of Derozio's influence on the minds of the young generation of his time. We have seen how liberal they became in their views, and how the noble principles of their natures were developed, and how, on the other hand, they imbibed the evil habit of drinking, which was wrongly regarded by them as one of the signs of civilisation. This habit in time became so general, and so overleaped the bounds of moderation, that English education progressed hand-in-hand with a morbid love for the bottle. Even students in their teens were known to be tipplers. According to them, Bacchanalian meetings in broad daylight, attended with feasting on meat cooked in Muhammadan shops, was thought to be the unmistakable sign of moral courage; and one's credit as a reformer depended on the degree in which one could indulge in these revelries. But you cannot safely play with a venomous reptile; and alcohol, which had as a reptile crept into the Bengali community, soon showed itself in its destructive character. The bodies and minds of many became injured, while the angel of death untimely cut short the career of some.

But Derozio is not solely to be blamed for the Bengalis' hostile attitude towards Hindu conservatism, or their predilection for everything English, including the vice of drinking. Another influence was at work—that of Captain

Shib Chandra Deb.

Richardson. He took his pupils through the works of Shakespeare in a way to enrapture them. They admired the Captain, and the race to which he belonged, and tried to imitate him; and as it is easier for human nature to copy vices rather than virtues our students made very poor attempts at the imitation of the Englishman's manliness, while they quickly adopted his vices—especially the vice of drinking.

Happily, the character of young Bengal was being moulded differently by circumstances of a different nature. Doctor Duff, to whose evangelistic work we referred in Chapter V., by his preaching created an ever-growing sensation. Several young men, respectably connected and well educated, embraced Christianity, greatly to the horror of the orthodox Hindus. We have spoken of the conversion to Christianity of Mahes Chandra Ghosh and Krishna Mohan Banerji. Subsequently Gyanendra Mohan Tagore, only son of Prasanna Kumar Tagore, became a follower of Christ; and he was followed by Guru Das Maitra, and several others, all of whom were of respectable birth. Christianity went on spreading, and the Church in Bengal was being gradually strengthened, in spite of great persecution. In 1845 one Umesh Chandra Sirkar, whose father was the Dewan of the Tagore family, left his paternal roof with his wife, and went to Dr Duff with the intention of being baptised. His father coming to know this tried by force to snatch them from the missionary's hands, but the latter was too strong and careful for such hindrance to his work. It was now that the members of the Brahmo Samaj commenced a war with Christianity. With the assistance of the well-to-do Hindus of Calcutta they founded a Hindu Mission School, which, having worked for some years, came to an end owing to the bankruptcy of its trustees. The *Tatwabodhini Patrika* violently attacked

Christianity; and the missionaries made bold retorts. They attempted to show that Brahmism had no reasonable basis, and that it was but an endeavonr to effect a compromise between Hinduism and Christianity; while the editor of the *Patrika* said that the religion the cause of which he advocated was founded on the infallible teachings of the Vedas. This caused great discord among the members of the Samaj; for Akhai Kumar Dutta, who had left off editing the *Tatwabodhini*, and his party did not believe in the Vedas as the word of God, and protested therefore against the position taken up by that journal; while the new school of thinkers, led by Ram Gopal Ghosh, was not backward in throwing taunts at the Brahmos as time-serving hypocrites.

In the midst of these agitations the Krishnagar College was opened, in the beginning of 1846, and Ramtanu was appointed second master of the Collegiate School. Before he left Calcutta his friends, Krishna Mohan Banerji and others, had a valedictory meeting, and presented him with a watch, which he kept till the end of his life, as a precious memento of their love for him.

CHAPTER VIII

RAMTANU'S LIFE IN 1846-1856

THE 1st of January 1846 was a memorable day for the people of Krishnagar, for it witnessed the opening of the Krishnagar College. Siris Chandra was now the Raja, and he encouraged the establishment of the institution. His predecessors had never thought of sending their boys to public schools; but he unhesitatingly sent his son, Satis Chandra to the College, and himself became one of the most energetic members of its Managing Committee.

Captain D. L. Richardson was appointed principal of the college, and Ramtanu Babu second master of the school. He entered with great earnestness upon his work, and rendered himself a general favourite. His old pupils, still living, say that, when engaged in teaching, the faces of his boys, and the lessons before him, absorbed his whole attention; and he seemed to be almost insensible to everything else. His method of teaching was unique. He was against cramming; and his chief aim was to put his pupils in the way of exercising their faculties on any special subject that might be presented to them. He never remained satisfied with teaching truths in the abstract, but illustrated them in their various relations in actual life. He would comment upon a single word in the lesson of the day so as to give a volume of information. Supposing he met with the word Arabia; he would not think it enough simply to say what or where it was; but would describe its physical features, the nature of the people dwelling in it, and their faith, winding up with a lecture on Muhammad and his times. Nobody can deny that, though his pupils made a tardy progress in their text-book, their minds were enriched by much useful information, and fully developed, so as to be able to grasp subjects of importance too difficult for young lads trained in a different way.

In Ramtanu the boys found not only a good teacher, but a loving friend also. He mixed with them in the play-ground and in the hours of rest, and his edifying company did much to call forth those virtues which in many cases adorned their characters during their subsequent lives.

The conflicts between the orthodox and the reformed Hindus in Calcutta, of which we have spoken in the last three chapters, were now renewed in Krishnagar. The first attack on the errors and superstitions of Hinduism was made by Sriprasad, the younger brother of Ramtanu. He had a free English School in his house; and here he preached against idolatry and the evil practices connected therewith. In course of time, there arose a number of young men in Krishnagar, who commenced a war against popular Hinduism. These had not to fight unaided. They received fresh recruits from the Missionary School close by, most of the students of which, under the influence of their teacher, Babu Brajanath Mukerji, a Brahmo, had publicly forsaken the religion of their forefathers and accepted the doctrines of Monotheism. And at length this young band of reformers, making no longer a secret of their religious convictions, openly announced their determination to put an end to idolatrous Hinduism. They attacked it with a force which its champions found difficult to resist, the more so as Raja Siris Chandra warmly took the side of the young reformers. He opened a Brahmo Samaj in the palace, and was delighted to see the spread of Vedic Theism in his Raj. We noticed in the first chapter how the appointment of Hazarilal, a Sudra, as the expounder of the Vedas in the Samaj offended him; and how he refused it the use of his own hall. But he still sympathised with the movement, and the Samaj was in a thriving condition even when its meetings, instead of being held in the palace, took place first in a small house at Aminbazar, and subsequently in one built for it in 1847. But the advocates of Puranic idolatry did not remain inactive. They, under the leadership of some wealthy citizens, established a Dharmasabha, or an association for the defence of Hinduism. But they could not do any harm to the new school, as the Raja was in its favour. In fact, he stood as the umpire between it and the old school. Many of the pandits of the latter were convinced by him of the propriety of worshipping the one God of the Vedas, but had not the moral courage to act up to their convictions.

Many may be surprised to hear that Ramtanu had no sympathy with the Brahmo Samaj. He was one of those that had entered the lists against the Calcutta Brahmos in their unreasonable attacks on Christianity, and attempts to give the Vedas the character of a Divine revelation, and he was still opposed to them on principle. The letter he wrote on 24th July 1846, to his friend Raj Narain Bose, in Calcutta, a zealous Brahmo, explains his attitude toward the society, to which the latter belonged. The letter runs thus:

"My Dear Raj Narain,—I cannot think much of the Vedantic movements here or elsewhere. Their followers merely temporise. They do not believe that the religion is from God, but will not say so to their countrymen who believe otherwise. Now, in my humble opinion, we should never preach doctrines as true in which we have no faith ourselves. I know that the subversion of idolatry is a consummation devoutly to be wished for; but I do not desire it to come about by employing wrong means. I do not allow the principle that means justify the end. Let us follow the right path, assured that it will ultimately promote the welfare of mankind. It can never do otherwise. I wish to request the Secretary of the *Tatwabodhini Sabha* to discontinue sending me the Society's paper [*Patrika*], as one cannot subscribe to it who is not a member of the Society. . . . I fear also that there is a spirit of hostility entertained by the Society against Christianity which is not credi-able. Our desire should be to see truth triumph. Let the votaries of all religions appeal to the reason of their fellow-creatures, and let him who has truth on his side prevail."

Though Mr Lahiri did not join the Brahmo Samaj, yet his appearance among the educated people of Krishnagar, and the healthy influence he exerted on them, infused into them new and noble sentiments. He had learnt from his teacher, Mr Derozio, how to appreciate truth. He had learnt from him, too, to respect freedom in thought and action; and, like him, he encouraged his pupils, whether in the class-room or out of it, to discuss freely the various topics he suggested. He had a regard for everyone's opinions; and was never ashamed to acknowledge it if his own judgment on any occasion seemed to him to be wrong. To the end of his life he sincerely believed that he might learn something from even the youngest. He was old enough to be our father, but he paid heed to our opinions out of the belief that God reveals His truth to "babes and sucklings." And great was his delight if he heard anything from our lips worthy of his approval. The young men of Krishnagar learnt from him to think freely, to discuss freely, and to act freely.

Now, at this time, a new subject came under discussion in Krishnagar—the remarriage of Hindu widows. Many believe that Ishwar Chandra Vidyasagara was the originator of this movement; but it was not so. Mr Derozio's pupils, in *The Bengal Spectator*, which they edited, had taken up the cause of Hindu widows, and ventilated the question of their taking, of course under particular circumstances, a second husband after the death of the first, and Pandit Ishwar Chandra Vidyasagara took his cue from them. The references to the sayings of the sage Purrashur, quoted by the latter as sanctioning widow remarriage, had first appeared in *The Bengal Spectator*. From its pages this important social question caught the attention of the public. Raja Siris Chandra entered into a discussion on it with the pandits of Nadia; and it was expected that he might do something in the noble cause. But the following unforeseen occurrences damped the Raja's enthusiasm, and he had to give it up.

Raja Siris Chandra was about to have the remarriage of widows sanctioned by the pandits, when the young reformers in the city held a meeting on the subject, on the premises of the college, and, after talking themselves hoarse on the pernicious customs of Hindu society, bound themselves by a solemn oath to fight on behalf of the widows of their country. They did not know the weapons their enemies were preparing to use against them. The latter spread a rumour that the college students had in the meeting butchered a cow, feasted on its meat, and made themselves drunk with wine. The rumour seriously compromised the young men themselves, the cause of widow marriage, and the college too. Many, regarding the college as a hot-bed of heterodoxy, withdrew their sons from it, and it would have suffered much but for the protecting hand of the Raja. The young men also got off unharmed, for the same hand was stretched out to screen them; but the question of widow marriage, being associated with their late alleged revelries, was looked at with suspicion by the pandits; so that the Raja Siris Chandra, afraid of incurring their displeasure, no longer sought their help in the movement.

Another incident had happened just before the above-mentioned meeting in the college, which brought upon Babu Ramtanu and his associates the stigma of beefeaters. Babu Kartik Chandra Roy writes thus about it:

"A friend of ours, Babu Kali Krishna Mitra, came to us from Calcutta. To do honour to him, Ramtanu Babu, his brothers, myself, and about ten others had a picnic at Anandabagh, a garden about three miles from our house. On our return from there we talked about widow marriage, and every one of us signed a bond to the effect that we would be its champion. The next day some malicious characters spread the false report that a calf's head, severed from the body, was lying hid under a stack of bricks near our house. It was then followed by the cry that So-and-so had lost his calf; and on the following day the alleged calf's head, and the loss of the calf, were explained by the bold assertion of our enemies that we had feasted on the calf at our picnic."

We have subsequently heard from some of our Krishnagar friends that the foundation on which the rumour was based was that the young men had killed a goat, and had left it for some time hanging from the branch of a tree. A good neighbour saw this, and hastened home to tell his friends that the Lahiris had killed a calf. His story got additions and exaggerations, till Ramtanu Babu and his companions in the picnic were branded as cow-killing beefeaters.

The events narrated above took place either at the end of 1850 or at the beginning of 1851; and they made Krishnagar too hot for Ramtanu. Unfounded public scandal, together with the grief it caused his father and friends, made him desirous of obtaining a transfer to another sphere of work. And this desire ripened into a resolution when, on the death of his first-born child, the neighbours cast in his wife's teeth that, in taking away his son, the gods had punished the father for the sin of beef-eating. He applied for a transfer, and was appointed headmaster of the Burdwan School in April 1851, on a salary of 150 rupees a month.

While Krishnagar was full of the agitations described above, measures were being taken in Calcutta by reformers to promote female education. Mr Drinkwater Bethune, President of the Education Council, and legal member of the Governor-General's Council, with the assistance of Pandit Ishwar Chandra Vidyasagara and Madan Mohan Tarkalankar, and with the approval of the Indian gentlemen of Calcutta educated in English, founded, on the 7th of May 1849, the girls' school, now raised to a college, which stills bears his name. Hare had been the friend of boys, Bethune was the friend of girls. When he visited the school—and this he did every day—he brought presents for the pupils. He often invited them to his house and gave them toys, sweetmeats, and valuable articles of dress. He was fond of frolics too, and sometimes, imitating a high-mettled horse, he trotted about with a Bengali girl, transformed into a Miss Sahib, on his back.

But the foundation of Bethune's School was not the first move towards female education. Similar endeavours had been made long before. As early as 1817 the School Society took up the question, and at the suggestion of Radhakanta Deb succeeded in getting the doors of its *patshalas* opened to boys and girls alike. This plan, after two years, appeared faulty to some of the members of the society, and the discussions on the point attracted, in 1819, the attention of a Baptist missionary, who made an appeal to the public on the lamentable ignorance of

Hindu ladies, and pointed out the desirability, nay, the urgent necessity, of giving the girls a decent education. The appeal was responded to by the European ladies belonging to Messrs Lawson and Pearce's Seminary, who, after mature deliberation, formed the "Female Juvenile Society," with the object of placing within the reach of their Hindu sisters the blessings of education. The members of the Female Juvenile Society, with the assistance of Raja Radhakanta Deb, established many girls' schools in Calcutta, and at their instance the British and Foreign School Society sent Miss Cooke, a lady of great attainments, to India, with the idea that she might take the lead in this new and difficult undertaking. She arrived here in November 1821, but unfortunately she had at first to meet with a rebuff. The School Society, now torn by factions, refused to support her, and she would probably have had to return home had not the Church Missionary Society in Calcutta received her with open arms, and promised to pay all her charges. Under this society she began in earnest her work among the benighted women of our country. In a short time ten schools were opened in Calcutta alone, and the number of girls attending them was 277. Miss Cooke soon became Mrs Wilson, and though in this changed position she could not devote so much time as before to the work for which she had left home and its dear associations, yet she remained as zealous a worker as ever.

Immediately after Miss Cooke's marriage some of the English ladies of Calcutta, under the auspices of Lady Amherst, established the "Bengal Ladies' Society," with the intention of forwarding the cause of female education in India. The society went on establishing schools in different places. It laid the foundation of a very large schoolhouse in the centre of Calcutta. Besides that

KALICHARAN GHOSH.

there were its girls' shools at Serampore, Burdwan, Kalna, and Katwa, and in Krishnagar, Dacca, Bakarganj, Murshidabad, Birbhum, and Chittagong. The schools in the *Mufasal* were nineteen in number, and the average attendance is said to have been 450. There is one noteworthy circumstance to be mentioned concerning these institutions. They were under Christian influence, and in them the preaching of the doctrines of Christianity went on along with the imparting of secular instruction.

The aim of the Bethune School was not to forward the cause of any particular religion. Its chief object was to train up girls in useful branches of knowledge so that they might discharge their various duties to themselves and to others, and that in future they might understand and meet their responsibilities as daughters, wives, and mothers. But yet it had to meet with a fierce opposition from the hands of prejudice. Though men like Madan Mohan Tarkalankar, Debendranath Tagore, Ram Gopal Ghosh, and others, sent their girls to it, yet the Hindu society at large, consisting mostly of the illiterate and superstitious, denounced it, saying that the education of women would cause a complete revolution, and that it would be impossible in any way to utilise the book-learned girls in the future who, instead of attending to domestic duties themselves, would assume the airs of "mem-sahibs," and fag their husbands to death.

It is, however, needless to say that the educated in the native community were unanimous in their gratitude to Mr Bethune for the establishment of the school. They loved him, too, and in the trying position in which he was soon to find himself he could count upon their love and friendship. That the heart of the educated native beat in unison with his was a sufficient comfort to him in the hour of his unpopularity with the majority of his countrymen in India. In the capacity of the Governor-General's legal counsellor he was called upon to prepare four drafts for the protection of natives from the lawless and flagrantly outrageous conduct of Englishmen in the *Mufasal*, nominally under the Supreme Court, but in reality answerable to no tribunal; for, as the law then stood, they were exempt from the jurisdiction of the district and subdivisional criminal courts. Cases against them could be brought before the Supreme Court, but the wronged had seldom the time and the means to seek redress there. He prepared the drafts, and thereby incurred the hatred of many Englishmen in Bengal, save a few officials of the East India Company. The drafts were as follows:—

1. Draft of an Act abolishing exemption from the jurisdiction of the East India Company's criminal courts.
2. Draft of an Act declaring the privileges of Her Majesty's European subjects.
3. Draft of an Act for the protection of medical officers.
4. Draft of an Act for trial by jury in the Company's territory.

As soon as these drafts were laid before the Governor-General's Council most of the Englishmen in India protested against them. They gave them the name of the "Black Acts," and spoke of the Governor General, Mr Bethune, and the other members of the Council in bitter terms. The Anglo-Indian newspapers raised a cry. At length the opposers of the Bills held a large meeting, in which it was resolved to lay the matter before Parliament, and the sum of 36,000 rupees was raised to enable them to keep the opposition alive here as well as in England. There was no one among Indians ready to use his tongue or pen in favour of the proposed legislation save Ram

Gopal Ghosh. The reader will see by reference to the "Life of Ram Gopal," in the Appendix, his point of view.

Mr Bethune's antagonists in the end got the better of him. The authorities at home ordered that the proposed Bills should not be passed; and the Governor-General was compelled to abide by their wishes. Mr Bethune, through excessive labour and anxiety, soon fell ill, and died on the 12th of August 1851. The success induced imitation, but on better lines and in a better cause. The educated gentlemen of Bengal resolved to combine, in order to criticise the measures of the Government, and to offer united representations to the authorities on all matters of importance. The organisation of a select body for the purpose was at once taken in hand. There were already the "Bengal Landowners' Association," consisting chiefly of the wealthy Zemindars of Calcutta, and the "Bengal British India Society"; and it was thought advisable that the two should be amalgamated. The desired amalgamation took place, and there rose into existence "The British Indian Association." That it was from the first a strong organisation is evident from the names of the members who formed the first committee. The names are as follows:—

Raja Radhakanta Deb, President.
 „ Kali Krishna Deb, Vice-president.
 „ Satyanarain Charan Ghosal.
Babu Hara Kumar Tagore.
 „ Romanath Tagore.
 „ Jai Krishna Mukerji.
 „ Ashutosh Deb.
 „ Hari Mohan Sen.
 „ Ram Gopal Ghosh.
 „ Umesh Chandra Datta.

Babu Krishna Kesor Ghosh.
,, Jagadananda Mukerji.
,, Peari Chand Mitra.
,, Shambhunath Pandit.
,, Debendranath Tagore, Secretary.
,, (afterwards Raja) Digambar Mitra, Assistant Secretary.

The British Indian Association proved a mighty lever in raising the social and political importance of Bengal. Its power was felt as soon as it was organised. Government was impressed with the fact that Indian gentlemen, of the highest rank in society, had united to make their wants known to their rulers, and to defend the rights of the people, and that it could no longer trifle with the feelings of their subjects. These in their turn perceived that they had a strong force to fight for them. So it may with truth be said that every class of men in Calcutta watched the work of the association with keen interest and hopeful hearts. None had ever before this stood by the poor and the oppressed, but now there was a powerful body to advocate their cause. The British Indian Association was formed on 31st October 1851.

We now return to our hero. We have seen that he was transferred from Krishnagar to Burdwan in April 1851. Here the hand of persecution was raised against him for his having cast off the Brahmanical thread. The orthodox Hindus hated him for this, and pronounced him an outcast. They succeeded in depriving him of the services of the washerman and the barber. He could not find even one from the lowest castes to do the menial work of the house. He himself had to shop, cut wood for fuel, and do other work of the kind, and his wife had to cook, clean the utensils, and sweep the house. He bore these privations

RAJA DIGAMBAR MITRA, C.S.I.
1817–1879.

calmly as far as he himself was concerned, but his heart bled for his weak partner in life, who, in addition to these discomforts, had often to smart under the taunts of her ignorant neighbours.

The news that Ramtanu had rejected the sacred thread soon reached Krishnagar, and many a bigot would have been pleased to kindle the torch to burn him had he been present on the spot. In his absence, however, his old father had to suffer for him. Taunts, abuse, and threats were used to wean his heart from his son, but all was in vain. The pious old man did not lose his equanimity. He did not resent the ill-treatment he received from his neighbours, nor was he at all influenced against his son. The mental anguish he had to suffer he bore in silence. But his son was in his sight a heretic; and this thought caused him so much shame that he could hardly hold up his head in public. Nor did the son remain indifferent to the sufferings of the father. Though absent from his side he tried to comfort him as much as possible in the circumstances. In Ramtanu there was a conflict at the time between the desire to act up to his convictions and the wish to please his father, which almost rent his heart; and he was in after years often seen to weep like a child when speaking of the incidents of this terrible trial.

The reader may be curious to know under what impulse Mr Lahiri finally broke with Hinduism by renouncing the sacerdotal badge, and we can do no better than relate the two incidents which, happening one after the other, and acting conjointly, made him take so bold and decisive a step.

Once when he was performing his mother's *Shradh* in Krishnagar, in the style of a genuine Brahman, a boy, pointing at him with a finger of scorn, said, so as to be heard by him, "Ha! You say you do not believe in

Hinduism; but what is this? You are engaged in your mother's *Shradh*, with your *Paita* fully displayed! A real Brahman! A clever hand you are at hypocrisy, I see!" This taunt cut Ramtanu to the heart. He was forced to admit that the boy was right in his criticism; and from that time he thought seriously of casting off the Brahmanical thread. Then again, in October 1851, when, during the Puja holidays, he was on a pleasant voyage to Ghazipur, to meet his friend Ram Gopal there, this thought of his became matured into a determination; and the corresponding action followed instantaneously. The story runs thus. One day, when he and his friends were enjoying the savoury dishes cooked for them by the Muhammadan boatmen, one of the party humorously said: "See, we are eating the food cooked by a Muhammadan, yet we wear the *Paita*, the emblem of Brahmanical purity? What hypocrites we are!" The words, though used in a jesting spirit, entered deep into Ramtanu's heart; and then and there he renounced the *Paita* for good.

Mr Lahiri remained in Burdwan only for a year. In 1852 he came to Uttarpara as headmaster of the English School there, where he worked till 1856. His son, Navakumar, was about two years old when he left Burdwan. His daughters, Lilavati and Indumati, were born at Uttarpara, Falgoon, in 1854 and in 1855.

He was an outcast here also; but through the assistance of his Calcutta friends he got on pretty comfortably, in spite of the persecution to which he was subject. Pandit Ishwar Chandra Vidyasagara sent him servant after servant. While here, he was advised by some of his friends to escape further persecution by taking again the Brahmanical thread; but he was determined not to yield. He said, "What I have done I have done."

At the end of 1853, or the beginning of 1854, the

Rajendra Datta.
1818-1889.

Hindu Metropolitan College was founded in Calcutta. It was set up with the object of injuring the Hindu College, the authorities of the latter having given umbrage to certain Hindu gentlemen of Calcutta by taking in as a pupil the son of a certain harlot, Hira Bulbul by name. Captain D. L. Richardson, no longer in Government service, was employed as principal of the new college in the palatial house of Babu Gopal Mullick at Sanduriapatty. The institution, under the able management of Babu Rajendral Datta of Bowbazar, soon attained considerable efficiency; and Keshub (Kesava) Chandra Sen and several other men of eminence were students here in their boyhood. But it worked only for a few years, and then became one of the things of the past.

To one more point of public importance we think it well to refer before closing this chapter—that is, the inauguration of the new educational policy of Government in 1855. The Court of Directors in 1854 sent a despatch, said to have been drawn up by John Stuart Mill, with the following instructions:—"The Governor-General should see: (1) that a separate Department in the administration of the country be organised as the Education Department; (2) that a University be established in each of the Presidency cities; (3) that Normal Schools be set up where expedient; (4) that the already existing Government educational establishments be kept going, and fresh ones be added to their number; (5) that middle-class schools be founded all through the country; (6) that a sound education be given to the natives in their vernacular languages, and measures be taken to found schools for the purpose; (7) that Government aid be given to schools and colleges founded by private enterprise.

The instructions of the Court of Directors were carried out the same year. The new Education Department was established, with a Director of Public Instruction at its head, and a body of functionaries, called Inspectors of Schools, to help him. In different places Normal Schools to train teachers were established; and the country became studded with Government and Government-aided high, middle, and vernacular schools.

Amidst these changes and improvements, Babu Ramtanu passed his time at Uttarpara, zealously and conscientiously discharging his duties. He modelled many a mind afterwards noted for its intellectual and moral excellence. Those who had learnt at his feet here in youth, deeply impressed with the nobility of his character, and attracted by his winning manners, showed their esteem and love for him when he was no more in the world by putting up in the Uttarpara School a tablet with the following inscription:—

This tablet to the memory of Babu Ramtanu Lahiri
is put up by his surviving Uttarpara School pupils
as a token of the love, gratitude and veneration that he inspired in them while Headmaster of the Uttarpara School from 1852 to 1856 by his loving care and by his sound method of instruction, which aimed less at the mere imparting of knowledge than at that supreme end of all education, the healthy stimulation of the intellect, the emotions and the will of the pupil, and above all by the example of the noble life he led.

Born, December, 1813; died, August, 1898.

CHAPTER IX

EDUCATIONAL WORK AND REFORM

In the period at which we have arrived a man stepped forth into the field of action whose noble courage, strong will, independent spirit, moral rectitude, and universal philanthropy have made his name famous in India. This was Pandit Ishwar Chandra Vidyasagara, who, born in circumstances most adverse, attained the pinnacle of fame and power by dint of high talents, and by his unwearied exertions in every good and laudable cause. On leaving college he devoted himself chiefly to the improvement of Bengali literature, which up to this time had been a medley of several tongues. We intend giving a summary of this great man's life in the Appendix. At this time there happened an event which convulsed the whole of India. This was the Mutiny of 1857, the cause of which was the groundless rumour that the Company Sahib (the East India Company), to make the Sepoys Christian, had prepared for them greased cartridges, so that neither Hindus nor Muhammadans serving in the Army could keep their caste. The rumour had its rise at Dumdum, whence it spread like wild-fire.

It is not our purpose to give a detailed account of the Mutiny. It is enough for us to say that it did not remain confined within the North-Western Provinces, but spread into certain parts of Behar.

Calcutta had had no real danger to fear, but the people at times were panic-stricken.

The Mutiny was soon suppressed, and Delhi and Lucknow were again taken possession of; and at last the whole country was again at peace. The British Sovereign, Queen Victoria, took the government in her own hands. Meanwhile, a new power had manifested itself among the educated in Bengal—the power of the Native (or Indian) Press. A weekly journal in English, named *The Hindu Patriot*, had been started in 1853, by one Madhusudan Roy, in Calcutta. He, unable to manage it properly, after a year or two sold the paper and his own proprietary right to Babu Haris Chandra Mukerji, then one of the leading men in the city. He was a man of great talents, keen sagacity, and a dauntless heart; and, thus equipped, he entered upon the discussion of the politics of the day. He boldly protested against Lord Dalhousie's policy of annexation, and with equal boldness he supported Lord Canning in his Liberal views. He tried to convince Englishmen here and at home that the Mutiny had had its origin in some shallow-headed bigoted zealots; and that the people of India, as a whole, were loyal to the backbone. Canning, by following a lenient policy, had incurred the displeasure of some of his countrymen, who even went so far as to recommend his being called upon to resign; and to combat his antagonists he often fell back upon the columns of *The Hindu Patriot*, the chief exponent of public opinion then in the country.

In *The Hindu Patriot* Haris Chandra Mukerji stoutly vindicated the cause of the ryots against the planters, at the time of the *Nil Darpan* troubles, and it was one of the results of his championship, that the Government appointed the "Indigo Commission," in 1860, to go round and collect evidence on the indigo question. Babu Haris Chandra gave his evidence in such terms as greatly to annoy some of the planters, and one of them brought a case of libel against him in the Supreme Court. The prosecution fell through, because the accused, living at Bhowanipur, was not under the jurisdiction of the Court. But the worry and anxiety attending it told so much on the already overworked constitution of Haris that he died, in June, 1861, at the age of fifty-seven years.

A chain of important events in Bengal made the time from 1856 to 1861 ever memorable. These were the widow-marriage agitation, the Mutiny, the indigo disturbances, the striking career of Haris Chandra Mukerji as a patriot and journalist, the rising of the vernacular paper *Som Prakas* into eminence, the starting of Bengali theatres, the fame and decline of the Bengali poet, Ishwar Chandra Gupta, the rise of Michael Madhu Sudham Dutt as the leading poet of Bengal, and, last but not least, Kesava Chandra Sen's joining the Brahmo Samaj and, in doing so, communicating to it a new force. Each of these events created a sensation throughout Bengal, and the circumstances in connection with each are worthy of our notice here. In the meantime let us say something about the growth of dramatic literature in Bengal. In the days when there was no drama in Bengali the educated Indian gentlemen of Calcutta used to attend the only English theatre in the city. But they soon felt the desirability of having actors from among themselves. Babu Prasanna Kumar Tagore once had the English translation of the *Uttararam Charita* played in his country house at Soorho, near Calcutta, by young Bengalis. In 1854 the Oriental Theatre was established, in which Indian actors played Shakespeare's *Macbeth* and other classical dramas. But the rich soon felt that such entertainments could not please the people in general, so one of them offered a prize for the best-written drama in Bengali, and the *Kulin Kuls Sharbassha Natak* was composed by Ram Narain Tarkaratna. Then followed

I

Sakuntala, in 1857, and then *Beni Shankar* and *Bikram Urbashi*, all these being translations from Sanskrit. They were played in several places, the house of Kali Prasanna Singha, the author of the last-named, being one of them.

It was at this time that through the joint exertions of Raja Protap Chandra, and Ishwar Chandra of Paikpara, and Maharaja Jotindra Mohan Tagore, that a Bengali theatre was inaugurated in the garden at Belgachia. It was here that Calcutta first came to know Mr Michael Madhu Sudhan Dutt, who, having returned from Madras in 1857, was working in the Calcutta Police Court. He was introduced to the patrons of the theatre, and he translated for them, in 1858, the *Ratna Vali Natak*, or the drama named *Ratna Vali*, after its heroine. Other works followed, which secured for him fame and popularity. Some there were, however, who, though quite fascinated by the flight of his genius, questioned the appropriateness of his versification. He was the first to use blank verse in Bengali poetry, and this offended their tastes, though there were others that lauded him for this innovation.

The rise of Mr Dutt at this particular time must be acknowledged to be a happy coincidence, following the decline of that witty poet of nature, Ishwar Chandra Gupta. The genius of Ishwar amused men much in the midst of the common surroundings of life, but that of Michael soared high and dealt with great and noble themes.

We now return to our hero Ramtanu. He was transferred from the Uttarpara School to that in Baraset in 1857, where he worked for about a year and a half; and where, being near to Calcutta, he could conveniently visit his friends and co-operate with them in their patriotic movements. The noble qualities of this good and great man were as conspicuous now as they had ever been before. He threw his heart and soul into his work. His great aim was to awaken in the minds of his pupils an earnest desire for knowledge, to help to the formation of good principles in them, and to excite in them a love of virtue. As for himself, he never spent a moment unprofitably. When free from school work he devoted himself to pursuits calculated to develop more fully his intellectual and moral faculties, among which were the study of botany in the flower garden and the laying-out of a piece of ground for horticultural purposes.

From Baraset Mr Lahiri was again sent to Krishnagar College in 1858. But he had another change of place soon. In 1859 he was appointed second master of the English School at Rassapagla, near Calcutta, established by the Government for the education of Tipu Sultan's descendants. While here he could very frequently call on his friend Ram Gopal, and others, and take part in their pursuits and enjoyments. He joined them in their literary labours, political agitations, and festive meetings.

Drinking wine, as we have said before, was the fashion of the day, and he relished this pleasure, though he was never known to go beyond the limits of moderation. Many a convivial gathering would have turned into a drinking-bout but for his presence. We have heard from his own lips that a circumstance happened at the time of which we are speaking which induced him to live as a teetotaller for years, till his health gave way, and he was, at the advice of doctors and friends, obliged to return to his former habit of drinking a glass or two of wine in the evening. One day a young relative of Ram Gopal, having drunk too much, lost all control over his own conduct and speech. This caused Ramtanu Babu to reflect on the bad and dangerous examples his friends and he were giving to the rising generation; and, addressing Babu Ram Gopal Ghosh, he said, "See, Ram Gopal, the boys are being spoilt by us. After what we have seen of your relative this evening let us resolve entirely to give up wine, so that we may not be stumbling-blocks to any." We do not know whether Ram Gopal Babu took this advice or not, but of this we are sure, that Ramtanu stuck to this resolution for a long time.

From Rassapagla Mr Lahiri was transferred to Barisal, as headmaster of the *Zila* School. Here he worked only for three months; but the impression he made on the minds of his pupils during this short time was as deep and lasting as if he had lived and worked among them for many years. He won their love and respect, and they used every evening to crowd around him, in spite of the opposition of their guardians, to discuss with him the questions of the day. Some of them are known now as men of distinction, and if anybody congratulates them on their success in life they invariably attribute everything they have to their great and venerable *Guru*, Ramtanu Lahiri.

Mr Lahiri came to the Krishnagar College for the third time in April 1861. He worked there till November 1865, when, his health failing, he applied for pension. Mr Alfred Smith, principal of the college, sent the application to the Director with the following remarks:—

"In parting with Babu Ramtanu Lahiri, I may be allowed to say that Government will lose the services of an educational officer than whom no one has discharged his public duties with greater fidelity, zeal, and devotion, or has laboured more assiduously and successfully for the moral elevation of his pupils."

The main secret of Ramtanu's remarkable success as a teacher was that his mind, instead of being stationary, was

SIR CHARLES CECIL STEVENS, K.C.S.I.
FORMERLY OFFICIATING LIEUTENANT-GOVERNOR OF BENGAL.

always learning; and every new truth he learnt was illustrated in all its bearings in the class-room.

Even when an octogenarian he would jump up with joy on hearing something new and interesting, stop the speaker, bring out his own memorandum-book, and then and there write down what he had heard. Knowledge from any source whatever was always prized by him. If a boy in his class ever pointed out any mistake of his, or suggested a better explanation of a passage than that which he had given, he, instead of being angry, as teachers generally are in such a case, gave calm attention to what the boy said, and was greatly delighted to have his own mistake corrected, or his faulty explanation superseded by a better one.

Here are some stories illustrating this admirable trait of his character. Without vouching for their truth, we give them just as we have heard them. Once Mr Lahiri, during his last connection with the Krishnagar College, was explaining a certain passage in the English text-book, when a boy, interrupting him, said, "Oh, sir, that isn't the correct meaning." To this Mr Lahiri replied, saying, "Well, what is your meaning?" At this the boy gave his explanation in such a satisfactory way that the master was quite delighted to hear him.

The second story more plainly shows Ramtanu Babu's modesty and desire to learn the truth. Once a boy doubted the correctness of his explanation of a certain passage. As he was sure on the point he explained it again, with illustrations to make it more lucid. But the boy's doubts were not removed. Then the modest teacher, having a fellow-teacher supposed to possess a very sound knowledge of English, Babu Umes Chandra Dutt, called him into the class-room, and said, "Will you please explain this passage to my boys?" and on Mr Dutt's explaining it he turned towards the boys, saying, "You see the meaning I gave to the passage was just the same as that given by Umes Babu [who subsequently became the Principal of the College, and still lives at Krishnagar]; but, as my knowledge of English is much inferior to his, I could not make myself as clear as he has done. There are very few Indians so learned in English as he."

Ramtanu was above the weakness of pretending to be omniscient. He had no false pride. If he did not understand a passage in the text-book he simply said so, and promised to be better informed the next day.

We must here notice the death of Mr Lahiri's father in 1857, and the birth of his second and third sons, Sharat Kumar and Basanta Kumar, in Bhadra, 1859, and in Magh, 1862, respectively. Babu Ram Krishna Lahiri had received a great shock from his son's renunciation of popular Hinduism, from which he never recovered, and to which he at last succumbed.

During Mr Lahiri's official career at Rassapagla, at Barisal, and for the third time at Krishnagar, four new forces came into existence in Bengal. These were, as mentioned before, the rise of Kesava Chandra Sen as a reformer, the appearance of Bankim Chandra in the field of Bengali fiction, of Dinabandhu Mitra as a dramatist, and of Dwarkanath Vidyabhusan as a journalist. These four men had a great hold on the people's hearts in Bengal. But the chief of them was Kesava Chandra. We will give a short account of the lives and doings of these great men in the Appendix; and so we will say no more about them at present.

Kesava Chandra Sen (Keshub Chundar Sen).

CHAPTER X

RETIREMENT IN KRISHNAGAR

MR LAHIRI's health had partially been injured at Barisal, but it became almost a wreck in 1862, while he was in Krishnagar. Malaria had got into his system; and to expel it he took a change, going with his family to Bali. On retiring from the service with a pension, in 1865, he went at first to Bhagalpur, for its healthy climate; and then, returning thence, settled in Krishnagar. Here, in February, 1868, his elder daughter, Lilavati, now grown up, was married to an assistant-surgeon, named Tarini Charan Bhaduri. The marriage was not celebrated with Hindu rites. The bride and bridegroom were united by the father of the former, who gave away his daughter, calling God to witness and bless the union. A large number of guests, consisting of all the European and Indian gentlemen of Krishnagar, and such great men as Kesava Chandra Sen and Pratap Chandra Mozumdar, were present on the occasion. The Roy brothers of Krishnagar, famous for their generosity, were in their relative's house, and took part in the preparations for the feast.

Mr Lahiri was greatly respected and loved, not only by his old pupils, but by all the common people too with whom he ever come into contact. The former loved and venerated him as a father: of these the late Kali Charan Ghosh was the foremost. What he did to show his devotion to his beloved teacher we will mention hereafter. There are many among them that learnt at his feet in youth, and who even now, when the old man is no more, are the best friends of his family, sympathising with them, and helping them in every way. Raja Peari Mohan Mukerji is one of these. But for his help, Sharat Kumar Lahiri, the second son of our hero, would never have prospered so well in his business.

The tablet in the Uttarpara School to commemorate Mr Lahiri owes its existence chiefly to the Raja. Happy the teacher who lives thus in the memory of his pupils; and happy are the pupils to retain in their hearts the image of their beloved instructor.

As to Mr Lahiri's hold on the hearts of the common people, we give below what we ourselves have personally witnessed. We were once on a visit to him in Krishnagar. Having spent the whole day with him, we were proceeding in the evening to another friend's house. When on the way we met some men belonging to the lower classes of society, who apparently were returning home from the bazaar. Curious to ascertain their opinion of the old man whom we so much revered, we entered into the following conversation.

We. Well, friends, do you live in Krishnagar?

People. Yes, sir, in a way—we live in the adjacent village.

We. Do you know Ramtanu Babu?

People. Whom?—our old Lahiri Babu? Who does not know him?

We. What kind of man is he?

People. Do you call him a man? He is a god.

We. How do you rank him among the gods who has cast off his Brahmanical threads, and eats fowls?

The men stared at me, and one of them said, "I see you do not belong to this part of the country, or you would not have spoken in this way. Casting off the thread and eating fowls are faults in others, but not in him. Whatever he does is good."

From the feelings of these illiterate people towards Mr Lahiri we can easily conjecture how greatly he was respected and loved by the educated portion of the Krishnagar community.

In August 1869 Mr Lahiri was blest with a grandchild: a son was born to Lilavati; and his *Annaprashan*, or the first putting of boiled rice into his mouth, was celebrated with great *éclat*.

About this time Ramtanu Babu was appointed guardian to the minors in the Mukerji family at Khetra Gobardanga. He was so well known for his high character and great abilities that the Government recommended him for this responsible post. We have already seen that wherever he went he did something worthy of being respectfully remembered, and this new place of his abode was not an exception. That he exercised a healthy influence on the minds of all classes of men there is apparent from the following lines quoted from the printed reports of the Khetra Brahmo Samaj :—"The well-known Babu Ramtanu Lahiri of Krishnagar was appointed by the Lieutenant-Governor as guardian to the minors in the family of the Zemindars of Gobardanga. During his stay here he was a great friend of a Brahmo youth of the Dutta family at Khetra, who found in him not only a wise adviser, but a ready helper too. It was a striking circumstance that an old and generally respected gentleman like Ramtanu Babu, setting at naught caste prejudices and all worldly distinctions, backed a young Brahmo in all his undertakings for the good of the village. Ramtanu's influence was felt by almost every villager. Those who never before came within the precincts of the Brahmo Samaj became its regular attendants at his exhortations. The long-standing breach between the orthodox Hindus and the Brahmos in the village was healed by him, a friend to both parties."

In 1869 Babu Ramtanu's connection with the Brahmos

and their Samaj became more intimate than before. The immediate cause of this was the marriage of Annadaini, the elder daughter of his departed cousin, Dwarkanath Lahiri, the genuine Christian, a short account of whom we gave at the close of the first chapter. She had after her father's death been living in Calcutta under Mr Lahiri's care, and as she had not embraced Christianity he gave her away in marriage to a Brahmo gentleman, named Haragopal Sirkar. Ramtanu visited Calcutta several times in 1869, and during these visits he came into a closer contact with the progressive Brahmos. In fact, there grew up an intimacy between him and them. We came to know him about this time. The first interview we had with him impressed us deeply with the loftiness of his sentiments, and this impression became stronger the more we knew him. Child-like simplicity was one of his characteristics. He was never sparing of praise or censure, as occasion required it. Whenever he found himself in the company of the Brahmos of Kesava Babu's school he would say to them, "Ah, if Ram Gopal and Rasik Krishna were alive now, I would place you before them as the fruit of their prayers for a band of real reformers."

We remember three incidents that happened at the time under review, which respectively show Mr Lahiri's unflinching resolution to glorify God at the sacrifice of everything personal, his dread of speaking God's name without due reverence, and the catholicity of his faith. To begin with the first. Immediately before Annadaini's marriage, we were asked by him to make a list of the intended guests. We did so; and on getting the list he added a few names, but struck off the name of one of the most respectable men in Calcutta, with whom he was very intimate, so much so that the two used to pass a few hours every day in each other's company. We were so surprised to see the name of such a great friend struck off that we could not help asking Ramtanu Babu the reason for it. But all he said was, "You need not know the reason, but please understand that I will on no account invite him to the wedding." We had, however, not to remain long in the dark. We heard from someone that the cause of this exclusion was the fear lest this gentleman should behave irreverently during the solemn marriage service, as he had once behaved at the wedding of one of the daughters of Debendranath Tagore—the irreverent behaviour on that occasion was that he did not join in the worship preceding the marriage, but remained smoking in a side room. Not to be able to invite this beloved friend on this joyous occasion caused Ramtanu sincere grief, but he would sooner a thousand times forgo the pleasure of his dearest friend's company rather than suffer his God to be insulted.

The second incident was as follows:—Once, a good singer being introduced to him when he was having his tea, he expressed a wish of hearing the man sing a Brahmo hymn. On this the latter commenced humming a tune by way of prelude. But he was too quick for Mr Lahiri, who had not finished drinking his tea, so he stopped the singer, saying, "Pray, sir, excuse me for a moment. I am not ready yet to hear my God praised." After this he had the tea-cup removed, and then, standing up with his chadar across his shoulders—the humblest and most devout attitude of an Indian when he approaches his Maker—he joined in the devotion with hearty sincerity. And this is the third incident. One day, while returning from his usual morning constitutional, he asked me if I would begin the day by calling on one of God's saints; and on my answering in the affirmative he took me to a Christian missionary living close by, whom he embraced most affectionately. I was quite moved at the sight of two of God's chosen people on earth making a mutual exchange of love and fellowship, which helped me in a great measure to realise the joyous meeting of God's children in heaven.

Thus we see that Mr Lahiri was not a sectarian. To him Godliness was Godliness, whether found in a Hindu, Brahmo, Christian, or Muhammadan. He was the friend of good men, no matter to what religion they belonged. It often happened that when, on hearing that he had come to Calcutta, we tried to discover where he was, we found him a guest in some Hindu, Brahmo or Christian house. He was at home wherever good or saintly conduct ruled.

In 1870 he had an addition to his family, by the birth of another son, whom he named Benoy Kumar. Another son had been born to him in 1866; but the child died in its infancy at Bhagalpur.

Every social reform, every movement tending to elevate life and morals, was countenanced by Mr Lahiri, and he zealously led the way in all endeavours for the welfare of India. Female emancipation was one of these. The progressive Brahmos began to fight for it in 1872, and Mr Lahiri backed them. It was during his attempt to break open the doors of the Zenana that he became first known to, and then familiar with, the late Sir John Budd Phear and his wife, two real friends of the women of India. But whilst he desired that ladies should mix freely in good society, he was very prudent in selecting the company in which they should move. He strongly disliked their associating with men unworthy of the privilege. Let us here relate an instance of this. Once he went to hear one of Kesava Chandra Sen's lectures in the Town Hall, with his nieces, and had them seated in the front. At this one of his old friends present there, whom we have often named, Peari Chand Mitra, sarcastically spoke thus to him, "Well done, old Ramtanu! You are greatly in-

Indumati Devi.

teresting the young men of Calcutta." Mr Lahiri bore the joke with his characteristic patience; but on his return home he said to me, "Peari evidently wished me to introduce him to the girls, but I thought his levity made him an unsuitable friend."

When the champions of women's liberty started the "Bangamohila School," or the school for Bengali ladies, Ramtanu Babu sent his second daughter, Indumati, there to receive her education. Miss Acroyd, subsequently Mrs Beveridge, who had come to this country to give education to the women at the request of Mr Manamohan Ghosh, whose guest she was, consented to superintend the working of the school. Mr Ghosh, as an inhabitant of Krishnagar, held Mr Lahiri in high esteem. Through him was the latter first introduced to Miss Acroyd. In time a great friendship grew up between Mr Lahiri and the lady; so much so that on the occasion of the misunderstanding that afterwards took place between her and Babu Kesava Chandra Sen he did not hesitate to speak to the latter very sharply.

Mr Lahiri was a great admirer of the feminine character. The ladies of the house where he used to stop while in Calcutta were very much attached him. They were always happy in his company; for it was his custom, after his short noonday rest, to get together all the ladies of the house in which he was guest for the time being and to be engaged with them in pleasant and instructive conversation. He would ask some one among them to read some portion of an interesting book; and was accustomed to use what was read as a text for an entertaining discourse. In this way the whole social and moral atmosphere of the house was benefited by his stay, even if only for a few days.

On the foundation of *Bharatasram*, or the "Indian Home," by Kesava Chandra Sen, Mr Lahiri sent two of his nieces there to make it their home. He himself would occasionally come to the "Home"; for he loved Kesava Babu as the son of his friend Peari Mohan Sen, and honoured him as a pious man. We remember many occasions when he was deeply impressed and quite transported by Kesava's eloquence in preaching. When any specially good and edifying words fell from the lips of the preacher Mr Lahiri, on quitting the hall of service, would, like a child, go about saying with great emotion, "Oh, what words of living truth come from Kesava!"

We have seen in Ramtanu the manifestation of no ordinary moral courage. It was this courage that bore him up in his many conflicts, social and religious. It gave him the pluck to be always frank and plain-spoken. No one, no matter how high his position might be, could do or say anything reprehensible in his presence without being instantly reproved by him. We have an example of this in the following anecdote:—One day he left the Brahmo "Home" with the intention of seeing a friend who was seriously ill. On his return from the visit some of the ladies of the "Home" crowded round him and asked many questions about the sufferer. One of them, hearing his name mentioned, burst forth into the exclamation, "What! You have been to visit a wretch like that? I never expected this." The lady's words jarred on the charitable feelings of Ramtanu. His friend, a retired Deputy Magistrate, had indeed been an ill liver in early manhood; but he had long learnt the error of his ways, and had been living a penitent, God-fearing life. So, irritated at the uncharitable remarks of the lady, Mr Lahiri said severely, "Madam, I know why you call my friend a wretch. But he is now quite changed. He has given his heart to God, and, even if it were not so, it would be wrong to revile him on his death-bed." Saying this, he went on recounting many instances of his friend's

Professor Peary Charan Sircar.
1823-1875.

fidelity to conscience and faithfulness to his Maker. As he finished recounting each instance he asked the lady, "Madam, could you have done so much?" Each time, she was compelled by conscience to answer, "No!" At length he concluded, "Look here, madam, we look at the dark side of our neighbour's character, and not at the bright. This is wrong. Man is frail, and so we should be judged as leniently as possible. Alas! it would be our ruin if God were as strict to mark, and severe to punish, our sins, as we are to notice the faults of our fellow-creatures."

Mr Lahiri passed his life in Calcutta happily. He enjoyed the companionship not only of the progressive Bramos, but of many highly cultured, educated, and public-spirited men also, who used to meet every evening at the house of Baba Kali Krishna Mitra of Baraset, then an invalid. One of these was the late Peari Charan Sarkar, who, after having held the headmastership of the Baraset Government School, and subsequently that of the Hare School in Calcutta, was at the time a professor in the Presidency College. Peari Babu has left an imperishable name in the social history of this country. The institutions that owed their existence chiefly to him were the Hindu Hostel, which has now been replaced by the Eden Hostel, the Girls' School at Chorbagan, and the first Temperance Society in India.

A man's happiness can never be uninterrupted in this world of suffering; and Mr Lahiri's comparatively smooth life at this time was ruffled by a circumstance the sad effects of which embittered the remaining days of his life This was the serious illness of his son, Navakumar, when he was well on the way to gain distinction as a medical student. The young man was attacked by phthisis, and as soon as his old father learnt this, while in Krishnagar, he hastened to Calcutta, and after consulting Dr Norman Chevers, Principal of the Medical College, had his son removed from his lodgings to Babu Kali Charan Ghosh's "Home." Every possible care was taken to obtain a speedy recovery, but no improvement was made. At length the patient was taken to Krishnagar, and Indumati left her studies and went home to nurse him. This change of scene, however, did no good to Navakumar, and the climate of Bhagalpur was next tried. Indumati was there too, to attend on her brother.

Troubles are said to have come in a chain; and such was the case in Ramtanu's family.

The master of the house had long been ailing. When in Calcutta before this he suffered from tertian fever, and had often to take to his bed. His daughter, Indumati, or one of his nieces, was always at his side reading something to him, or entertaining him by conversation. We remember an occurrence, at the time of which we are speaking, which showed that ill health had not in the least diminished the vigour and ardour of his soul. One day, when lying on his bed, he was hearing Annadaini read the *Dharmalata*, a Brahmo Bengali journal, and these words caught his ear: "There seems to be a close kinship between the passions; so that when we break the neck of one the others take fear and become weakened." Casting off his lethargy, he got up from the bed; and with great excitement praised the thought in the passage, and went on repeating every word in it a hundred times. He asked his daughter and nieces who had used these words, and on their being unable to tell him he sent for me, as I was then living in the house. On my appearance the passage was at his request read to me; and I was asked who had expressed the sublime truth in it. I said it was Kesava Chandra Sen. Language fails to picture the delight with which he heard this. He loved Kesava, and great was his pleasure to find that it was his favourite orator who had given expression to such a beautiful thought.

The change to Bhagalpur at first proved beneficial to Navakumar. He recovered sufficiently to begin practising as a doctor. So, when Sharat Kumar came to Bhagalpur in July 1875, to recruit his health, his elder brother could join Indumati in caring for him.

Mr Lahiri was now happily living with the rest of the family at Krishnagar. But a calamity, the like of which he had not yet had to cope with, soon overtook him. One day in November, the same year, a telegram announced to him that his son-in-law, Tarini Charan, had committed suicide. Navakumar and Indumati, being informed of this, came to Krishnagar, and took the family thence to Bhagalpur. But nothing could repair the loss they had sustained. Mr Lahiri in a short time returned home with his wife and children, leaving Navakumar and Indumati at Bhagalpur. The former soon had a relapse; and the treacherous disease that had so long been preying on his system manifested itself in its worst form. Indumati's devotion at this time was exemplary. Not to mention her denying herself every comfort while nursing her brother, she often had to fast for hours together, till at length her health gave way. In a short time she too was seized with consumption. We may well imagine the agony and grief of Mr Lahiri and his family when they received the terrible news that not only Navakumar, but Indumati also, were on the verge of the grave. They both were suffering from the same insidious disease, though in the one its fell work was slow, but not less sure, while in the other it progressed rapidly. In the middle of 1877 Mr Lahiri took both of them to Arrah for change. Here there was no sensible improvement. But at this time another dire calamity burst on the troubled family. Mr Lahiri's youngest daughter, a girl of about two years and a half, died of acute fever. Indu grew worse rapidly after the shock of this catastrophe. In a month the doctors gave her up; and she was brought back to Krishnagar, there to sleep her last sleep. The whole family, including Navakumar, at this time again returned to their paternal roof.

The anguish which now tore the mother's heart is beyond description. In addition to her mental sufferings she had, alone and unaided, to keep the house, besides nursing her dying children, so soon to pass beyond her care. It is a sad consolation to know that Navakumar and Indu, though knowing that their end must be approaching, were each most anxious for the other's comfort. Many a time was each heard to ask his or her parents to give greater attention to the other. The brother knew that he was the cause of his sister's untimely death; for if she had not undermined her health by incessantly watching by his sick-bed, and suffering so much privation, she might have had many years of life and its joys in store for her. And this thought made his heart bleed. He was unremitting in his inquiries about her, and in his prayers to his parents to look after her comforts. Indu, in response, put her brother's claims before her own. She, too, would ask her parents not to give so much time to her, but to attend to him whose life, she said, was much more valuable than hers. If Navakumar could have saved his sister's life, or even prolonged its span a little, by giving his life for her, he would gladly have done so. Nor would Indu have been less ready to sacrifice her own little remnant of life to snatch her brother from the jaws of death. But they were soon parted, to meet again in a land where there would be no separation. At length the 4th of December dawned, the last day of Indu's sojourn here. She wanted

Gangamati Devi.

to see her father, who was called in by Lilavati. Finding the dying girl in her last struggles he sat by her side; and by way of diverting her mind from her sufferings said, "Darling Indu, why did you send for me?" Indu opened her eyes and said, "Papa, sit by me. I am very restless." On this Ramtanu, lovingly taking one of the girl's hands in his, said, "Indu, we have done everything in our power; and do not know what more we can do for you. Pray to God that he may soon give you relief." Indu, putting her clasped hands on her bosom, and looking up, said, "My God, give me a speedy deliverance." Then looking at her father she said, "Farewell, papa." The father said, "Farewell, my darling"; and then Indu's spirit left its tenement of clay, and flew to its Maker.

It was while under the shadow of this trial that Mr Lahiri showed to the world of what stuff he was made. The fading away of a daughter like Indu from his sight rent his heart, but did not break his courage. When, at the moment of her daughter's death, the mother wept and bewailed her sad fate, as it was natural she should do, her husband bravely consoled her. He prayed her to trust in God. He said: "You are putting your wishes before God's. Bless His name that He, after giving our daughter a happy and peaceful deliverance from this world of suffering, has taken her into the home of peace. Do not lose the firmness of your mind. There is another child of ours, almost dying. We must devote ourselves to him. If you give way to grief in this way he will be neglected, and his life will be shortened. Come, let us go to him." Ramtanu indeed knew the Divine secret of resignation to the will of God, by which man can master his grief. He believed that to mourn for the departed was a weakness, and that it betokened a heart rebellious against God. I have heard from a friend that Mr Lahiri, shortly after

Indu's death, invited a number of his friends, of whom my informant was one, to assemble in worship in remembrance of her. In the middle of the service the afflicted father uttered the girl's name with a deep sob. He understood that he had betrayed a weakness; and so after service he spoke to his guests thus, "We say God is good; but our conduct hardly tallies with what we say. I just now showed unbelief in shedding tears for Indu. Why should I weep for her, when I remember that she is in His good keeping?"

Indu's death accelerated Navakumar's. From the moment of her death he never spoke another word. Every minute he thought of the sacrifices his sister had made for him. He was, as it were, stunned by grief, and then he would weep bitter tears of sorrow. Once a slip of paper with "Darling Sister," and one or two lines written below, was found on his bed. His grief was violent, and his shattered frame succumbed under its weight. On the 15th of September 1878 he left this world of sorrows to meet his dear sister beyond the valley of the shadow of death. And that was a day of despairing grief, never to be forgotten by the Lahiri family. But it was also a day, too, that called forth all Ramtanu's feelings of pious resignation. He showed a fortitude the like of which has seldom been known. When Navakumar's dead body was in the house, and the bereaved mother lying swooning and senseless by its side, the father was whispering words of kindly solace into the ears of one of Babu Kartik Chandra Roy's sons, who had been attached to the young man, and was bitterly mourning for him. At this very moment some young men arrived with whom Ramtanu had been accustomed to hold a religious service in his house on a certain day in the week, and this was the day for it. The young men had come in, not knowing the calamity that had befallen the inmates of the house. Mr Lahiri, seeing them step into the courtyard, ran up to them, and said, "I am sorry we cannot have the meeting here to-day. I made a mistake. I should have informed you of this before. Please excuse me." On their asking him the reason he said, "Navakumar is just dead. His body lies in yonder room. Don't go in, the sight will pain you." They were all amazed to hear this from a father whose son was lying lifeless at that moment, but this pious man knew how to gain the victory over grief. Hearing of Indumati's death I wrote a letter to him, blotted with many a tear, and expected that, in reply, he would give expression to thoughts of violent anguish. But I was wrong. The reply was thus worded:

"MY DEAR SHIBNATH,—Thank you for your grief at our loss. Let us unite in thanking God for His having given Indu a deliverance from her sufferings."

Another instance of his uncommon fortitude I mention here for the edification of the reader, that he may in this world of death and sorrow follow the footsteps of this great man. He had a friend at Bhagalpur to whom he regularly reported Indu's condition when she lay on her death-bed at Krishnagar. One day his report was thus worded, "You will be glad to know that Indumati has no more to suffer. She is quite happy now." The friend thought that by some unforeseen agency the girl had recovered. He was under this impression when the news of her death was brought him by some other person. Sages say that one should not shed tears for the departed; and Ramtanu did more than live up to this advice. He rejoiced in the sure conviction that the death of his dear departed children had made them partakers of the joys of heaven; and to lament their loss was in his opinion an unpardonable folly, combined with ingratitude of the blackest dye to the merciful Disposer of events. Actuated by this belief he would visit scenes of death and administer comfort to the bereaved.

I may mention an incident that occurred when I visited him one day in his lodgings in Calcutta, after the death of Navakumar and Indumati. I found him rather excited, and on my asking him the cause he said, "A few days ago a child in the adjacent house died, and since the occurrence my neighbours, male and female, have been lamenting their loss. I have been in there, and, calling the men to me, I have tried to console them. I have shown them that, as their dear one has been taken away from them by God for His good purposes, it is not right for them thus to lament their loss as those without hope. They reply by speaking of the transmigration of souls, and of the teachings of the Sastras; and so I have had to come away acknowledging my ignorance of these. Now, Shibnath, you know the Sastras, can you go and show the men from the teachings of their own sacred books that inordinate grief is a sin?" But I felt that it was useless to argue with them at such a time.

On the other hand, Mrs Lahiri was overwhelmed with grief at the loss of her dear children, and it became very painful for her to live any longer at the house in Krishnagar, where everything reminded her of them. So Mr Lahiri, giving up his guardianship of the young Raja, came to Calcutta in 1879, and took up his abode in a house at Champatola.

CHAPTER XI

RAMTANU'S LIFE IN CALCUTTA

RAMTANU'S pecuniary position now was not at all enviable. The drain on his purse during Navakumar's and Indu's illnesses had almost emptied it, and when there were no former savings for him to fall back upon the small pension of seventy-five rupees a month hardly enabled him to make both ends meet. But he was not helpless. Many a friend sympathised with him and came forward to relieve his wants. Among the first to do so was his old pupil, Kali Charan Ghosh, who had before this regularly aided him in various ways. Navakumar had been sent to Bhagalpur and Arrah at Kali Babu's cost; and this gentleman now hired the house for Mr Lahiri and his family at Champatola. Their daily wants, too, were largely provided for by him. We shall give some account of this benevolent friend in the Appendix.

Mr Lahiri's second son, Sharat Kumar, having read for the First Examination in Arts of the Calcutta University, thought at this time of giving up his studies and earning something for the family. This became the more necessary as business called Babu Kali Charan Ghosh away from Calcutta, and prevented him from supplying the wants of the Lahiri family as he had hitherto been accustomed to do. Pandit Ishwar Chandra Vidyasagar, to lighten to some extent Mr Lahiri's burden, appointed Sharat as the Librarian of the Metropolitan Institution. This gave the young man a good opportunity for increasing the stock of his knowledge from the rich library in his charge, and for fitting himself in this way for the battle of life.

One of the most important events in the history of the Brahmo Samaj at the time was the secession of the majority of its members from the communion of Kesava Chandra Sen. This was the immediate result of the latter having married his daughter to the Maharaja of Kuch Behar, in circumstances which occasioned much controversy. The Sadharan Brahmo Samaj was founded in 1878 as a consequence of this friction. Ramtanu was strongly opposed to the marriage.

He loved and practised truth in thought, word, and deed, and warmly deprecated the least violation of it. From the following dialogue between him and a visitor the reader will find that he was even over-scrupulous on this point:—

Visitor. Well, sir, you seem to be rather disturbed and excited in mind; may I know the cause of this excitement?

Mr Lahiri. For some time a thought has troubled me a good deal. I see our Brahman cook preparing for the sick members of our family dishes which his religion tells him not to touch, without the least reluctance. But I am afraid he makes a denial of all this when interrogated by the public. Don't you think that we are in a way teaching him falsehoods, and therefore murdering truth indirectly, and committing sin?

Visitor. Your fears are groundless. The public would not bother their heads with what your cook does in your house. And again, you can extricate yourself from this delicate position by dismissing the Brahman and employing a man of a lower caste as your cook.

Mr Lahiri. I have many times thought as much, but my wife does not like it.

There are several anecdotes current in Bengal as illustrating Ramtanu's uncommonly strict adherence to truth, even in small matters. We give two of them here. Once the servant who looked after Navakumar when he was a baby, finding him in a bad humour, tried to cure him of it by promising some sweetmeats. Mr Lahiri, overhearing the promise made, and wishing that it should be fulfilled, so that the boy might not learn to make false promises, ran up to the servant, and putting some pice in his hands said to him, "When you have promised to give my son sweatmeats you must buy some from the bazaar and redeem yonr word, or you would teach him to deal falsely."

Again, during his stay at Bhagalpur, Mr Lahiri, going to Babu Atul Chandra Mullick's house, saw that the servant of the latter had prepared a hooka for his master, and was about to place it before him; and that Atul Babu, seeing Mr Lahiri approach, beckoned the servant to remove it. This did not please the visitor; so, calling his friend aside, he said to him, "If smoking tobacco be a vice, and you do not dare indulge in it in my presence, do not smoke at all, but if otherwise you need not be ashamed of your hooka. You must not do anything on the sly. Your present conduct may be construed as an attempt to impose upon me."

Next let me give an anecdote which illustrates his regard for justice, and his readiness to acknowledge his own errors. One day, when working in the Krishnagar College, he found some money missing from his drawers. His suspicion fell on a servant named Madhu, and he communicated it to others, and began looking upon Madhu with distrust. The lost money, however, was discovered in a few days; so then Mr Lahiri, finding that he had wronged the servant by suspecting him of a crime he had never committed, made a public apology to him.

We now return to Sharat Kumar. The post of librarian failing to bring him enough income, he, in 1883, set himself up as a publisher and bookseller. He was backed in the business by an old pupil of his father, a well-to-do gentleman of Konnagar, Babu Khetra Mohan Bose. Sharat's business prospered; and the main secret of this was his father's name and influence. Hearing that the worthy son was working so hard to place his father beyond the reach of privation, people from all sides, acquaintances and strangers, gave him plenty of work. When he found, two years afterwards, that his connection with the Metropolitan Institution interfered with his duties in the publishing house, he took leave of Vidyasagara, with his consent and approval, not without expressions of deep thankfulness to his benefactor.

For want of sufficient funds young Sharat had at first taken Khetra Babu's nephew, Purna Chandra, as his partner, but in 1887 he was able to buy up Purna Babu's share, and to carry on the business as the sole proprietor.

From a pecuniary point of view Ramtanu's family fared well now. But the hand of death, which had snatched away two of its brightest jewels, was still heavy upon it His youngest son, Bijai, died on the 23rd of August 1885, at the age of fifteen, of malarious fever, at Krishnagar, where the family had gone for a change.

On Mr Lahiri's return to Calcutta, some friends, on a visit of condolence, said to him, "It is a sad thing, indeed, that so many of your children have died so early." He replied, "Why do you say so? Rather thank God that He has kept so many of my children alive. A wretched sinner, such as I am, can have no claims on Him, and I should have no right to murmur even if He were to deprive me of these also."

Time healed the wound inflicted by Bijai's death. Happier days were in store for the Lahiri family, and the auspicious marriage of young Sharat Kumar shortly followed. The marriage was in 1889 blessed with a daughter, and greatly did Mrs Lahiri rejoice in the birth of a grandchild. But by the Divine will she was not destined long to enjoy this happiness: she passed peacefully away only a fortnight after her granddaughter's birth.

The partner of his joys and sorrows, his helpmeet in this world of trouble, being no longer by his side, Ramtanu was utterly desolate. He resolved to devote the remainder of his life to meditation and prayer, so as to prepare for a peaceful end. But this was not to be, and many a sword was still to pierce his heart. The first wound he received was from the death of Vidyasagara, on 28th July 1891. Next came the death of his younger brother, Dr Kali Charan Lahiri, on the 7th of October in that year. Great was the blow he received from this; and we all feared that his shattered body would not withstand it. But he received it apparently unmoved. His heart was no doubt lacerated, but not a word of anguish escaped his lips. There was now the same calm resignation, the same trust in the Divine mercy that had made his heart proof against earlier griefs. He felt that the departure of his brother was a prelude to his own, and he awaited his end patiently.

The last and most overwhelming blow at length came from the death of his old pupil, friend, and benefactor, Kali Charan Ghosh, who all along loved him as his own son, and served him as a faithful servant. Ramtanu's soul after the departure of this dear friend must have yearned to follow him, and indications of speedy decay became apparent.

His son, Sharat Kumar, had, in the meantime, attained an ample competence in Calcutta. He had built for himself a fine house in Harrison Road, and there Mr Lahiri lived till his death, surrounded by all possible comforts. His sons, and his widowed daughter, Lilavati, were unremitting in their attentions to him. But the earth seemed to have lost all its attractions for him; and as a bird, in spite of its comforts in the cage, hankers after the companionship of its mate outside, so his soul, in the midst of the affectionate care of his children, longed to join his loved ones in the regions above.

Men are sometimes inclined, in advanced age, to complain of being neglected by their friends and relations, on imaginary grounds. But Ramtanu was not one of these. On the contrary, he feared lest his failure, through infirmity, to call on those who cared to see him might be construed into wilful neglect; and that was the reason why, even when it was not thought wise for him to quit the house, he tottered to the houses of his relatives and friends, to make kind inquiries about them. Let me give an instance in my own case. Pressure of business had once prevented me, for a few days, from calling on him. One day, however, I found time to seek his society. While at the threshold of his house I was rather abashed to make my appearance after such delay, and thought out a suitable apology; but as soon as I had made the customary obeisance to my *Guru* I found that I had been anticipated. He broke forth into words of self-accusation for having allowed so much time to pass without coming to our house. He said, "Oh, Shibnath, of what omissions of duty I have been guilty of late! The ladies of your family are so fond of me, and I have not been to see them for so long! You are always busy, and so you cannot be expected to come to see me. I should go to you." I was quite surprised to hear him talk in this strain. I had expected to be taxed with neglect, but instead of that he was making an apology for a fancied omission of duty. It is the sign of a lofty soul to overlook the shortcomings of others and to be over-strict in judging itself.

Mr Lahiri, even when almost bedridden, was not unmindful of the claims of his departed friends. As an instance, we may refer to the complaints he often made of nothing being done in honour of the memory of David Hare since he had been unable to take an active part in observing the anniversary of that great man's death. It was at length at Mr Lahiri's instance that Babu Umes Chandra Dutt, Principal of the City College, called a meeting, to be held in College Square on the 1st of June every year, to pay the tribute due to Hare's memory. To show his full sympathy with the movement, Ramtanu used to have himself carried in a palanquin to the meeting, where he showed himself absorbed in the contemplation of the virtues of the noble educationist and reformer in whose honour it had been convened.

In 1898 an accident happened which made Mr Lahiri quite helpless. By some means he chanced to fall out of bed, and his leg was broken. This made him quite helpless, and most probably accelerated his death. His mind became weak as well as his body, and his memory showed signs of failing him. The dire event, which we had for years dreaded, at length became a reality; and he passed away quietly on the 18th of August 1898.

When the news of his departure from this world spread

through the town people thronged to poor Sharat's house in Harrison Road. Its gates were crowded. Language fails to describe our feelings at the time, when we looked at that face, which had ever glowed with devotion, or flashed with anger at anything done or said amiss, now placid in death. A long funeral procession attended the remains on the road to the place of cremation; and all all along the route we continually heard the bystanders reverently say, "Alas! a saint has gone to his eternal rest."

In course of time his *Shradh* was performed by Sharat and Basanta according to the Brahmo ceremonial. Many friends were invited, among whom were Raja Peari Mohan Mukerji, Dr Mahendra Lal Sirkar, and Mr K. P. Gupta.

Thus closed this eventful life—a long life dedicated to the glory of its Maker, and to the service of the world at large. Ramtanu Lahiri has left an imperishable name in the annals of the world's moral heroes. His footsteps are worthy of being followed by all, and many a bruised heart will find a balm in the contemplation of his placid and resigned character. Even when removed beyond our ken, he tells us the blessedness of those who can trust in God and tutor their souls to a perfect submission to His will. May his sons, and all others that were under his influence, with God's help ever follow his bright example! It was not his to achieve any uncommon distinction in the rich and rugged domains of learning. He had neither the opportunity nor the desire to take any prominent part in the political arena. Wealth or power had no charms for him. But far better than all this, he had true manliness, a bold heart to fight for truth, a determination to advance the cause of virtue, and courage to repress everything that was immoral. He was a giant in true Godliness. He fulfilled his great mission, he fought the good fight, and is now in the enjoyment of his reward. May it be our lot to live and die like him, that so we may share with him that great reward in the eternal Hereafter! Amen.

APPENDIX I

NOTES BY SOME PUPILS AND FRIENDS

The following Note on the Life of Ramtanu Lahiri was drawn up by Babu Kshetra Mohan Basu, and is given here to illustrate the view taken of his life's work by his friends and pupils

1. Ramtanu Babu came to Uttarpara as headmaster of the school in 1852. He was forty years of age then, though he looked older. In 1856, to recruit his health, he took leave for a year, and went with his family in a boat to the north-west.

The Mutiny breaking out he had to return earlier than he had expected. In 1858 he was appointed first assistant-master in the Russa School, whence, after a few months, he was transferred to Barisal, as headmaster. After working here for about a year he next served as second master in the Krishnagar Collegiate School. But his health again gave way, and he had to take leave for two years and go to Bhagalpur again for a change. Thence he sent in his application for pension. His great desire was to pass his life in his newly-built house at Baludanga—a suburb of Krishnagar; but fate ruled otherwise. Owing to his children's death, and the prevalence of malarious fever there, he left the neighbourhood of Krishnagar for good. Calcutta became his last home.

2. On his appointment to the headmastership of the Uttarpara School he found a very valuable assistant in Dwarkanath Bhattacharjya, who resigned a higher class scholarship simply in order to serve under him. The two in a short time came to know the boys so well that they had the names of these, their fathers' names, and the places where they lived, at their fingers' ends.

To describe his method of teaching:

3. Ramtanu was always present in the playground, watching over the conduct of the boys, and sometimes acting as their umpire.

4. His presence among the boys signified a great deal. There were about 250 pupils, and all kept quiet when he made his appearance.

5. Hard work immediately after taking food being supposed to be injurious to the health, he made it a rule that during the first half-hour every day the boys should write copies. He, being an excellent writer himself, corrected these.

6. Then came the lessons in the text-books. Each boy was made to read aloud the lesson of the day till he got the proper pronunciation of every word and minded the stops. Mr Lahiri's custom was to read a passage to the boys so that they might catch the proper accents and sounds of words. Then, after they had read it to his satisfaction, there came an explanation, which from him was not merely a substitution of synonyms for the words in the text, but a full rendering of the passage read into plain language. Next followed a close questioning on the matter it contained, and answers were elicited from the boys in such a way as to impress on them the author's ideas; then, last of all, came such general information as each word in the text might suggest.

7. His chief object was to awaken in his pupils a love for knowledge, and to put them into the way of thinking for themselves. He took a pleasure in reading with them standard works in English poetry. He was always bright and buoyant when reciting selections from them.

8. Every pupil was made to feel that there was work for him to do, that his happiness as well as his duty lay in doing that work well. Hence an indescribable zest was communicated to a young man's feeling about life. A strange joy came over him on discovering that he had the means of being useful, and thus of being happy; and a deep respect and ardent attachment sprang up towards the tutor who had taught him thus to value life, his own self, and his work and mission in this world.

All this was founded on the breadth and comprehensiveness of Ramtanu's character, as well as on its striking truth and reality;

on the unfeigned regard he had for work of all kinds, and the sense he had of its value, both for the complex aggregate of society and for the growth and perfection of the individual. It would not be exaggerating Ramtanu's merits were we to call him the "Arnold of Bengal," a description often applied to him.

9. He was always lenient to his pupils. He felt their weaknesses, and tried his best to render them the required help.

10. It was he who opened our eyes to the sacred relation between the teacher and the taught, aud to the gravity of our position as students. It was while under his instruction that we learnt that all our future prospects depended on the way we worked during our school life.

11. There were many headmasters like him then, the foremost among whom were Babus Peari Charan Sirkar at Baraset; Ishwan Chandra Banerji in Hughli; Haragobinda Sen in Boalia, and Bhudeb Mukerji in Howrah. They were possibly of higher attainments than Ramtanu, but he was regarded as their superior in teaching capacity.

12. The great secret of this was that he studied hard to qualify himself as a teacher before he began to teach. He never came to the class unprepared. The acquisition of knowledge was his chief object in life, and as the profession of a teacher was best suited to promote it, he not only took to teaching for a time, but made it his chief and favourite work for life. Even after he had retired from the Government service he used to call boys, girls, men, and women around him, and impart to them instruction on useful topics.

13. The country then chiefly needed good teachers; and it was to supply this need that he refused to take more lucrative work, and became a schoolmaster.

14. Half-a-century ago he elaborated a system of education which, even yet, is not excelled in our Government institutions.

15. Ramtanu was of middle stature and well built. He was tolerably strong in youth. But anxiety, aided by the malaria that had given him fever, made him prematurely old. His portrait taken when he was a young man bears no resemblance to the original as seen in later life. His face as seen by us was oval,

while in the youthful picture it was long. The difference between his appearance in youth and that in age is very striking.

16. He was very careful of his health. He was extremely moderate in eating and drinking. Abstemiousness was the rule of his life, and to it he owed his longevity and the unimpaired soundness of the senses. He lived long, but did not lose a single tooth. The power of hearing remained uninjured to the last.

17. During his waking hours he never remained unemployed. From his diary we see that he spent his leisure hours in talking with friends, playing with little boys and girls, or feeding crows or sparrows with crumbs of bread. When ill-health prevented him from seeking these recreations he meditated on the happiness of those who had gone before him to a better world. Ram Gopal Ghosh was a beloved friend of his; and at Ram Gopal's death-bed he wept like a child. Rupik Krishna was another whose early death he bitterly lamented; and last, but not least, was Mr Derozio, whose memory he devoutly cherished till he drew his last breath.

18. Mr Lahiri was remarkably gifted with the power of recognising men and remembering their names. At one time two of his old pupils came to see him. He recognised their faces, but their names had slipped out of his memory. But when they had said that they were inhabitants of Barisal, and had read in the school there about twenty-seven years ago, his memory came to his help, and he could at once tell who they were, and all the particulars of their school life during his headmastership.

19. His countenance was always tranquil and cheerful. Many were his troubles, but none ever found his equanimity ruffled. Grief often upsets a man, but it was powerless in the case of Ramtanu. He wrote to me of the loss of Navakumar as if he had been giving me some intelligence in which he was not concerned. He simply said, "Poor Navakumar died yesterday."

20. English literature was his favourite study. When age and infirmity had deprived him of the power of reading he had the works he liked best read by one of his children or friends; and then if any passage especially caught his fancy he would have it reread several times, and admire it with childlike rapture, so great was his love for the grand and sublime.

21. One day, some months before his death, I found him rather melancholy. He did not give me that hearty reception which was his wont. Evidently weakness had got the better of him; so, to divert his mind, I repeated the first sentences of a famous speech on Liberty. It had the intended effect. It was a spark to set his thoughts on fire; and, repeating one or two sentences following, he again felt the natural ardour of his soul, and went on expatiating on the speaker's ideas. Thus the meeting ended, on that occasion, happily both for him and me.

22. I used often to call on Ramtanu Babu at his house at Baladanga, and was pleased to meet there with him also his brother, Dr Kali Charan Lahiri, and his cousin, Kartik Chandra Rai. They were both men of great talents and winning manners. The latter was a good musician.

23. Ramtanu belonged to no religious sect; but he was none the less a pious servant of God, glorifying Him in thought, word, and deed. He had no particular place or hour fixed for his devotional exercises. He, like the poet, said: "I lose myself in Him."

24. He had cast off the *Paita* (Brahmanical thread) before he came to Uttarpara, and had had to put up with much persecution. It was a great trial for him. On the one hand, there were the natural ties of affection and friendship, while on the other there was the sense of duty. The latter was victorious. Conscience got the better of his affections. It falls to the lot of few to fight a battle like this. "Do what is right, and leave the rest to God" was his favourite motto through life; and people first saw its effect in this bold step he took against priestcraft.

25. His life, to the superficial observer, was apparently a smooth current, silently and calmly moving towards its end; but who fully knows what agitations there were beneath the surface? This we can say, that, in spite of his many and great calamities, under the pressure of which many an ordinary mind might have given way, he maintained the peaceful tenor of his course, with a heart full of hope and joy, centred in his God.

26. This is but a poor sketch of his life. It is a matter of regret to me that I have been unable fully to realise how great he was, and that I cannot find language adequate to express a thousandth part even of that little which I have realised.

27. When our dear country shall be free from its superstitions and prejudices, when educated men here will be organised in a strong body to fight for what is right in religion and morals, we shall turn our eyes again, and to more purpose, upon this zealous and dauntless soldier of a forlorn hope, who waged against the conservatism of the old impossible world so fiery a battle—waged it till he fell—waged it with such sincerity and strength!

(Signed) KHETRA MOHAN BOSE.

CALCUTTA, 1310 (B.S.). 30*th Kartic*.

Notes by Ramendranath Chakravartti, on a meeting between Ramtanu Lahiri and Debendranath Tagore

We remember to have read that the Rishis of old used to hold fraternal meetings in some shade where congenial spirits happily interchanged their thoughts to mutual edification. We ever longed to witness a meeting of the kind in our days, though we feared that a thing such as this would never come to pass. At length it so happened that two of God's saints met before our eyes. They were Ramtanu Lahiri and Maharshi Debendranath Tagore, the former lying on his sick-bed, at the age of eighty-five, and the latter, five years his junior, seated by his side.

Making inquiries about Mr Lahiri's health, Debendranath said, "Dear Ramtanu, virtue protects the virtuous. You have so long fought for virtue that she has always been your friend." Now a little daughter of my friend Sharat Kumar Lahiri made her appearance, and her grandfather thus spoke to her, "Bow down to this friend of mine. We all honour him, for he holds his God in great honour." Both the gentlemen were old and infirm, and so their conversation ended here. At the time of bidding farewell, Maharshi Debendranath said, "One thought is uppermost in my mind and I cannot help giving expression to it. The saints are waiting for you in heaven, and as soon as you join them they will take you to the Supreme God." Ramtanu, whose feelings must have been overwrought at the time, with his usual simplicity said, "What can I say to this? I cannot find words to express my feelings." He then made an attempt to touch his friend's feet, by way of honouring him, but the latter, stopping him, took his hands between his own. At the time of the Maharshi's departure the ladies of the house made the due reverential obeisance to him, and thought themselves thrice blessed when he pronounced his parting benediction. If these two great hearts had thus met when in the vigour of manhood, and the flow of their thoughts and speech had not been interrupted by age and weakness, how much more material should we have had for our edification! The meeting of the two holy men had made Sharat's house a place of sanctity.

(Signed) RAMENDRANATH CHACKRABUTTY.

CALCUTTA, 1310 (B.S.). *3rd Magh.*

The late Professor Max Müller thus wrote of Ramtanu Lahiri in his "Auld Lang Syne" (second series):

"Ramtanu was born in 1813, and therefore must have been older than Debendranath Tagore, who is generally considered as the Nestor of the Brahmo Samaj. He was a pupil of David Hare, who had undertaken the philanthropic work of educating native youths; and after spending a few years at Hare's School he was admitted into the Hindu College at Calcutta, which was established in Calcutta in 1817 as the first fruit of the annual vote of £10,000 for educational purposes insisted on by the English Parliament. The teacher who chiefly influenced the young men was Mr Derozio, who, though branded by the clergy as an infidel, and as a devil of the Thomas Paine school, was worshipped by his pupils as the incarnation of goodness and kindness. It was Christian morality, as preached by Derozio, that appealed most strongly to the heart of Ramtanu and his fellow-pupils, many of whom, distinguished in later life, were the fathers and grandfathers of the present generation of Indian reformers. Ramtanu became a model among his friends in all matters relating to morality and conscience; penitence and sincerity being the watchwords of his early career, vice and hypocrisy the constant objects of his denunciation both among his equals and among those of higher rank and authority. Even the founder of the Brahmo Samaj did not escape his reproof, on account of what he considered want of moral courage to act up to his convictions. As to himself, he denounced caste as a great social and moral evil, and silent submission to superstitious customs as reprehensible weakness. In order to show those who denounced beef-eating as sinful, he and his friends would actually parade the streets with beef in their hands, inviting the people to take and eat it. The Brahmanical thread, which was retained by all the members of the Brahmo Samaj at late as 1861, was openly disregarded by him in 1851. And we must remember that, in those days, such open apostasy was almost a question of life or death; and that Rammohan Roy was in danger of assassination in the very streets of Calcutta. It is true that European officials respected and supported Ramtanu; but among his own countrymen he was despised and shunned. However, he continued his career undisturbed by friend or foe, and guided by his own conscience only. Poor as he was, he desired no more than to earn a small pittance as a teacher in public and private schools. Later in life he was attracted to the new Brahmo Samaj, and became a close friend of Keshub Chandra Sen. When he saw others who spent much time in prayer he considered them the most favoured of mortals, for, pure and conscientious as he was, he felt himself so sinful that he could but seldom utter a word or two in the spirit of what he considered true prayer before the eyes of the Lord. While cultivating his little garden he was found lost in devotion at the sight of a full-blown rose, and when singing a hymn in adoration of God his whole countenance seemed to beam with a heavenly light. One of his friends tells us that one morning early he rushed into his room like a madman, and dragged him out of bed, saying that when the whole of nature was ablaze with the light and fire of God's glory it was a shame to lie in bed. He took the sleeper to the next field, and, pointing to the rising sun and the beautiful trees and foliage, he recited with great rapture—what? Not a hymn from the Vedas, but some verses from Wordsworth. When his end approached, his friend, Debendranath Tagore, went to take leave of him, and when he left him he cried, 'Now the gates of heaven are open to you; and the gods are waiting with outstretched arms to receive you to the glorious regions.' Did the old Vedantist really say 'the gods'? I doubt it, unless he used the language of *Maya*, as we also do sometimes, knowing that his friend would interpret it in the right sense."

The remaining sentences of Professor Max Müller's *Note*, about half-a-dozen in number, do not refer to Ramtanu or his times, but are merely certain criticisms on the Vedantist's belief in the gods: and so we omit them here.

APPENDIX II

A short sketch of the lives of some of the leading men in Bengal, who have been introduced to the reader in the foregoing narrative as friends of Ramtanu Lahiri

1. RAJA RAMMOHAN ROY

1774-1833

THIS great social and religious reformer was born at Radhanagore. near Khanakul, in the Burdwan District, in 1774. After he had learned the rudiments of his mother tongue at the village *patshala,* he was sent by his father, Ramkant Roy, to Patna to learn Persian and Arabic, in which languages he attained great proficiency at the early age of sixteen or seventeen. It is said that in Patna he read through the Koran, which for the first time impressed him with the absurdity and sinfulness of idol worship, and that the result was the publishing by him of a pamphlet in Persian exposing the superstitions of Hinduism. This caused a breach between him and his father; and he went about as a traveller in the company of some ascetics. Having reached Thibet, he denounced the idolatry and superstition prevalent among the Buddhists there. This made the place too hot for him; and returning to India he went to Benares to learn Sanskrit. His object was fulfilled; and the very fact of his having attained a sound knowledge of the language of the gods softened his father's heart, and he invited him home. There he learnt English, and at the age of twenty-two entered Government service. Working in various lower capacities, he was promoted to the Sheristadarship or Dewanship of the Collector of Rungpore. His father was then alive, and quite happy in the prosperity of the son whom he had once turned out as an outcast. But Ramkant was not permitted long to enjoy this

Raja Ram Mohan Roy.
1772–1833.

happiness, for he died soon afterwards. For ten years more Rammohan worked under Government; and then in 1813 retired, with the title of Raja, to devote his whole time to the moral and religious regeneration of his country. He came to Calcutta, and permanently settled there in 1814. He had in the meantime written many books on Monotheism. While at Rungpore he had given publicity to his Theistic doctrines, and thus incurred the bitter hatred of a host of orthodox Hindus of rank and eminence. It was his favourite amusement while there to invite Hindu Pandits and Maulvies to his lodgings, almost every evening, to listen to their discussions, and then to express his own opinions.

In Calcutta he got a few adherents from among the thoughtful and intelligent; though there were some men there who joined him from the selfish motive of having their worldly interests promoted by so clever and businesslike a man as he. The Alm's Sobha, or the Association of Friends, was organised by him, in which the doctrines of Vedantism were expounded and discussed. Here is an anecdote illustrating Rammohan Roy's command of Vedic and Vedantic lore. One day in 1819 a Madrasi Pandit, Shubrahmanya Shastri, came to Calcutta and challenged him to a controversy, saying that, from the Vedas and Vedantas themselves, he would prove the reasonableness and the necessity of idol-worshipping. The challenge was accepted, and a day fixed for discussion. A vast meeting was held at the house of one Beharilal Choulay. Leaders of the Hindu Society, such as Radhakanta Deb, were present at the discussion; and Rammohan Roy expressed his views so convincingly that his antagonist had to acknowledge himself in the wrong.

The cause of Vedantic Monotheism became now stronger, and its advocate bolder. He founded the Brahmo Samaj for the worship of the one living and true God, and fearlessly declaimed against idolatry and superstition. But his attention was not monopolised by religious questions alone; he took a prominent part in the discussion of social matters as well.

In some of the preceding pages we have described how firm a stand he had made against *Sati*, and how he had done all in his power to promote a more liberal and enlightened system of education in this country. We described, too, what a bold front he had presented when his bigoted countrymen combined to persecute him. We followed him in his voyage to England; and, as we have said, he died at Bristol on the 27th of September 1833.

2. MAHARAJA SIR JATINDRA MOHAN TAGORE BAHADUR, K.C.S.I. (A PUPIL OF RAMTANU LAHIRI)

THERE is no name more familiar in Bengal, or for that matter in India, than that of Maharaja Sir Jatindra Mohan Tagore, the subject of this sketch. The Maharaja, who is the acknowledged head of the Tagore family, is the son of Hara Kumar Tagore, the eldest brother of the well-known Prasanna Kumar Tagore. The Maharaja was born in Calcutta, in the year 1831. In 1840 he married Srimati Troilukokali Devi, daughter of Babu Krishnamohan Mullick of Jagaddal, 24-Perganas. He is as sound a vernacular as he is an English scholar, and received his early English education in the Hindu College, where he studied till the age of seventeen, thereafter passing under the private tuition of Captain D. L. Richardson, the well-known scholar and poetical writer; the Rev. Dr Noah; Herman Geffroy (barrister), and other competent European educationists. The Tagore family has always been known for its devotion to Sanskrit learning, and the Maharaja is an accomplished student of that language. From an early period in life, it is said, the Maharaja displayed a marked taste for literary composition, both in English and the vernacular, and especially for poetry, as the verses contributed by him to the *Provakar* — then edited by the well-known Bengali poet, Isvarchandra Gupta—and to *The Literary Gazette* testify. His "Flight of Fancy"—which was printed strictly for private circulation, among friends only—contains verses written during his youthful days. Some of these pieces have received the special commendation of well-known European authorities.

Few men have done more to improve and raise the character of the native stage in Bengal than the Maharaja, who has spent large sums of money in this direction. His interest in the native drama has not been confined to a mere patronage, for he has contributed by his pen a number of Bengali dramas and farces, among which the *Bidya Sundar Natak* occupies a foremost place, and has long been considered one of the classical compositions of the day. His talents have also been conducive to the improvement of the orchestras, and have helped much in popularising Bengali drama in its modern form. In fact, the series of theatrical entertainments given at the Maharaja's residence in Calcutta in past years really paved the way for the establishment of public native theatres.

But vernacular literature and the improvement of the native stage are not the only subjects which have engrossed the Maharaja's attention, for he has lent his powerful influence, all through his busy and distinguished life, to raising the standard of Hindu society in Calcutta. He has always taken a deep thoughtful interest in the progress of the country, contributing to objects of public interest.

Maharaja Jatindra Mohan Tagore, who is at present one of the leading members of the native community of Calcutta, and is one of the largest Zemindars in these provinces, owning estates in eighteen different districts, came to the notice of the Government by his liberal treatment of his tenantry during the famine of 1866, by the interest he took in all movements affecting native interests, and by the assistance he rendered to Government in his capacity as Honorary Secretary to the British Indian Association. He has, in fact, from the commencement of his public career, been an active member of the British Indian Association, for, after filling for some time the office of Honorary Secretary, he was, in 1879, elected its President, an honour which has been conferred on him several times since. In 1870 the Maharaja was appointed a member of the Bengal Council, by Sir William Grey, and the services which he rendered in that capacity were so much appreciated that in the following year, when Sir George Campbell became Lieutenant-Governor of Bengal, he was nominated for a further term of membership, the high opinion entertained of him being thus expressed in a flattering letter :

"Belvedere, Alipore,
"*October 5th*, 1871.

"My dear Raja,—I hope you will allow me to nominate you for another term in the Bengal Legislative Council. Your high character and fair mode of dealing with all questions render your assistance especially valuable, and I have much confidence that you are a man not bound to class interests, but prepared to look to the good of the whole community, high and low alike.

"Believe me, very truly yours,
"(Signed) G. Campbell.

"Raja Jatindra Mohan Tagore, etc."

Giving expression to a strong recommendation of Sir William Grey, Jatindra Mohan Tagore received the title, on the 17th March 1871, of Raja Bahadur. Sir William Grey's recommendation was made in the following terms:—

"Babu Jatindra Mohan is a man of great enlightenment, and has had a thoroughly good English education. He is one of the leading members of the native community, is of unexceptionable private character, and is held by his fellow-countrymen in the highest respect. He is a useful member of the Council of the Lieutenant-Governor, and takes a deep interest in the progress of the country. He has estates in the districts of Midnapore, Faridpore, Murshidabad, Rajshahi, Nudea, and the 24-Perganas, and during his lifetime enjoys the revenue of the large estates of his uncle, the late Honourable Prasanna Kumar Tagore, in Rungpore and other places. He has always been found ready to contribute liberally to schools, roads, and other objects of public interest, both in Calcutta and in the districts in which his estates are situated, and has helped to promote science and literature amongst his countrymen by large contributions to that end. He regularly maintains eighteen poor students in Calcutta, and he fully accepted the obligation of his position in the famine of 1866, remitting the rents of his ryots, and feeding 250 paupers daily in Calcutta for a period of three months."

The ceremony of investiture was performed by Sir George Campbell, who thus addressed Raja Jatindra Mohan Tagore on the occasion:

"I have to convey to you the high honour which His Excellency the Viceroy, as the representative of Queen Victoria, has been pleased to confer on you. I feel a peculiar pleasure in being thus the channel of conveying this honour to you.

"You come from a family great in the annals of Calcutta—I may say great in the annals of the British Dominions in India—conspicuous for loyalty to the British Government and for acts of public beneficence.

"But it is not from consideration of your family alone the Viceroy has been pleased to confer the high honour upon you. You have proved yourself worthy of it by your own merits. Your great intelligence and ability, distinguished public spirit, high character, and the services you have rendered to the State deserve a fitting recognition.

"I have had the pleasure of receiving your assistance as a member of the Bengal Council, and can assure you that I highly appreciate the ability and information which you bring to bear upon its deliberations. Indeed, nothing can be more acceptable to me than advice from one like yourself. It is true we have had occasion to differ, and honest differences of opinion will always prevail between man and man; but, at the same time, I can honestly tell you that when we have been on the same side I have felt your support to be of the utmost value, and when you have chanced to be in opposition, yours has been intelligent, loyal, and courteous opposition."

In April 1871 Raja Jatindra Mohan was exempted from attendance in Civil Courts. Six years later—*i.e.* on the 1st January 1877—on the occasion of the assumption of the Imperial title by her late lamented Majesty Queen Victoria, Lord Lytton conferred on him the title of Maharaja, the *Sanad* of which was presented to him by Sir Ashley Eden at a Durbar at Belvedere, in which he occupied the place of honour, on 14th August following.

The Maharaja was first appointed a member of the Supreme Legislative Council in February 1871, and so valuable was the help rendered by him in its deliberations, especially in the description of the provisions of the Civil Procedure Code Bill, that he was reappointed in 1879, and in 1881, as a member of the Legislative Council of the Governor-General.

In the course of the debate on the above Bill, Sir A. Hobhouse, the legal Member of Council, said:

"Whatever can be said on that subject will be said by my friend, Maharaja Jatindra Mohan Tagore; for in committee he has supported the views of the objectors with great ability and acuteness, and, I must add, with equal feeling and moderation." And again: "If the clause stood as in Bill No. IV. I confess I should not be able to maintain my ground against such an argument as we have heard from my honourable friend, Maharaja Jatindra Mohan Tagore. I have shown that conviction in the most practical way, by succumbing to his arguments in committee, and voting with him on his proposal to alter No. IV."

The Maharaja had by this time become a "power in the land," which he continues to be to this day, and there was scarcely a subject of public importance in which he did not take part, or upon which his advice and opinion were not sought. The Maharaja Bahadur was elected, by the unanimous voice of the European and native community of Calcutta, the President of the Reception Committee for the entertainment given to His Royal Highness Prince Albert Victor, during his visit to Calcutta. Honours thoroughly well deserved also commenced to fall on him fast. He was, in quick succession, created in 1880 a Companion of the Most Exalted Order of the Star of India. On the 1st of February 1890 the title of Maharaja Bahadur was conferred on him, as a personal distinction, and at the Durbar held at Belvedere, Sir Stuart Baily formally invested him with the new title, and presented him with a jewelled sword as a *khillat*. In 1891 the title of Maharaja was, in the Foreign Department notification, declared to be hereditary, and in 1892 the Maharaja Bahadur was formally invested with the hereditary title of Maharaja at a Durbar held in Belvedere, when a jewelled *peshkach*, as a *khillat*, was presented to him by Sir Charles Elliott.

The Maharaja was a Justice of the Peace for the town of Calcutta; he is a Fellow of the Calcutta University; was Trustee of the Indian Museum (of which he was elected President in the year 1882); is one of the Governors of the Mayo Hospital; a member of the Asiatic Society, and a member of Committee and one of the Trustees of the Central Dufferin Fund. He was Vice-

President of the Faculty of Arts in 1881-82. In 1882 he was elected President of the Faculty of Arts of the Calcutta University and of the Indian Museum, and was appointed by the Government of India to be a member of the Education Commission. He took a most active part in the discussion which preceded the Bengal Rent Bill of 1885. He has, besides, held, and continues to hold, many offices of trust and distinction. One of the wealthiest landowners of Bengal, he has been a liberal donor and subscriber to numerous works of public utility, among which may be mentioned the free gift to the trustees of his interest in the land on which the Mayo Hospital at Pathuriaghatta is built. He has also subscribed liberally towards the cause of native education, not only in Calcutta, but in Bengal generally, several scholarships being founded to perpetuate the names of his distinguished father and uncle. He presented to the Calcutta University the marble statue of his uncle, the Honourable Prasanna Kumar Tagore, which is placed in the portico of the Senate House. Jointly with his brother, the Raja Sir Sourindra Mohan Tagore, he presented a piece of land to the Municipality of Calcutta for the construction of a square (to be named after his father), in which he has, at his own expense, placed a marble bust of his father. He has also founded, in memory of his mother, an endowment for the benefit of the Hindu widows of one *lakh* of rupees, under the name of the "Maharajmata Sivasundari Devi Hindu Widow Fund." In 1893 the Maharaja Bahadur was appointed to be a member of the committee to inquire into the working of the Jury System.

In the debate in the House of Lords on the Indian Import Duties, on the 20th July 1894, Lord Roberts of Kandahar, in quoting a letter he had received from Maharaja Sir Jatindra Mohan Tagore, declared that "there was no more loyal subject or enlightened gentleman in Her Majesty's Dominions." He is a man of mild disposition, but extremely independent in his views and liberal in thought. The late Sir Richard Temple said of him that "he combined the polished politeness of the old school of native with the educational accomplishments of the new," without the forwardness and self-assertion which sometimes characterises the latter.

A devout Hindu, a man of cultured tastes and polished manners, the Maharaja is universally popular, and is ever ready to assist in every good movement. He is a well-known social entertainer, and no one of distinction, either European or native, has ever passed through Calcutta without participating in his refined and cultivated hospitality. His recreations are mainly literary pursuits and musical entertainments, both vocal and instrumental, for which purpose he employs about a dozen musicians in his establishment. The Maharaja's library is one of the most complete private collections in India; while his art gallery contains many fine pictures, including some genuine "Old Masters." Latterly, owing to advancing years, he has not been very much in evidence, but he still takes a keen interest in all public movements of the day.

The Maharaja Bahadur, who has adopted his nephew, had four daughters, of whom only one is now living. He has five grandsons—namely, Babu Kumudprakash Gangoli, Babu Nalinprakash Gongoli, Babu Jaladhi Chandra Mukerji, Babu Kiranmali Mukerji and Babu Sheshprakash Gangoli, of whom Babu Nalinprakash and Jaladhi Chandra went to England, in company with the Maharaj-Kumar, on the occasion of the coronation of H.M. King Edward VII.

3. RAJA SIR RADHAKANTA DEB, BAHADUR, K.C.S.I.

1784-1867

THIS Indian grandee, the grandson of the famous Maharaja Nava Krishna Deb, Lord Clive's Persian secretary, was born in March 1784. He received his English education at the Calcutta Academy, a private school, and learnt Sanskrit and Persian at home under Pandits and Maulvies. He was a lover of learning, and encouraged the study of English and Sanskrit literatures. He was the first Hindu to take up the cause of female education. He made himself famous as the author of the Sanskrit dictionary, "Subdakalpdrum," for which the learned societies of Europe conferred titles and honours on him, and Her Majesty the Queen awarded him a gold medal. He also took part in politics.

In religion he was a bigoted Hindu—a strong supporter of the many prejudices and superstitions of his country. It was he who opposed—though in vain—the abolition of *Sati*, the suppression of polygamy, and the passing of the *lex loci* (the law conferring on native Christian converts the right of inheritance when their fathers died intestate).

He stood foremost in almost all educational movements. He was a director of the Hindu College and secretary to the School Society.

He was an Honorary Magistrate and a Justice of the Peace in 1855, and President of the British Indian Association from 1851 to his death.

The Government honoured him with the title, Raja Bahadur, in 1837; and he was the first Bengali gentleman that was invested with the title and decoration of the Star of India. He died on the 19th of April 1867, at the age of eighty-three.

4. DWARKANATH TAGORE

1794-1846

Dwarkanath was born in 1794. During his boyhood he was educated in English in Mr Sherbourne's school; and he also acquired a good knowledge of Persian and Arabic. When a young man he read law with a barrister named Fergusson; and thus learnt Court business. Trading in indigo for some time, and not finding the business sufficiently lucrative, he left it when an opportunity for bettering his circumstances presented itself. Mr Plowden, then the salt agent, appointed him as his Dewan. After a few years' service he returned, having saved money enough to start a mercantile firm, under the name of Carr, Tagore & Co. Besides that, he became the chief manager of a bank called the "Union Bank." He was well known for his generosity and other qualities of the kind. He was very successful in making money, and was noted for his munificence. He soon became one of the wealthiest citizens of Calcutta, and the right hand of Rammohan Roy in all works of public utility. On his return from England, in 1842, he refused to perform the expiatory rite of *Prayaschitra*. He made two voyages to England, where he died, in 1846.

5. RAMKAMAL SEN

1783-1844

RAMKAMAL SEN was Babu Keshub (Kesava) Chandra Sen's grandfather. He was born at Goriffa, a village near Hughli, in 1783. When seven years old he came to Calcutta for his education. But through lack of means he had to leave his studies rather early, and get into the way of earning something for himself. He worked for several years in a Hindustani press, after which he was appointed as a clerk in the Asiatic Society. But the posts which brought him wealth, rank, and honour, were the Dewani of the Mint, and the treasurership of the Bengal Bank. He joined in almost every endeavour for public good. He was a member of the Hindu College Committee, and the superintendent of the newly-established Sanskrit College. He was a member of the Medical Commission appointed by Lord William Bentinck. He compiled a very comprehensive English and Bengali dictionary. He died in 1844.

6. MATI LAL SEAL

1791-1854

MATI LAL SEAL, the founder and patron of the institution called Seal's Free College, was born at Colootola in Calcutta in the year 1791, and his position in society by birth was humble. But vast wealth, acquired solely by his own exertions, and the application of a considerable portion of it to charitable purposes, challenged the respect of all, the proud Kulin Brahman not excepted. His father, a dealer in cloth, died, leaving Mati Lal, then a boy of five years old, comparatively destitute. So the boy could get no better education than that available at a common *patshala*. But he knew how to make the best of small opportunities; and he soon got a thorough knowledge of the vernacular, and of accounts. He got married at the age of seventeen, and accompanied his father-in-law in his pilgrimage to the shrines in the North-west. His travel matured his mind, and gave him a great deal of practical wisdom. Returning to Calcutta, in 1815, he managed to get some insignificant post at Fort William. But while here he hit upon a plan which became the foundation of his future fortune. This was the idea of buying and profitably selling bottles and corks. He carried on this business together with his work in the fort, and soon he became the possessor of capital enough for more venturesome and profitable transactions. One of these was the "banianship" of foreign ships lying in harbour in Calcutta—a business that brought large returns. He was always honest; not a single rupee came into his hands in an unfair way. He was polite, affable, and benevolent. "Seal's Free College," founded in 1842, and supplied with ample funds, bears testimony to his liberality. He died in 1854, at the age of sixty-three. The Seals of Colootola (who only a few years ago ranked in wealth next to the Maharaja of Burdwan) were his descendants and heirs.

7. HENRY LOUIS VIVIAN DEROZIO

1809-1831

THIS clever Eurasian was born at Entally, in Calcutta, in 1809. He was of Portuguese extraction. His father held a respectable post in a mercantile firm in the city, and was respected by the community. Vivian had two brothers and two sisters. Both his brothers were older than himself. Their end was sad. The eldest became spoiled and useless. The second, Claudius, was sent by his father to be educated in Scotland; what became of him there is not known. The elder sister died when seventeen years old, but the younger, Amilia, lived with Vivian, and was a devoted sister.

Young Derozio was brought up at a school at Dharmtala, kept by a Mr Drummond, a man deeply learned in literature and science. Drummond was a poet too. It was said of him that difference in religious opinions had caused a breach between him and his relations, and that consequently he had made India his home. The freedom of thought that had been the cause of the French Revolution was fully developed in him, and the European residents of Calcutta were afraid to send their sons to his school. Derozio's genius, of which we have said so much, bore the deep impress of Mr Drummond's influence.

Vivian Derozio, leaving school at the age of fourteen, worked in his father's office for some time, and then went to Bhagalpur, to live with his aunt. It was his custom, while here, to ramble along the banks of the Ganges, deep in meditation, and to pore over the pages of all manner of works in literature and science. He wrote articles for *The Indian Gazette*, edited by Dr Grant. It has been said that he at this time also wrote such a clever criticism on Kant's philosophy as to astonish everyone. It has been sometimes observed that a philosopher cannot be a poet, but Derozio was an instance to the contrary—he was both a philosopher and a genuine poet.

On returning to Calcutta he was appointed to the fourth mastership of the Hindu College. How he did his work, in what friendly relations he stood with his pupils, how their minds were broadened under his influence, and how he sent out a band of young Bengalis as harbingers of light to their benighted countrymen, we have already mentioned. He died on the 23rd of December 1831. The reader has already been told how anxiously and affectionately he was watched and nursed by his pupils while on his death-bed.

8. THE REV. DOCTOR KRISHNA MOHAN BANERJI

1813-1885

THE growth of the banyan-tree, with its far-spreading branches from a tiny seed, is hardly more wonderful than the development of the humble Kulin Brahman boy, Krishna Mohan Banerji, into the Rev. Dr K. M. Banerji. He first saw light in 1813, in his maternal grandfather's house at Shampukur, Culcutta. His parents being very poor, he had in his childhood to endure every sort of privation. At the age of six he was sent to one of Mr Hare's *patshalas*. Here his talents were noticed, and

Mr Hare, in 1822, took him into the "School Society's School," at present known as the "Hare School." From here the young lad went to the Hindu College in 1824.

His love of learning, even when a boy, was so great that he never willingly absented himself from school. Many a morning would he trudge thither without even a handful of rice to fortify him for the hard work of the day. To relieve his mother he often cooked the evening meal.

He belonged to the first class of the Hindu College when Mr Derozio got his appointment there, and an intimacy soon grew up between them. When the Academic Association was organised, Krishna Mohan took the most active part in it. When he finished his collegiate education, in 1829, Mr Hare appointed him second master of his school. While here he took up journalism, and in May 1831 he started *The Inquirer*. to wage war against Hinduism. In the month of August, the same year, he had to suffer expulsion from home, being the scapegoat of his beef-eating friends. Not that he was less forward than they in ridiculing Hindu prejudices and superstition; not that he refrained from offending the orthodox community by eating and drinking what was abomination to them; but on the evening in question he was absent from the scene of a disturbance which his friends created by throwing beef from his house into his neighbour's.

Expelled from home he sought shelter in his friend Dakhinaranjan's house. How long he remained there is not known, but we suppose that he had soon to leave his friend's roof through fear of causing a dissension between him and his father, who did not like his son to associate with him, much less to receive him as his guest.

Krishna Mohan was homeless for some time, but never dispirited or down-hearted. He edited *The Inquirer* still, and gave vent to his rancour against Hinduism in language more bitter than ever. He boldly attended Duff's and Dealtry's lectures, and freely ate and drank with them. The 17th of October 1832 witnessed his baptism. Dr Duff's and Mr Dealtry's influence, conjointly with that of Captain Corbyn and Colonel Powney, who were sincere Christians, and with whom Krishna Mohan freely mixed, brought about his conversion.

This was the turning point in his life. His countrymen now hated and opposed him more than ever; but, undaunted by all their attempts to crush him, he rose higher and higher, till he attained a position of great public influence. His wife, after hesitating for about four years, joined him. She too accepted Jesus as her Saviour, and the husband and the wife lived peaceful Christian lives for many years.

Krishna Mohan was one of Dr Duff's converts; but, believing the doctrines of the Church of England to be more Biblical than those of the sister Church of Scotland, he soon joined the former; and was ordained deacon in 1837. He was then appointed pastor of Christ Church, Cornwallis Square. He made two converts: his younger brother, Kali Charan, and Ganendra Mohan Tagore, the only son of Prasanna Kumar Tagore.

Mr Banerji left Christ Church in 1852, for a professor's chair in Bishop's College, which he occupied till 1860. Here is a list of the chief works which have made him famous in Bengal:

1. Thirteen volumes of the *Encyclopædia Bengalensis*, in English and Bengali.
2. An essay on female education.
3. The six Darsanas, or Schools of Hindu Philosophy.
4. *The Aryan Witness.*
5. Numerous text-books and pamphlets in Sanskrit, and lectures in English.

He resigned the professorship in the Bishop's College in 1868, and became a pensioner of the Society for the Propagation of the Gospel. Subsequently, he became the Bishop's Honorary Chaplain.

In 1867 the Calcutta University conferred on him the title of Doctor of Laws. In 1878 he acted as President of the Index Association. In 1880 he was elected a Municipal Commissioner, but he resigned the commissionership in 1885, when the Bengal Government interfered with the sanitary arrangements of the Corporation. He died on the 11th of May in that year.

Dr Banerji was a very eminent linguist. He was learned in English, Latin, Greek, Hebrew and Sanskrit; and in Bengali and Uriya he was an acknowledged authority. He was for many years an examiner in Bengali, both for the Government and for the University of Calcutta—in 1869 the editor of this work had the privilege of being examined by him, and passed, in this language. In *The Aryan Witness* he showed an acquaintance with the chief Semitic and Coptic languages. He understood business well; and ably managed his son-in-law Ganendra Mohan Tagore's property during his absence in England. He managed also his own affairs so well as not only to be comparatively wealthy himself, but to be able also to meet with a free hand the calls of charity. He lived and died respected and loved by all.

9. RAM GOPAL GHOSH

1815-1868

THIS early friend of Dr Banerji, and not unlike him in intellectual capacity and reputation, distinguished himself chiefly in the domain of politics. He was born in October, 1815, in Bechu Chatterjee's Street in Calcutta, and was the grandson of Dewan Ramprosad Ghosh, and son of Gobinda Chandra Ghosh, a dealer in cloth in the China Bazaar. Their family house was near Trebeni, in the Hughli District. Ram Gopal prosecuted his studies in the Hindu College, and was one of the first to follow Mr Derozio's teachings with regard to the superstitions of his country, denouncing the religion of his forefathers, and living rather an Anglicised life. Before finishing his college course he, in 1832, secured a good position in the business world, through Mr Hare's recommendation, with a merchant who wanted an assistant. He not only served his master to his satisfaction, but before he was twenty gained so much experience in mercantile affairs as to write a series of articles on Inland Transit Duties. He soon became a partner in a European firm; and a few years afterwards, probably in 1848, he started business independently, under the name of R. G. Ghosh & Co.

He did not, however, in the cares of his extensive business, forget his duties to his country or to his friends. He played the most important part in all social movements; and he was ever ready to help those whom he loved, to the best of his power. Once, Babu Ramtanu Lahiri being in straits, his friend Ram Gopal Babu unable to render him enough pecuniary assistance, got him appointed as a Munshi to a merchant. Besides this, when another friend of his, Rasik Krishna Mullick, of whom we have often spoken in our narrative, was seized with an illness from which he never rallied, and came to Calcutta, Ram Gopal Babu took him in and entertained him in his garden-house on the river bank, and made lavish arrangements for his treatment and comfort. But the crowning act of his liberality and friendship was that, when lying on his death-bed, he called for the bonds his friends had given him for the loans advanced to them, and tore them to pieces, thereby freeing those friends from all liabilities. The sum covered by the bonds was about 40,000 rupees.

Ram Gopal was truthful and honest, as well as liberal. To show this we will relate the following incidents :—

When his grandfather died, and his father had to perform the *Shradh*, the orthodox Brahmans and Kayasthas threatened that they would neither eat at the latter's house, nor receive his gifts, because his son was a heretic and a *Mlechchha*. This was the greatest disgrace a Hindu could imagine; and the old man, with tears in his eyes, told his son that matters might be mended if the latter would only disown having done anything anti-Hindu. But Ram Gopal was too conscientious to yield. He burst into tears and said, "Father, I am prepared to suffer everything for your satisfaction, but can never tell a lie." This instance of firm adherence to truth was noised abroad; and he rose the higher for it in the estimation of the world.

On another occasion, when, through failure of business, he was involved in debt from which he seemed powerless to extricate himself, some of his friends advised him to make all his property *benami*. But he would not entertain the idea, and said firmly, "I would be the last man to deprive my creditors of their due."

Babu Ram Gopal Ghosh, as we have said before, always directed his energies to the improvement of his countrymen. He edited the journal called *Gyananneshur*, and organised a "Society for the Acquisition of General Knowledge." He founded the "Epistolary Club," and started *The Bengal Spectator*, which we have previously mentioned. He supported Dwarkanath Tagore and Dr Goodeve in their proposal to send Bengal medical students to England to complete their education there; and when the four selected students were about to embark he cheered and encouraged them to try the perilous voyage.

He was a genius in politics, and took a leading part in all political movements of the day. Mr Adams established the "Indian Association" in England, and managed it according to the plan suggested by him. But we have yet to mention the most brilliant gift he possessed—namely, that of genuine oratory. He was the Demosthenes of India; and his speech against the Government Resolution not to permit the burning of the dead at the Nimtala Ghat, also that on the renewal of the Charter Act of 1853, that on the memorial to be raised in honour of Sir Henry Hardinge, and that on the administration of Lord Canning, were masterpieces of oratory.

Government appreciated his merits, and as a reward offered him the second judgeship of the Small Cause Court in Calcutta, but he respectfully declined the offer. He was a member of the Calcutta Police Committee of 1845, of the Small-pox Committee, of the Central Committee for the Collection of Works of Industry and Arts for the London Exhibition in 1851, the Paris Exhibitions of 1855 and 1867, and the Bengal Agricultural Exhibitions of 1855 and 1864. He was a member of the Council from 1848 to its dissolution, in January 1855; a very active member of the Bengal Chamber of Commerce; a Fellow of the Calcutta University, the Agri-Horticultural Society, and the District Charitable Society; an Honorary Magistrate; and a Justice of the Peace for Calcutta, and a member of the Bengal Legislative Council from 1862 to 1866.

As a promoter of education, a patriot, a politician, a speaker, a social reformer, and a successful merchant, Babu Ram Gopal Ghosh was one of the foremost men of his time, and he did much for the advancement and enlightenment of Hindu society. We have derived the information on which this memoir is founded from Mr Buckland's "Bengal under the Lieutenant-Governors."

The career of this great man closed in January, 1868.

10. RASIK KRISHNA MULLICK

RASIK was born in 1810. He was a *Tili* by caste, and belonged to a very respectable family. There is unfortunately not much to write of this man. Not that his life was barren of incident, but that we have not a full and reliable account of it. He may have been less forward that Krishna Mohan and Ram Gopal in demolishing the fortress of Hindu prejudices and superstitions, but none the less zealous in fighting for what seemed to him to be right. Ram Gopal's speeches against Hinduism were fiery and stirring, Krishna Mohan's were full of humour and satirical eloquence, while Rasik Krishna's were calm and thoughtful. That he was a true disciple of Derozio, and could not tolerate idolatrous Hinduism, is evident from the following incident, that happened in his student life:—Once, when summoned as a witness before the Supreme Court, and, according to the custom, required to ratify his deposition by swearing on a copper vessel containing a few leaves of the *tulsi* dipped in a little Ganges water—the most sacred symbols with Hindus—he boldly said that he was not a Hindu, and would not take the required oath. The whole court was thunderstruck to hear this. The Hindus present shut their ears with their hands, and hissed in scorn.

When Rasik, on leaving college, enrolled himself as one of the zealous workers in the cause of social and religious reform, his mother tried by every means, reasonable or unreasonable, to throw obstacles in his way. She thought him possessed of some wicked spirit, to destroy whose influence she once contrived to make her son eat a white powder, which proved to be poison. Poor Rasik fell insensible, and while in this condition arrangements were made to send him by boat to Benares. But when the boat was in readiness, and his hands and legs were tied, to make him incapable of resistance, fortunately his senses returned. He broke the bonds asunder, ran out of the house, and took lodgings at Chorbagan, which eventually became the rendezvous of all the young men of Derozio's school.

Rasik Krishna began the world as a teacher in the Hare School. Then he got an appointment as Deputy-Collector of Burdwan. Here he worked for many years, with a good name for probity and fairness. He was often offered bribes by the *amlas* of the Burdwan Raj; but nothing could induce him to swerve an inch from an impartial course.

By a fortunate coincidence, Babu Ramtanu Lahiri came to Burdwan when his friend Babu Rasik Krishna was Deputy-Collector there. They lived there again in close companionship. Ramtanu would not take any important step without consulting Rasik. The one held the other as his guide, philosopher, and friend. In after years, long after Rasik Babu had departed this life, we have often heard Mr Lahiri quote him as an authority.

In 1858 Babu Rasik Krishna came to Calcutta as an invalid, and lodged in Babu Ram Gopal Ghosh's garden-house at Kamarhatti. It was there that he breathed his last, leaving Ram Gopal and Peari Chand Mitra his executors.

11. SHIB CHANDRA DEB

Babu Shib Chandra Deb was born at Konnagar, on the 10th of July 1811. His father was a well-to-do gentleman of good character. After receiving some education at home he was, at the age of thirteen, sent to the Hindu College, where he finished his studies. He was one of Mr Derozio's pupils and admirers.

After leaving college he worked for some time as a computer in the Survey Office, at a salary of thirty rupees a month. Then as Deputy-Collector he was posted to Balasore, in 1838, and to Midnapur in 1844. From there he was transferred to Alipur, in 1850.

Having served the Government for twenty-five years he retired, in 1863. But in this last period of his life he was most active in improving the condition of his native town—which had, even before that, been benefited by him in many ways. It was to his endeavours that the Konnagar schools, both English and vernacular, the railway station, post office, Brahmo Samaj, and dispensary owed their origin. He established a Girls' School there at his own cost.

He died on 12th November 1890, leaving a widow and a large number of children and grandchildren.

12. HARA CHANDRA GHOSH, BAHADUR

HE too was a student of the Hindu College and a disciple of Derozio. He was born in 1808, and he died in 1868. He took a leading part in the Academic Association.

Lord William Bentinck offered him his Dewanship, but he could not accept it owing to the opposition of his mother. In 1832 he became Munshi of Bankura, and proved himself so trustworthy that he was promoted within a year to the rank of *Sadar Amin.* In 1838 he was transferred to Hughli. He gradually rose in rank, and in 1844 he came to Alipur as principal *Sadar Amin.* In 1852 he became Junior Magistrate of the Police Court in Calcutta, and in 1854 Judge of the Small Cause Court there.

He was a learned man himself, and encouraged the progress of learning in general. He was a friend of the cultured, and joined in every undertaking for the intellectual and moral improvement of his country. He took under his tutelage the youthful Kristo (Krishna) Das Pal, afterwards famous as the editor of *The Hindu Patriot*, and treated him as if he had been his own son, and he supported many other poor and helpless boys.

There was great lamentation among his friends and relatives on his departure from this world, on the 3rd December 1868. On 4th January 1869 a monster meeting took place, in the Town Hall, to devise the best way of perpetuating his memory. A marble statue was erected and placed at the Small Cause Court. It still stands there, as a tribute of public gratitude to a man who devoted his life to the faithful service of Government and his countrymen.

13. PEARI CHAND MITRA

1814-1883

THE reader has often heard in the foregoing chapters of this man, famous for his intelligence and his warm desire for the public good. He was born in Calcutta, in 1814, and educated at the Hindu College, where, in 1835, he gained all the honours and distinctions within his reach. He then got employment as Deputy-Librarian in the Calcutta Library, which now is housed at the

Metcalfe Hall. From Deputy-Librarian he became Librarian, then Secretary, and at length Curator, and the Curator's post he held till the end of his life. His connection with the library gave him an excellent opportunity of acquiring knowledge and developing his mind, and he was a regular contributor to all those magazines that were edited by Ram Gopal Ghosh and Rasik Krishna Mullick.

It was Peari Chand who gave a happy turn to the Bengali literature of the time, by editing, conjointly with Radhanath Sirkar, a small monthly journal in good colloquial Bengali. This was in the nature of a reaction against the highly classical and Sanskritised style of Pandit Ishwar Chandra Vidyasagar and Akhoy Kumar Dutt, who, by using too many long and pompous Sanskrit words in their Bengali writings, had given the language, in the opinion of many, a heavy and ludicrous character. Peari Chand, under the *nom de plume* of "Tekchand," also wrote in the same style the first Bengali tale, "The Spoiled Pet in a Rich Family," which is still regarded as a good sample of light and pleasing literature. He subsequently wrote many works in Bengali, neither in this light style, nor in the pedantic Johnsonian style that had become unpopular with the majority of the reading public, but with an easy and graceful flow of language.

He, with his brother, Kessori Chand, wrote in English the biographies of David Hare, Ram Kamal Sen, and Mr Grant.

He understood mercantile matters thoroughly. He at first carried out some successful speculations in partnership with his friend, Babu Tarachand Chakravartti, and on the death of that gentleman, in 1855, he took the business into his own hands. His profits were great, and so wide was his reputation in the mercantile world that he was appointed to be a director of many firms.

He was public spirited, and took a leading part in all movements for the public good. He was a member of the Social Science Association, the Agri-Horticultural Society, the District Charitable Society, the School Book Society, and of the Society for the Prevention of Cruelty to Animals. For two years he served his country as a member of the Bengal Legislative Council. After his wife's death, in 1860, he, to some extent, lived a retired life, and devoted much of his time to the study of Spiritualism. When Colonel Olcott and Madame Blavatsky founded the Calcutta Theosophical Society he joined it. He died on the 23rd of November 1883, to the regret of his many friends, who put up to his memory in the Metcalfe Hall his portrait in oils, and in the Town Hall his bust in marble.

14. RADHANATH SIKDAR

1813-1870

HE was one of the pupils of Derozio, and an intimate of Ramtanu. He was born in 1813, of a Brahman family, which had gained considerable distinction during the latter years of the Mughul rule. Sikdar means "Police Commissioner," and the family had this name because the heads of it were successively the Heads of the Police under the Nawabs of Bengal.

He was a student of the Hindu College, where he gained a Senior Scholarship. He had a great taste for mathematics, and had Dr Fuller, then the first mathematician in India, for his teacher. He, like all other followers of Derozio, came forward as a deliverer of his country from the trammels of ignorance and superstition. He was always true to his word. Neither fear nor self-interest could induce him to swerve an inch from what he thought was right. He always detested what he felt to be wrong; and a proof of this was the celibate life he lived, in spite of the wishes of his mother, whom he both loved and revered, for his early marriage. He believed that it was wrong to force a girl eight or ten years of age, through her parents, into a wedlock entailing responsibilities the nature of which she did not understand; and as young Hindu maidens of a riper age were not available in those days he altogether shelved the question of marriage.

He left the Hindu College on being appointed a computer in the G. F. Survey on thirty rupees a month. He gradually rose in the Survey Department, and was transferred to the North-west. His strong will, great self-respect, and exceptional cleverness, secured for him the esteem and friendship of both the European and the Indian gentlemen with whom he came into contact.

That he was not a man to be easily snubbed is evident from the following incident, which happened when he was a surveyor at Dehradun. The District Magistrate, Mr Vansittart, on one occasion, while on tour, forced some of Mr Sikdar's men to work as his coolies. Mr Sikdar, greatly offended at this, rushed out of his bungalow and brought the coolies back, with the Magistrate's things on their shoulders, protesting against the illegal proceedings of the latter. Mr Vansittart was in a fury, and he prosecuted Mr Sikdar for having obstructed a public servant in the discharge of his duties. The case came up before another magistrate, and, fearful of the consequences, many of Mr Sikdar's friends advised him to apologise; but he did not yield at all. He remained firm to the end; and, though he was fined 200 rupees for the offence, his resistance gave rise to a strong agitation, the result of which has been that the practice of forcing men to labour has died out among Government officials.

The highest post he occupied was the head computership, the monthly salary for which was 600 rupees. When he returned to Calcutta, a few years after his father's death, in 1853, his friends found that he was perfectly anglicised in customs and manners.

We have in Peari Chand's "Life" referred to Mr Sikdar as his colleague in improving Bengali literature. To write chaste Bengali in a style so easy that even illiterate people might understand it became the latter's chief aim; and before sending his articles to the monthly periodical of which he was joint-editor he would first read them to the ladies of his house, whose understanding of them was the criterion for their admission into its columns.

He died in 1870 at his garden-house near the French station of Chandernagore.

15. RAJA DAKHINARANJAN MUKERJI

1814-1878

THE career of Dakhinaranjan was not of much importance, and we give his life only because he was an early friend of Mr

Lahiri, and a year or two older. He was born in the Tagore family, the son of Babu Surjya Kumar Tagore's daughter. He cared very little for his father, who, living as a dependant on his father-in-law, was rather looked down upon by his son. In fact he cared for none of his relations; and, therefore, in eating and drinking with Europeans, and imitating their manners, he was more forward than many of his friends.

He had an affectionate heart; and he loved his early friends sincerely. Here are two instances of it. When Krishna Mohan Banerji had to leave home Dakhinaranjan gave him shelter, and on his father having one day, in his absence, driven his friend away he left home and lodged in a house near Mr Derozio. The other instance was his making an anonymous gift of 1000 rupees to Babu Tarachand Chakravartti, when the latter was in some difficulty. Tarachand Babu was for some time in the dark as to whence the help came; and it was only after much inquiry that he found out who his benefactor was.

As long as Mr Derozio lived Dakhinaranjan was as well behaved and pure in principles as his companions; but after his death Dakhinaranjan became a changed man. He became intemperate and licentious, and his early friends all forsook him. To redeem his character to a certain extent, it was said that this change or deterioration in him was the result of his having been poisoned by his relations with a drug similar to that administered to Rasik Krishna. The strain on his intellect was too great, and he gave way to temptation. After some time he seemed to have regained his former strength of mind and a mastery over his passions, and was again hailed by his friends as their lost brother reclaimed. But again a circumstance happened which for good alienated them from him. Into the well-known details we need not here enter. His friends shunned him now, never to receive him back. He felt greatly pained at this, and left Calcutta. When he did so is not known to us. It seems likely that he left Calcutta for Lucknow in 1851 or 1852. He was at Lucknow during the Mutiny, and as a reward for his having helped the Government to restore peace he received a *jagir*, and the title of Raja. In old age his noble sentiments and aspirations, which seemed to have been long dead, revived, and he once more devoted himself to the good of his country. Through his exertions was founded the Talukdar's Association of Oudh, on the model of the British Indian Association; and he did much to remove the racial antipathies between the English and the Indians. He edited a periodical dealing chiefly with political matters. But a change of fortune embittered his last days. He somehow lost the Government's favour; his honours were taken away from him, and he died of a broken heart, in 1887.

16. TARACHAND CHAKRAVARTTI

WITH the life of Tarachand Chakravartti, we will close the biographies of Mr Derozio's pupils and disciples. Born in Calcutta in 1804, he received his early education in a *patshala*. Then he was taken into the Hindu College as a free student. Having gone through the final course there, he worked for some time as a teacher, and then as the Deputy-Registrar of the *Sadar Diwani Adalat*. Subsequently, he went to Ichanabad as *munsif*. But he did not long work in this capacity. He gave up Government service and undertook the translation of "Manu Sanghita" from Sanskrit into English, and the preparation of an Anglo-Vernacular dictionary. *The Quill*, a journal to criticise the policy of Government, was at this time started by him, and he conducted it in a way that incurred the displeasure of the authorities. He was one of the foremost in all matters relating to his countrymen's progress in knowledge and civilisation. He was one of Rammohan Roy's favourite adherents, and was appointed by him secretary to the newly-established Brahmo Samaj. During the latter part of his life he was the chief counsellor of the Raja of Burdwan, who had an implicit faith in him, and never took any important step without his consent. The Raja honoured him as an elder brother, and on his demise took his children under his protection, and allowed each of them an annuity. We are not certain as to the date of his death.

17. PANDIT ISHWAR CHANDRA VIDYASAGAR

1820-1891

THE name of this illustrious man will never be forgotten. It has been the lot of few in India to leave such a bright example after them as he has left. He was born in 1820, in the Midnapur district. His parents were very poor. He had a great desire to acquire knowledge, and underwent many privations when a student. He studied in the Sanskrit College from 1829 to 1841, and then became head pandit in the Fort William College. In 1848 he published the translation of the "Vetal Panchabinsati," or the twenty-five stories related by a demon to Vikramaditya. In the same year he was appointed assistant-secretary to the Sanskrit College, but resigned his post in a year owing to the Council of Education not accepting some of his proposals. In 1849 he was appointed head assistant to the Fort William College, and the next year he became a professor in the Sanskrit College, of which he got the principalship in 1851. The college is largely indebted to him for the prosperity it enjoys. In 1855 he was appointed special Inspector of Schools for the Hughli, Burdwan, Midnapur, and Nadia districts. The new appointment did not interfere with his duties in the Sanskrit College; and he received a total salary of 500 rupees. It was under his auspices that many vernacular schools, both for boys and for girls, were established in the districts under his inspection; and it was in connection with these that some friction arose between him and the then Director of Public Instruction. The differences grew into a serious misunderstanding, and he resigned his appointments in 1858. But he continued to enjoy the confidence of the Government. On the establishment of the Calcutta University he was nominated as one of its Fellows and a member of the Board of Examiners. In January 1880 he was created a C.I.E.

Miss Mary Carpenter, in her mission to Indian ladies in 1866, chose him as her chief counsellor; and while driving with her from the Bally Station to the Uttarpara Girls' School he had a bad fall, the effects of which lasted till the day of his death, which happened on the 29th July 1891. Vidyasagar was a great educationist. He opened the Metropolitan Institution, and its branch schools in different parts of Calcutta, with the object of training the young on an improved system. He wrote a graduated series of school-books in Bengali and Sanskrit. The greatest reform, for which he will always be remembered with admiration, was that made with regard to Hindu widows. He showed from the *Shastras* that the remarriage of these was not anti-Hindu. Great was the battle he had to fight with his fellow-pandits, many of equal rank with himself, and bitter was the persecution that he had to endure. But undaunted he carried on his noble work, and the remarriage of widows was sanctioned by legislature.

He was a great philanthropist. Distress in any form always touched his heart, and he was quick to remedy it. The upper and the lower classes were equally the objects of his charity. He opened his purse to Michael Madhusudan Dutt as readily as to the poorest creature that drew breath in the slums of Calcutta.

He was a good disciplinarian. He knew how to punish intentional neglect of duty. Under the simplicity of a child he hid the sternness of a judge, which won him the respect of everybody. His death was felt as a national calamity. He was a first-class educationist, reformer, and philanthropist, and we fear India will never see his like again. His life has supplied materials for many a voluminous treatise; and lest we should be lost in the immensity of the subject we have confined ourselves only to the simple enumeration of some of the most important events in this great man's career, and the most salient points of his character.

18. AKHOY KUMAR DUTT

1821-1886

Ahkoy Kumar has left a name behind him for his literary works and the improvements which Bengali society owes to him. He was born in 1820, at a village in the Nadia district. After he had obtained a rudimentary education in Bengali he was, in 1830, taken by his father to Kidderpur, his place of business. Akhoy's guardians and friends were for teaching him Persian; but the boy showed so great a desire to learn English that they had at length to decide in its favour. For some time he learnt it at home, with the help of his father's English-speaking friends; but he felt that his progress was by no means satisfactory, and therefore got himself, without his father's knowledge, admitted into the Free English School at Kidderpur started by missionaries. His guardians, afraid of keeping him under missionary influence, made arrangements for him to go to Calcutta and to attend Gaur Mohan Addy's school, then one of the most efficient educational establishments in the city. This was when he was in the sixteenth year of his age. While here he showed an insatiable thirst for knowledge, and eagerly grasped every kind of information within his reach. But his father's death, three years after, compelled him to leave school. Poverty, with all its concomitants, made life miserable. But the young man did not give in. While working for his mother's and his own subsistence, he tried as hard as before to acquire knowledge. He made Sanskrit his chief study, and made great progress in it. In 1840 he succeeded in getting a teachership in the *Tatwabodhini* School. He began with the monthly salary of eight rupees, which in a short time rose to fourteen rupees. In 1843 the *Tatwabodhini Patrika* was started, and he became its editor. His connection with this paper was the source of his future greatness. To acquire a sound scientific knowledge he, as an ex-student, studied botany, physiology, and chemistry in the Medical College. Besides this, he devoured the contents of the useful works in the *Tatwabodhini* Library, and he edited the *Patrika* in a way that showed that the right man was in the right place. His style was superior to that of any other Indian journalist of the day. The books he wrote were full of profound thought, clothed in chaste though somewhat bombastic language; and in a short time he became an authority on Bengali literature. His chief ambition was to spread the light of knowledge among his benighted countrymen. Rank and wealth had no attraction for him.

But the most important of his achievements was to free the Brahmo Samaj from its thraldom to the Vedas, which it had hitherto held to be of Divine inspiration. The falsity of this position struck Akhoy Babu; and after much conflict with Babu Debendranath Tagore he, in 1850, was able to convince his friends of the fact that the Vedas were not the word of God. He was chiefly instrumental in reducing the Brahmo creed to its present form.

On the establishment of the Calcutta Normal School he was appointed one of its teachers; but this new employment did not materially interfere with his editing the *Tatwabodhini Patrika*. His constitution however, never a strong one, gave way one day in 1855, when he was worshipping in the Brahmo Samaj. He fell down in a fainting fit. With great care he was brought to; but his brain was affected, and he was compelled to give up writing. Even in this invalid state, however, he compiled his famous and learned work, "The Worshippers of God in India," with the help of an amanuensis.

He passed his last days in retirement in his bungalow at Bally. Here he died on the 14th of Jaishta 1886, leaving behind him many thoughtful and instructive works in Bengali.

19. RAJA DIGAMBAR MITRA, C.S.I.

1817-1879

THIS eminent man was born at Konnagar in 1817, educated in the Hindu College, and began life as a teacher in the Nizamat School. After holding several posts of trust under Government, in 1838 he became manager to the Kasimbazar Raj, under Krishnanath Kumar, husband of the late Maharani Surnamai. He so ingratiated himself with the Kumar as to receive from him a present of a *lakh* of rupees. With this large sum of money Digambar got on well in speculations in indigo and silk; but the failure of the Union Bank gave an overwhelming blow to his prospects. From the effects of this, however, he recovered by selling off his garden-house at Bagmari, and buying with the proceeds of the sale the Sunderban lot Dabipur, in the 24-Perganas. He was a Zemindar now, and gained distinction in public life by taking a prominent part in the political questions of the day. He began as assistant-secretary to the British Indian Association;

and in 1864 he sat on the Malarious Fever Commission appointed by Government, and in the Bengal Legislative Council. He extended his estates by purchasing some lots of ground in Orissa, in 1866; and, learning in his visits the ravages that famine was making there, he urged upon the Government the necessity of relief, and himself rendered valuable services as a member of the Relief Committee. In 1869 he became Vice-President of the British Indian Association, and in 1870 again took his seat in the Lieutenant-Governor's Council. When the local Government entered into an investigation of the causes of the epidemic fever that had for years been ravaging Lower Bengal he showed that the chief cause had been the obstruction to free drainage offered by railways, and roads connected with them. In 1872 he was appointed, for the third time, a member of the Legislative Council, and acting President of the British Indian Association. He became Sheriff of Calcutta in 1874, and was made a C.S.I. in 1876. The title of Raja was conferred on him the next year. Before this he had succeeded in getting himself appointed President of the British Indian Association.

Raja Digambar Mitra left this world on the 20th of April 1879, after a brilliant career. He rendered eminent services to his country through the British Indian Association; and with the chief Government officials his opinions were of great weight. A few years before death he had to suffer a great bereavement in the accidental death of his only son. Another calamity which embittered his last days was the permanent insanity of his wife.

20. BABU PRASANNA KUMAR TAGORE, C.S.I.

THIS worthy member of the illustrious Tagore family was born in 1803, and received as good an education as was available in the country for one of his parentage. He at one time thought seriously of taking up the work of social reform; but the conversion of his only son to Christianity produced in him a reaction; and after that he became averse to all radical changes in society.

Though the property left by his father was very large, and though he had considerably increased it by the intelligent management of his Zemindaries, still, to enrich himself further, he practised as a pleader in the *Sadar Diwani Adalat.* His success in his profession was remarkable, and his annual income as a pleader ranged between one *lakh* and one and a half *lakhs* of rupees. He did much for the spread of English education. He was a member of the Hindu School Committee, and of the Council of Education; and when the Calcutta University was founded he became one of its Fellows.

Lord Dalhousie appointed him clerk-assistant to the Imperial Legislative Council. Subsequently, he sat as a member of the same Council. He was made a C.S.I., and died in 1868.

He has left a name behind him for charity. He not only patronised the Mayo Hospital, but, at his own cost, established charitable dispensaries in his Zemindaries in the Mufasal. He placed three *lakhs* of rupees in the hands of the Calcutta University, for a Law Professor to lecture on Hindu Law. To commemorate him, a marble statue has been placed in the vestibule of the Senate Hall of the university.

21. MAHARSHI DEBENDRANATH TAGORE

1818-1905

Maharshi Debendranath Tagore, the son of Dwarkanath Tagore, was born in 1818, in the family mansion in Calcutta. Having received his early education in the school founded by Raja Rammohan Roy, he joined the Hindu College, and was one of the fellow-students of Ramtanu, though he was not one of those attached to Mr Derozio. In the formation of his early religious impressions he was influenced not so much by the broad and reformed views of his father as by the nursery tales and traditions held sacred by the old ladies presiding over his father's house. And so he grew up a quiet young man, holding the religion of his forefathers in great reverence, and practically mindful more of his worldly than spiritual interests. But certain unexpected circumstances, which we need not mention here, wrought a change in him on attaining to manhood. Thinking little of the world and its attractions he devoted himself, as he thought, to the service and glorification of his Maker.. In 1839 he founded the *Tatwabodhini Sabha*, or Society to Promote the Knowledge of Truth, and in 1840 the *Tatwabodhini* School for the study of the Vedantas. The religious movement that originated in him was purely national, for amidst all the preference that was then being given by the educated to the manners and customs of the West, and the air of defiance young Bengal had assumed against the old religion of his country, Debendranath's principle was strict conservatism. He tried to establish the belief that Monotheism was the religion of the Vedas and Vedantas, and that following the doctrines propounded in them was the surest way to salvation. To him, ancient India was the cradle of all that was good in religion and morals, and he bent his whole soul upon the revival of that spirituality which had marked the Vedic ages.

In 1842 Debendranath joined the Brahmo Samaj, and finding that, through want of proper management, it had lapsed into a comparatively lifeless society, he devoted all his energies to its improvement. The number of its members gradually increased, till it rose to 573 in 1847.

But a difference of opinion crept into the Samaj, and after a good deal of discussion the majority of its members, in 1850, decided that neither the Vedas nor the Upanishads were to be accepted as infallible, and that the natural intuitions of the soul, together with the highest spiritual ideals reached by philosophy and religion in India, or anywhere else, should be regarded as man's guides.

Maharshi Debendranath gave an example of commendable integrity when he impoverished himself by paying off certain heavy debts which he was not legally bound to pay. The debts had been contracted by his father in a way to leave him free from all liability, and he could have repudiated them. But conscience told him of his moral duty, and he paid them off to the best of his ability. The consequence was that he had to part with much valuable property.

We judge of a *Guru* generally by the pupils he brings up; and so in Debendranath's case we must make obeisance to the greatness of his mind, and to the spirituality of his soul, when we bear in mind that Kesava Chandra Sen received his religious instruction from him. Saintly, philosophic, and gifted with oratorical powers of the highest description, he commanded general respect and admiration.

By dint of economy and good management he recovered his fortune, and again took his place among the richest in Calcutta. Some of his sons have made great names for themselves—Dwijendra as a philosopher, Satyandranath as the first Bengali civilian, and Robindranath as a poet and prose writer in Bengali. The title Maharshi, given to Debendranath by his people, means the great *Rishi*. He died on 19th January 1905.

22. KESHUB (KESAVA) CHANDRA SEN

1838-1884

KESHUB's natural powers were extraordinary, and his eloquence wonderful. He would have taken a place among the really great if there had been in him less of a zealot, and if he had a little clipped the wings of his imagination. But, on the whole, he is worthy of our admiration, as having left his mark on his time.

He was born in 1838, and admitted into the Hindu College in 1845, which he left in 1853 to join the newly-founded Metropolitan Institution. On the failure of this he returned to his old *alma mater*, in 1854.

An incident now happened which had a great effect upon him. He was caught using unfair means to pass one of his college examinations, and turned out. He had all along been quiet and well behaved, and great was his shame and bitter his grief at the occurrence. He forsook his former companions, repented of his folly, and spent much of his time in prayer and meditation. He joined the Hindu College again as an ex-student.

At this time he often sought the society of the Reverend James Long, of the Church Missionary Society, and Dr Dutt, the Unitarian Missionary, and with them he founded an association called the "British India Society." A night school in Keshub's dwelling-house at Colootola was an offshoot of this.

In 1857 he, with a few friends, organised a religious association, called the "Good Will Fraternity." It was at the meetings of this society that his oratorical powers were first called forth and improved. It was here also that Maharshi Debendranath Tagore first came to know him. Soon after this Keshub formally joined the Brahmo Samaj. In 1859 the Brahmo School was founded, and here both Debendra and Keshub used to lecture in English and Bengali to college students, the subjects being always religious. This was the means of attracting many intelligent young men towards the Brahmo Samaj.

In 1860 the *Sangit Sabha*, or "Association for Mutual Improvement," was established by Keshub Babu in his house. It met once a week, and the members talked over their spiritual experiences. It was about this time that, urged by his guardian, he accepted a post in the Bengal Bank at a monthly salary of thirty rupees. But though tied to the desk his energy remained undiminished, and showed itself in the publication of many pamphlets, of which "Young Bengal, This is for You" was one. It was about this time also that he started *The Indian Mirror* and a Bengali newspaper, both of which he ably conducted.

The year 1865 saw a great revolution in the Brahmo Samaj. Keshub, though he had for so many years sat at the feet of Debendranath, could no longer put up with his conservatism. Debendranath maintained that widows should not remarry, and that caste distinctions should not be done away with, while Keshub held exactly opposite views, and thus a breach took place between them.

In 1866 the Brahmo Samaj of India was started, with Keshub as secretary. It had no connection with Debendranath or his Samaj, which now became designated as the Adi Brahmo Samaj. It was purely eclectic, taking its doctrines from the Bible, the Koran, the Zendavesta, and the Hindu Shastras; and eight missionaries were appointed to preach this new faith.

The erection of the Brahmo Mandir in Machua Bazar Street, Calcutta, was completed in August, 1869, and since then the Samaj founded by Keshub Babu has met there.

In 1870 Keshub went to England, and was favoured by Her Majesty Queen Victoria with an audience. After his return he established a training school for Indian women, an industrial school for young men, and the Brahmo Home. The cause of temperance, too, had his attention. It was chiefly through his exertions that the Civil Marriages Act became law in 1872.

The hitherto uninterrupted success attending Keshub's career as a reformer put him rather above himself, and it is said of him that, during the latter part of his life, he tried to impress the belief on his fellow-Brahmos that he was their spiritual *Guru*, appointed by God to bring them into his fold, and that he was to command and they were to obey. Giving his daughter in marriage to the Maharaja of Kuch Behar, in May 1878, against the representations of his friends and admirers, was the first step he took in that direction.

From this event dated his claims to superhuman powers, his visions like those vouchsafed unto Jewish prophets of old, and his rhapsodical addresses.

In 1881 he proclaimed the *New Dispensation*, a medley of many religions and of Hindu *Joga* and *Bhakti*. Referring to this time Max Müller said, "He sometimes seems to me on the verge of the very madness of faith." Pouring ghee over a blazing fire, Keshub thus addressed Agni: "Thou art not God; we do not adore thee. But in thee dwells the Lord, the Eternal, inextinguishable flame. O thou brilliant Agni, in thee we behold our resplendent Lord." (Buckland's "Bengal under the Lieutenant-Governors.")

To Keshub's credit as a preacher be it said, that but for him Brahmoism could never have made so much progress in India. Though he seemed to revere Christ, he opposed somewhat the spread of Christianity. When many a Hindu mind had been cleared of the superstitions of ages, and prepared to receive the seed of the Gospel, in came Keshub, dispossessed the Christian missionary of the soil he had fitted for cultivation, and used it for his own purposes.

Before taking leave of him let us quote a few words about him from Buckland's "Bengal under the Lieutenant-Governors." These are: "His neo-Hinduism was never fully developed, but had he lived a few years longer it is more than probable that he would have discarded his earlier conceptions and risen to the rank of a powerful reformer, like Chaitanya. But as it has happened, Chaitanya's followers are counted by the million, those of Keshub by scarcely as many hundreds."

Hard labour, and anxiety to regain the prestige he had lost, told on his constitution, and he died of diabetes on the 8th January 1884.

23. ISHWAR CHANDRA GUPTA

Ishwar Chandra Gupta was born at Kanchrapara, in B. S. 1218. His father was very poor, and maintained his family with the small salary of eight rupees he got by working in a factory. Having lost his father at the age of ten, he lived at his maternal grandfather's house in Calcutta. It is said that while here he wilfully neglected even the very slender opportunities he had for acquiring knowledge, and he entered the world with a smattering of Bengali—his sole stock-in-trade. His muse, though unschooled, enraptured me with her melody, and through her inspiration he ranked as one of the greatest poets of the day. His compositions in prose, also, were equally charming. He had a ready wit, and an inexhaustible stock of humour, together with the power of giving a solemn turn to the commonest things in nature.

In 1830, at his friend Jogendranath Tagore's instance, he started the *Probhakar*, a Bengali weekly, containing excellent contributions in poetry and prose. But he had to give it up after two years, owing to the death of his friend and patron. It was then brought out as a daily; and it was as its editor that he attained his highest fame and influence. There grew up in Bengal a school of poets after his fashion. Bankim Chandra Chatterjee, the Sir Walter Scott of Bengal, and Dina Bandhu Mitra, the famous dramatist, and writer of the "Nildarpan, or the Indigo Planters' Doings," received their first lessons as writers from him.

Ishwar wrote many learned books too in Bengali, in a style both easy and eloquent. He was a favourite not only in all literary circles, but in the Zenana too, and ladies were often heard repeating his poems with great delight. He died in 1865.

24. MICHAEL MADHUSUDAN DUTT

1824-1873

THE name of Michael Madhusudan Dutt will ever remain enshrined in the memory of his countrymen. He has given the Bengali language a new life and a new power, and adorned Bengali literature with a new store of gems, largely gathered from the Persian. He was born on the 25th of January 1824, in his ancestral home at a village in the Jessore District. He was much petted by his parents; they never said nay to whatever he wanted, and this over-indulgence was the chief factor in the composition of his impulsive and volatile character in manhood. In his very boyhood he learnt to seek his own comforts, and to gratify his own inclinations, entirely disregarding the wishes of his parents. His father, Rajnarain Dutt, a Vakil of the *Sadar Diwani Adalat*, brought him at the age of twelve to his lodgings at Kidderpur, and had him admitted into the Hindu College, where he read till 1842. During his career as a student he took the foremost place in every class through which he passed and distinguished himself as a writer in verse and prose. Mathematics he detested. He had many frailties. He lived after the lusts of the flesh; but he never allowed his propensities to interfere with his acquisition of knowledge. The one great peculiarity in his nature was that he scorned to tread the beaten track. To do something new and unprecedented was always the goal he had in view.

He left the Hindu College in the highest class, and became a Christian in February, 1843. He then joined the Bishop's College as a theological student. During the four years that he studied there he attained proficiency in Greek, Latin, and Hebrew. Later on he acquired French, German, and Italian. But his restless nature was still dominant in him, and ambition led him to Madras. While in Bengal he was, through the munificence of his kind father, never in want; but bereft of this while in Madras he had to suffer more or less from poverty. He could, however, though with difficulty, manage to make both ends meet by writing for the newspapers. He had married an English lady, but he forsook her for a countrywoman of hers, and came back to Calcutta, in 1856, to find that his parents had died during his absence, that his nearest of kin had cast him off as an apostate to the faith of his fathers, that his ancestral property had been seized by others, that many of his college friends had left Calcutta, and that their places had been taken by strangers. His prospects were indeed gloomy now; but he was soon helped out of his difficulties by one of his early friends, Gurudas Baisak, who got for him a clerkship in the Presidency Magistrate's Court, from which he soon rose to the post of interpreter. It was Gurudas again who introduced him to the Raja of Paikpara, and to the Maharaja Jotindra Mohan Tagore, when they started the Belgachia Theatre. An English translation of the Sanskrit drama *Ratnavali*, from the pen of Michael, was acted with success on 31st July 1858. This was followed by two Bengali dramas, *Sarmistha* and *Padmavati*. His next undertaking was a poem in blank verse, "Tilottama Sambhab." This was the first attempt at Bengali blank verse, and its novelty, together with its true poetic sentiments, startled the public. Next followed that stirring poem of his "The Megnadbadha Kaliya," the most precious treasure in Bengali literature; and the farces *Akaylkibole Sabhayata* and *Bura Salikar Gharhe*, exposing respectively the vices of young Bengal and the hypocrisy of the old Hindu. To the list is to be added his later productions, *Biranagana Kalya* and *Krishna Kumari*.

It was a lucky circumstances that his occupation as an author did not entirely take away his mind from worldly concerns. He put forth his claim to his paternal property, and succeeded in proving it. His circumstances were prosperous now; and if he had been less extravagant, and less ambitious, he might have passed life in ease. But rest he was never to enjoy. His whims got the better of him again, and he embarked for England in June 1862. There he entered Gray's Inn. He passed five years in Europe in great want and privation. He was involved in debts, and life seemed a burden to him and to his family. They had not the means of paying their passage back to India, and their bones would have lain far away from its shores if Pandit Ishwar Chandra Vidyasagar had not helped them with the sum necessary for their voyage home.

Michael came back to Calcutta as a barrister in 1867. But law was not his proper element. He was literally a briefless barrister; and, after a period of untold misery, he died, in the Alipur General Hospital, in June 1873. It is said that when about to die he sent for the Rev. Krishna Mohan Banerji, and received absolution from him.

25. HARISH CHANDRA MUKERJI

1824-1861

We have in Harish another self-made man. From the humble position of a Kulin Brahman's son, born in the most indigent circumstances, he rose to an eminence which many might covet. He first saw light in a humble house at Bhawanipur, a suburb of Calcutta. He attended a Free School for five years, and was obliged to leave it at the age of seventeen years, with an unfinished education, in order to earn his own livelihood. The first post he got was worth ten rupees a month. But he soon found how to improve his circumstances. He gained admission to the office of the Military Department as a clerk on twenty-five rupees a month. Here he worked uninterruptedly for many years, his salary before his death being 400 rupees a month.

Being comparatively free from the cares attending poverty, he could devote his time and attention to the pursuit of knowledge. He became a subscriber to the Calcutta Public Library, and with avidity studied numerous works in English literature on subjects legal, historical, political, and scientific. It is said that in five months he had read over fifty-seven volumes of *The Edinburgh Review* two or three times, and then got their contents by heart, and that he could repeat many passages from Gibbon's "Rise and Fall of the Roman Empire," and from Kant's philosophical writings.

Harish became first known to the public through his contributions to *The Hindu Intelligencer*, edited by Kasiprosad Ghosh, an old student of the Hindu College. When *The Bengal Recorder* was brought out, in 1849, he often wrote articles for it also. In 1852 he rose so high in public estimation that he was elected a member of the British Indian Association. *The Hindu Patriot*, his own paper, was started under the nominal proprietorship of his elder brother, Haran Chandra, in 1855. It was after the issue of this powerful journal that Harish's influence became so very strong with the Government. After he had fulminated bold denunciations against Dalhousie's annexation of Oudh he upheld the pacific policy of Canning during the Mutiny, and vindicated the Bengali character from all imputations of disloyalty. He stood as the champion of the ryot against the planter. He not only ventilated the grievances of the ryots in *The Patriot*, but also gave them legal advice, and drew up their petitions to Government. In spite of the opposition of the planters, and of their advocates in the English Press, he succeeded in drawing the attention of the Government to the indigo question, and obtaining reforms.

Harish Chandra, amidst all these pursuits, did not neglect his own and his fellow-men's spiritual interests. He was a Brahmo himself; and he established the Bhawanipur Brahmo Samaj.

Many of the highest rank in the land were his friends, and valued his company much. They loved and honoured him; and great was their grief when he died, on the 14th of June 1861. To perpetuate his memory they established the Harish Chandra Library, and placed it in the British Indian Association buildings.

One word more before we take leave of Harish. He fell a victim to hard work and intemperance. Amidst all his manly qualities he had one failing—and that was his love of drink. To find relief in hours of weariness, and lighten the grief occasioned by the death of his beloved wife, he tried the experiment of drinking. And, unhappily, what was tried at first as an experiment soon grew into a habit. His vital energies soon gave way, and he died a premature death. Let young Bengal learn, from the example of this man, to shun alcohol.

26. RAI BANKIM CHANDRA CHATTERJI, BAHADUR, B.A., B.L., C.I.E.

1838-1894

Bankim Chandra Chatterji was the first B.A. from Calcutta University, and the first novelist in Bengali. When writing of Ishwar Chandra Gupta we said that Bankim had sat at the feet of the poet in the hope of being initiated into the mystery of his art. But the young man's heart misgave him when he saw Michael becoming so famous, and so he retired from the field of poetic honours, to show his genius as a prose writer.

He was born on 27th June 1838, at Kantalpara, near Naihati, in the district of the 24-Perganas. Having read for some time in the Vernacular School at his village, and then in the Midnapur English School, he studied in the Hughli College till 1856. From here he went, with a scholarship, to the Calcutta Presidency College, in 1856. He passed as B.A in 1858; and was appointed a deputy-magistrate. He held Government service till 1891, and was regularly promoted to ranks involving great responsibility and trust.

But we honour Bankim not so much for his distinguished career as a public servant as for what he has done for the literature of his country. For his achievements in this direction alone he received titles from Government. Even in boyhood he practised writing poems and essays. When fifteen years of age he gained such command of Sanskrit as to be able to criticise works in it.

Bankim cast the Bengali language into a new form. He bridged over the immense gap between the laboured Johnsonian style of Vidyasagar and Akhoy and the over-colloquial style of Peari Chand Mitra and Radha Sikdar. His Bengali was chaste, forcible, and pleasing. He was the first novelist, and his "Durges Nandini," the first historical novel in Bengali, took people by surprise. Next followed other works of the same kind. The latter part of his life he devoted to the figurative and philosophic exposition of idolatrous Hinduism. But in these writings there is not that vivacity and that clearness which mark his works of fiction. Here is a list of his chief works. 1. "Durges Nandini."

2. "Kapala Kandala." 3. "Mrinalini." 4. "Bisha Brikkha." 5. "Krishna Kanta's Will." 6. "Chandrasikhar." 7. "Debi Chaudhurani." 8. "Ananda Math." 9. "Sitaram." 10. "Raj Sinha." 11. "Rajani."

These are all fiction; and in plot and language they are alike beautiful.

Bankim's *Banga Darshan* was a monthly literary magazine; and his "Krishna Charita" a philosophical exposition of Krishna's life, character, and teachings. He died 8th April 1894.

27. RAI DINA BANDHU MITRA, BAHADUR

1829-1873

As a writer of dramas Dina Bandhu Mitra has a high place in the gallery of Bengali authors. He was born in 1829, at a village near Calcutta. He was not born in a position of wealth, so, after finishing his studies in the village school, he had to work as an apprentice in a Zemindari kachari. But he was far from being happy in this situation. He had a yearning for knowledge, especially that of the English language, and so he ran away from this work to Calcutta, took shelter in a relation's house, and commenced learning English. In a short time he came into contact with Ishwar Chandra Gupta, and the beginnings of poetic genius that he possessed were encouraged, and he wrote a Bengali poem on human character. Other poems came from his pen, and were published in the *Probhakar*, and he soon made a name for himself as a poet. But, like Bankim, he gave up poetry for dramatic literature.

Finishing his education in 1855, he began service in the Postal Department, and soon rose to positions of trust. During the Lushai War he received the charge of making the requisite postal arrangements; and for the conscientious discharge of his duties he was honoured with the title of Rai Bahadur. In the course of his service he had visited many strange places, and mixed with many strange peoples; and this gave him extensive opportunities of increasing his knowledge of men and manners. It was this knowledge that stood him in good stead in the choice of his dramatic characters.

His first drama was the *Nildarpan*, directed against the indigo planters. Then followed the *Nabin Tapashini*, the *Biapugla Burha* ("The old Fool mad after Marriage"), the *Sadhabar Ekadashi*, and the *Jamaibarik* (or "A Hostel full of homeless Sons-in-law"). The last two of his works were *Surodhani Kalya* and *Kamala Kamini*.

He lived in Krishnagar for many years, and thus came to know Ramtanu Lahiri well.

Here is the purport of a few lines in the *Surodhani* written by the author in acknowledgment of Ramtanu's uncommon qualities:

"Here is a noble-minded, pious man, with a genuine love of truth, and a desire for universal good. He is full of simplicity, and, like the *Rishis* of old, he remains unmoved by pleasure or pain. He is wise and pure, with a complete mastery over his passions. If the most wicked pass but a single day with him, they are sure to receive lasting good impressions from him. He is charitable in every way, and his great delight is to place the benefits of sound instruction within the reach of all. This man is Ramtanu Babu—one who is generally known as the paragon of virtue and goodness." Dina Bandhu died in November 1873.

28. DWARKANATH BIDYABHUSAN

DWARKANATH has left a name behind him as a journalist. Before we give the principal events in his life let us summarise the history of journalistic literature in Bengal.

The first Bengali newspaper was the *Darpan*, issued by the Serampore missionaries. Being published by foreigners, it bore marks of foreign authorship. Its style was a jumble of Bengali and English idioms. Then followed, in 1821, the *Shangbad Kaumadi*, a weekly, edited by Raja Rammohan Roy, and full of general information; then a rival to this, the *Chandrika*, was started by the Hindus, when the Raja preached the abolition of *Sati*. The *Kaumadi* survived its editor for a brief period, but nothing is known of the *Chandrika*. The *Probhakar* next came into existence, and then, in 1845, the *Tatwabodhini Patrika*. In 1850 numerous Bengali periodicals made their appearance, which were notorious for the vulgar language in which the editors abused one another. *Probhakar*, in spite of the noble end it had in view—the diffusion of useful knowledge and the awakening of public interest in poetic literature—caught the infection, and so indecent and vulgar was the tone it adopted in its warfare with the *Bhaskar*, edited by Gauri Sankar, nicknamed for his dwarfish size "Goorhgoorhay Bhuttacharjee," that the number of its readers considerably fell away. To undo what he had done, Ishwar Chandra Gupta issued the *Shadu Ranja*, with the object of pleasing the public. But journalistic controversy in vile language did not cease here. Every week, nay, every day, the public were disgusted with the vulgar trash that came into their hands. It was just at this time that the *Somprakas* was started by Dwarkanath Vidyabhushan. It was the right thing at the right time. Journalistic literature had been tainted by the ills of which we have been speaking, and to clear the air was the chief object of Dwarkanath. His language was chaste and sweet, his sentiments were liberal, and his arguments solid. He expressed his views with an earnestness that carried everything before it. He bluntly pointed out the shortcomings of Bengali society, not caring in the least whom he might offend. The chief attraction of the *Somprakas* was its fearless advocacy of what was right, and its denunciation of what was wrong; and so great was its popularity that the number of its subscribers rose rapidly. The yearly subscription was ten rupees—a rate very high for a Bengali newspaper—and yet there was continually an increase of subscribers. Vidyabhushan wielded a mighty influence on the minds of the Bengali community; and many still acknowledge this influence in their life. We deem that it may not be out of place here to trace the history of this powerful mind from its first appearance to the full development of its powers.

Dwarkanath was born in 1820, in a village ten miles to the south of Calcutta. His father was a good Sanskrit scholar, and had a *tol* of his own in Calcutta. At the age of twelve Dwarkanath was admitted into the Sanskrit College, where he studied till 1845. His acknowledged merit subsequently secured for him the professorship of grammar in the college. The authorities were so pleased with his work as to promote him to higher ranks, but his useful career as professor closed in 1873, when, owing to ill-health, he was obliged to retire. To recruit his health he went to Satara in 1886, and it was here that he breathed his last.

In 1856 his father had bought a printing-press, with the object of publishing his own and his son's works in Sanskrit; but he died soon after, and left it to his son. The latter first gained distinction as the author of a "History of Greece," and also one of Rome; and he also wrote certain useful text-books in Bengali. The *Somprakas* was started in 1858, the idea having been first suggested by Ishwar Chandra Vidyasagar, to give work to a certain deaf pandit, their friend. Dwarkanath became its editor, and it was published from his press. Many learned Sanskrit pandits had at first offered to contribute to the paper, bnt there was hardly anybody to help him when the time for action arrived. He was left unaided, and the sole responsibility rested on his shoulders. He wanted a few hours for rest after his hard work in the Sanskrit College; but those hours he greatly curtailed in the interests of the *Somprakas*. He was scrupulously conscientious in the discharge of his duties, devoting the days to teaching, and spending the nights in plodding through a mass of literature in preparation for his editorial work. Those that lodged with him said that there was no hour at night when they did not find him awake and working.

There was a great friendship between Ramtanu Lahiri and Pandit Dwarkanath Vidyabhushan. They had often met in youth, when the former received his lessons in Sanskrit from the latter's father; and their early association ripened into intimacy as they grew older.

29. RAJENDRA LAL DUTT

1818-1889

THE name of Rajendra Lal Dutt is associated with the spread of homœopathy in India. Born in 1818, in the Dutt family of Bowbazar, he possessed all the advantages that wealth and education could give. He was a fellow-student of Ramtanu, and one of those whose minds were moulded by Derozio. Having finished his education in the Hindu College, he attended for some time the Medical College as an ex-student, with the object of being able in future to render medical help gratis to the poor and needy. The desire for mitigating the sufferings of these was cherished by him, even when he worked for some time as a banyan in a mercantile firm; and, with the help of the late Dr Durgacharan Banerji, he opened a charitable allopathic dispensary in his own house.

It was at this time that Dr Tonnerre, the distinguished homœopathist, afterwards the first health officer of Calcutta, came to the city. Rajendra Babu helped him to establish a Homœopathic Hospital, which, however, for some cause or other, failed to be lasting. But the impression that Rajendra Babu then received of the superiority of homœopathy as a system of treatment was permanent; and it was under this impression that he devoted his whole life to the promotion of its cause. It is well known that he achieved wonderful success as a homœopathic practitioner.

In the active part he took in the foundation and management of the Metropolitan College, we get an inkling of the jealousy with which he tried to maintain the prestige of birth and caste. But he was far from being a proud aristocrat. When, during the latter part of his life, in conjunction with Dr Berigny, he went round visiting the sick, he made no distinction of creed, caste, or rank. The Mehtar received as much attention from him as the high-caste Kulin Brahman; and he entered as readily the dingy hut of the pariah as the mansion of the twice-born.

To relieve the sufferings of diseased humanity was his chief end in life, and his achievements were considerable. His visits were not only professional, but friendly also. He would sit by his patients in friendly chat with them; if ever he found any of them without means to procure the necessary diet, or other essentials, he would place his own purse at their disposal.

Rajendra Babu was really a philanthropist, worthy of living in the memory of posterity. God gave him a long life, and that life he devoted to good and useful works. He died in June 1889.

30. DR MAHENDRA LAL SIRKAR, C.I.E., M.D., D.L.

1833-1904

No one has done so much for the advancement of scientific learning in Bengal as the late Mahendra Lal. He was born in 1833, in a village in the Howrah district, of a *Satgop* family (a family belonging to the cultivating class). Having lost his father when a mere boy, he was looked after by his maternal uncles, who put him into the Hare School at the age of seven. He left this institution in the seventeenth year of his age, with a junior scholarship, and was admitted into the Hindu College, which was soon changed into the Presidency College. He studied here for five years, and then joined the Medical College, in 1855. When a second-year student he delivered a series of lectures on optics to his fellow-students, which made his career in the college a marked one. He passed the final examination in 1860, with the highest distinction in medicine, surgery, and midwifery, and got his M.D. in 1863. In the same year he joined the Bengal branch of the British Medical Asssociation. For three years he was secretary to the association, and after that he was elected one of the vice-presidents. He was a hater of homœopathy at the time, and once delivered a long and impressive lecture exposing it as a sort of quackery. But his views with regard to this mode of treatment soon underwent a change, and he declared his faith in it at the annual meeting of the Medical Association in February 1867. A year later he started *The Calcutta Journal of Medicine*, to give publicity to his opinions. With the support of Sir Richard Temple he established, in 1876, the Indian Association for the Cultivation of Science, which has survived him, and is still doing its good work. The Calcutta University conferred on him the degree of Doctor of Laws in 1890.

He was appointed Sheriff of Calcutta in 1887, and was a member of the Legislative Council from this year to 1893. In 1883 he was made a C.I.E. for his successful labours in the cause of science.

Dr Sirkar was always loyal to Government. Though a

patriot in every sense of the word, he always supported the influence of authority. He took pains to impress on the minds of his countrymen the benignity of their rulers.

He was abstemious in his habits and very simple in his manners. His regard for the interests of his friends was sincere. They reposed a great confidence in him, not only as a doctor, but as one ready to help them in every emergency. The family of Ramtanu Lahiri, whom he revered very much, received every attention from him, both in health and in sickness. His life, says Buckland, was devoted to toil for science for his fellow-men. He died in 1904.

31. KALI CHARAN GHOSH

KALI CHARAN GHOSH was probably the greatest friend and benefactor that Ramtanu Lahiri had. He was one of Mr Lahiri's pupils, who served him to the best of his abilities, regarding it in no other light than as a return for the intellectual and moral training he had received from his teacher. Kali Charan was born in May, 1835, at a village in the Jessore district. He lost his parents when very young, and was brought up by his uncle. He received his education in the Krishnagar College, whence he passed the Senior Scholarship Examination, in 1857. He then joined the Presidency College, and graduated as B.A., in 1860. He was enrolled as a pleader in the Judge's Court in Krishnagar, but the profession not suiting him he gave it up for a deputy-magistrateship. He got his first appointment in 1861. The Bengal Government, pleased with his work, deputed him to save the encumbered estates of the Zemindar of Narail in East Bengal from ruin. After this he was posted in Calcutta, in 1882, and was entrusted by Government with funds for purchasing lands on its behalf for the construction of Harrison Road and the Kidderpur Dockyard. His honesty and talents secured for him the esteem of all who came into contact with him, and he retired from Government service in April 1892. He was not long to enjoy his pension, for he died in 1895.

Kali Charan, in spite of rank, wealth, and influence, had little domestic happiness. His wife, a lady of rare accomplishments, became raving mad; and he was in constant dread of losing his life at her hands. But he was not on this account the less assiduous in caring for her wants and comfort. We mention here an incident in connection with this trouble which illustrates Vidyasagar's kind and obliging disposition. Kali Babu's wife, Kunti Debi, once refused to take her food unless Vidyasagar fed her with his own hands. The generous man, being informed of this, came to Kali Babu's house, and fed Kunti as desired. This he did not once only, but for months together.

Kali Charan Babu lived an austere life. Home had no attraction for him, and luxury no hold on his nature. He devoted his life to the acquisition of knowledge, and to the service of his friends.

32. KESHORI CHAND MITRA

Keshori Chand, the younger brother of Peari Chand, was born in 1822. He was one of the greatest English scholars of his time. His "Life of Rammohan Roy," in *The Calcutta Review*, attracted the favourable notice of Sir F. Halliday, the then Secretary to the Government of Bengal; and he was offered by him a deputy-magistracy at Rajshahi. He commanded general respect there, and he induced the Zemindars of the district to do many works of public utility, such as the founding of schools and dispensaries, the construction of roads and the excavation of tanks.

Keshori Chand was brought back to Calcutta by his patron, Sir F. Halliday, as the junior magistrate. For some years he worked creditably to himself, but he lost his appointment for reasons we need not here mention. Then he had recourse to a life purely literary. He edited *The Indian Field* for several years; and *The Calcutta Review* received regular contributions from him. He was at home in a large range of subjects—biography, politics, theology, sociology, and agriculture.

He was a great social and moral reformer. When a police magistrate, he started a "Social Reform Association," through which he waged warfare against the evil customs of his country.

Keshori Chand had one prominent failing. He was rather

intemperate in food and drink. His premature death was supposed by the public to be the consequence of immoderate drinking. He was an agreeable companion, a hearty friend, and a zealous supporter of what was manly. Of him *The Hindu Patriot* of the 11th August 1873 said, "One thing, however, must be said of him—that whatever his faults he injured only himself and nobody else. As an accomplished writer, a fearless advocate of his country's interests, and a zealous worker, he has left a void which, we fear, cannot be easily filled up." He died on the 6th of August 1873. A biographer thus shows the contrast between Keshori Chand and Peari Chand—"Both were reformers. But while the elder brother inculcated enlightened precepts by gentle means, the younger shocked the feelings of the majority of the people by doing violence to their time-honoured customs. While the one reads and respects our *Shastras*, the other did not think it worth his while to go through them, simply from a feeling of supreme contempt. The one is a thorough spiritualist, the other was to all intents and purposes a sturdy materialist, probably an honest Epicurean."

33. RAJA PRATAP CHANDRA SINGH

PRATAP CHANDRA was the great-grandson of Ganga Govinda Singh of Paikpara by adoption. Ganga Govinda was the Dewan of the East India Company in the time of Warren Hastings. Pratap and his brother Ishwar, both adopted by Dewan Srinarain Sing, actively participated in every public movement. Bengali dramatic literature and performances on the stage owed their introduction to the two brothers. The Government rewarded both of them with the title of Raja for their donations to the Medical College Hospital and other charitable institutions. They paid 25,000 rupees to the widow remarriage fund; and established a higher class English School at Kandi, near Murshidabad, the original seat of the family. Pratap was made a C.S.I. He died in 1868, leaving a son, who survived him only nine years. Ishwar had died in 1863. His son, Indranarain, lived till a few years ago, as the head of the Paikpara family.

APPENDIX III

Notes on the English Friends of Ramtanu Lahiri

RAMTANU LAHIRI had, as the narrative of his life shows us, a mind so liberal, so tolerant, and so many-sided, that there was probably no Indian gentleman of his time who numbered among his intimate friends so many Englishmen. As we have given, in Appendix II., a brief account of the lives of some of his chief Indian friends, we now proceed to give a few notes on the English gentlemen who completed the circle of his friends and admirers.

1. MR DAVID HARE

WE have shown in the text how great was the debt of Ramtanu, as a boy, to the kindness, and the wise insight into character, of the great pioneer of English education in Bengal, David Hare.

This philanthropist was born in Scotland, in 1775. He came to India in 1800, as a watchmaker, and a great friendship grew up between him and Rammohan Roy after the latter had settled in Calcutta. We have already in this work dwelt on his efforts to give young Bengalis a sound and thorough education in English, and the gentle and affectionate way in which he carried on this work, so we need not recur to those points here. The whole of his life spent in India he devoted to the promotion of the welfare of the people of the country. We have mentioned in the body of the book every public movement in Calcutta in which he took part, and the good offices he did to all, especially to the young; and all that now remains for us is to take the reader to the last scene of his useful life.

He, as the reader has already been told, was seized with

cholera at one o'clock in the morning of 31st May 1842. Even in the incipient stage of the disease he guessed that its effects would be fatal; and so told his bearer to ask Mr Grey to have his coffin ready. His old pupil, Prasanna Kumar Mitra, then a qualified doctor, attended him, and did all in his power to check the course of the disease; but all his attempts were futile. On the second day Mr Hare asked Prasanna not to increase his sufferings by further application of blisters. The few remaining hours of his life he passed peacefully, and breathed his last on the 1st of June, before nightfall.

2. SIR FREDERICK JAMES HALLIDAY, K.C.B.

1806-1901

Sir Frederick Halliday, the first Lieutenant-Governor of Bengal, and one of the greatest men in India during the period covered by this Biography, was a firm friend and patron of Mr Lahiri during the whole of his career. The events of his life are too well-known to demand any recapitulation in this place. His official life in India lasted from 1825 to 1859; and he took a leading part in such great historical events as the suppression of the great Mutiny, in the creation of the Lieutenant-Governorship of Bengal, in the suppression of the Santal Rebellion, in the introduction of the education policy founded on the famous Despatch of 1854, in the early formation of the railway system of Bengal and Upper India, and in various great reforms in rent and revenue legislation. He was a member of the Council of the Secretary of State for India from 1868 to 1886; and died on 22nd October 1901.

3. THE HON. SIR ASHLEY EDEN, K.C.S.I.

1831-1887

This famous Indian administrator, who throughout took a warm interest in the various reforms associated with the name of Ramtanu Lahiri, was more closely connected with the Government of Bengal than almost any other civil servant. He served under Sir Frederick Halliday in the suppression of the Santal Rebellion in 1855, and was Chief Secretary to the Government of Bengal for many years. He went to Burma in 1871, and during his absence from Bengal also acted, in 1875, as a member of the Supreme Council of India. From 1877 to 1882 he was the Lieutenant-Governor of Bengal, and attained signal success in that capacity. On his retirement, in 1882, he was appointed to the Council of the Secretary of State in London—where he died in 1887.

4. SIR RIVERS THOMPSON, K.C.S.I.

1829-1890

It is interesting to note that all the Indian officials most closely associated with the history of the district of Nadia and the city of Krishnagar during the lifetime of Ramtanu Lahiri—including, among many others, Sir Augustus Rivers Thompson, Sir William James Herschel, baronet, Sir Charles Cecil Stevens, Sir Roper Lethbridge, Professor S. Lobb, and Mr William Benjamin Oldham—were each and all numbered among Mr Lahiri's intimate friends. Sir Rivers Thompson, who was the great-grandson of Warren Hastings, and in boyhood a renowned Eton "Blue," was the Collector and Magistrate of Nadia during the early period of Ramtanu's retirement, and the friendship then formed lasted through life. In 1882 Sir Rivers became Lieutenant-Governor of Bengal; and was often known to take counsel with Mr Lahiri during the troubled times of his rule. He retired in 1887, and died at Gibraltar in 1890.

5. SIR WILLIAM HERSCHEL, BART.

Sir William Herschel, who was a member of the Bengal Civil Service from 1853 to 1878, and is now living in retirement at Oxford, was the Judge of Nadia, and remarkably popular at Krishnagar at the time when Ramtanu was resident for the last time in that district. Mr Lahiri, to the last day of his life, spoke with warm affection and respect of the encouragement he had derived from the friendship and support of this distinguished man.

6. SIR JOHN BUDD PHEAR, KT.

1825-1905

HARDLY any other official of the renaissance period in Bengal was more closely associated than Sir John Phear, at that time a Puisne Judge of the High Court of Calcutta, with every movement of reform; and it was in this way that, during Mr Lahiri's residence in Calcutta towards the close of his life, a warm friendship sprang up between these two noble-minded men. Sir John, after serving for some years as Chief Justice of Ceylon, retired to England, in 1879, and lived at Exmouth, in Devonshire, until his death, in 1905. On the sad occasion of the death of Ramtanu, in 1898, Sir John Phear wrote from Exmouth in the following appreciative terms to Mr Sharat Kumar Lahiri:—

"I had seen an announcement of your father's death in a newspaper before your letter reached me, and I felt that I had sustained a great personal loss. I valued Babu Ramtanu's friendship very highly and held him in sincere esteem. Permit me to assure you that I sympathise deeply with you and your relatives in your sorrow. Time is sadly shortening the list of old friends remaining to me in India, but they will ever live in my memory."

7. SIR WILLIAM WILSON HUNTER, K.C.S.I.

1840-1900

SIR WILLIAM HUNTER, the most widely read and most picturesque Anglo-Indian writer of modern times, during the time that he was editing *The Imperial Gazetteer of India*, was an intimate friend of Ramtanu Lahiri. In a letter written on the occasion of the death of the latter, in 1898, Sir William wrote thus of the loss sustained by Bengal and India:

"I take the opportunity of expressing my sympathy in the death of the late Babu Ramtanu Lahiri. His decease must have left a sad blank, and I beg to assure Mr S. K. Lahiri that I share his sorrow for the loss of his respected father."

8. SIR CHARLES CECIL STEVENS, K.C.S.I.

SIR CHARLES STEVENS, some time acting as Lieutenant-Governor of Bengal, and now living in retirement in London, was one of those Krishnagar notabilities of whose friendship and help Mr Lahiri always spoke in warm terms of gratitude. During the time that Sir Charles was the Collector and Magistrate of Nadia, and afterwards, when he was successively Chief Secretary to the Government of Bengal, member of the Bengal Board of Revenue, additional member of the Governor-General's Council, and, finally, officiating Lieutenant-Governor of Bengal—there were many occasions when he was able to show his sympathy for Ramtanu's earnestness in the cause of reform. Shortly before the death of the latter Sir Charles thus wrote of him from Belvedere:

"It is many years since I had any intercourse with him, but I used to know him when I was in Nadia. He was distinguished in those days for having had the courage of his opinion and for a degree of enlightenment surpassing all but a few of his countrymen."

And similarly, on the occasion of Mr Lahiri's death, Mr Sharat Kumar Lahiri received from Sir Charles Stevens a most sympathetic letter of condolence, which contained the following striking appreciation of the reformer's work, which is particularly weighty as coming from an authority more competent to speak on the subject than almost any other:—

"Whenever the history of social reform in Bengal is adequately written your father's name will have an honourable and conspicuous place in it. He was a reformer in days when reform was novel and unfashionable, and to preach it, and still more to practise it, involved serious sacrifices. The social progress of later years must have been most satisfactory to him, as both justifying and rewarding his efforts."

9. SIR ROPER LETHBRIDGE, K.C.I.E.

ALL that need be said of the warm friendship and deep respect felt for Mr Lahiri by the editor of this Biography has already been said in the Introduction.

10. SIR HENRY COTTON, K.C.S.I.

LIKE so many other English friends of Mr Lahiri, Sir Henry Cotton was first known to him when serving in the Nadia district. Throughout the whole of a distinguished official career, Sir Henry's interest in the veteran reformer never flagged. At the time of Ramtanu's death Sir Henry Cotton was Chief Commissioner of Assam; and he thus wrote to Mr Sharat Kumar Lahiri from Shillong:

"Your father died in the fulness of years and was, I believe, the last of a generation who profoundly influenced modern thought in Bengal more than sixty years ago. Probably there is now no man alive who was personally associated with Derozio and David Hare. It is a pleasure to me to remember that I met your father on several occasions and to recall the kindly manner in which he would speak to me of bygone days. Babu Ramtanu Lahiri led a blameless life, and his exemplary character remains as a guide and beacon to your countrymen at the present time. I offer you my sincere condolence in your loss."

11. MR WILLIAM BENJAMIN OLDHAM, C.I.E.

MR OLDHAM, another valued friend of Ramtanu Lahiri, was at one time an official in Nadia, and was a member of the Bengal Board of Revenue in 1900.

12. SIR JAMES WESTLAND, K.C.S.I.

1842-1903

SIR JAMES WESTLAND, who was Finance Minister of India from 1893 to 1899, thus wrote of Mr Lahiri on the occasion of his death, in 1898:

"Before receipt of your letter I had seen a newspaper notice of the death of your venerable father, Babu Ramtanu Lahiri, and it recalled to my mind the occasion on which I first made his acquaintance—namely, the marriage of his daughter at Krishnagar, somewhere about 1867, at which I was present. Babu Ramtanu Lahiri was even then a man advanced in years, and he was one for whom I entertained a great respect, in common with many others of my friends at that station.

"I feel it an honour that his family should so far have remembered the past days of my acquaintance with him as to invite me to the memorial service, and I would certainly have been present had I been in Calcutta. I shall be much obliged by your communicating to the deceased gentleman's family my sympathy with them in the loss they have sustained."

13, 14, 15, 16. Professor Norman Chevers, Professor S. Lobb, Professor Rowe, the Hon. Mr Grimley.

Among the English sympathisers with Ramtanu Lahiri in his work of reform in Bengal, the names of these gentlemen ought to be included.

APPENDIX IV.—GENEALOGICAL TABLES.

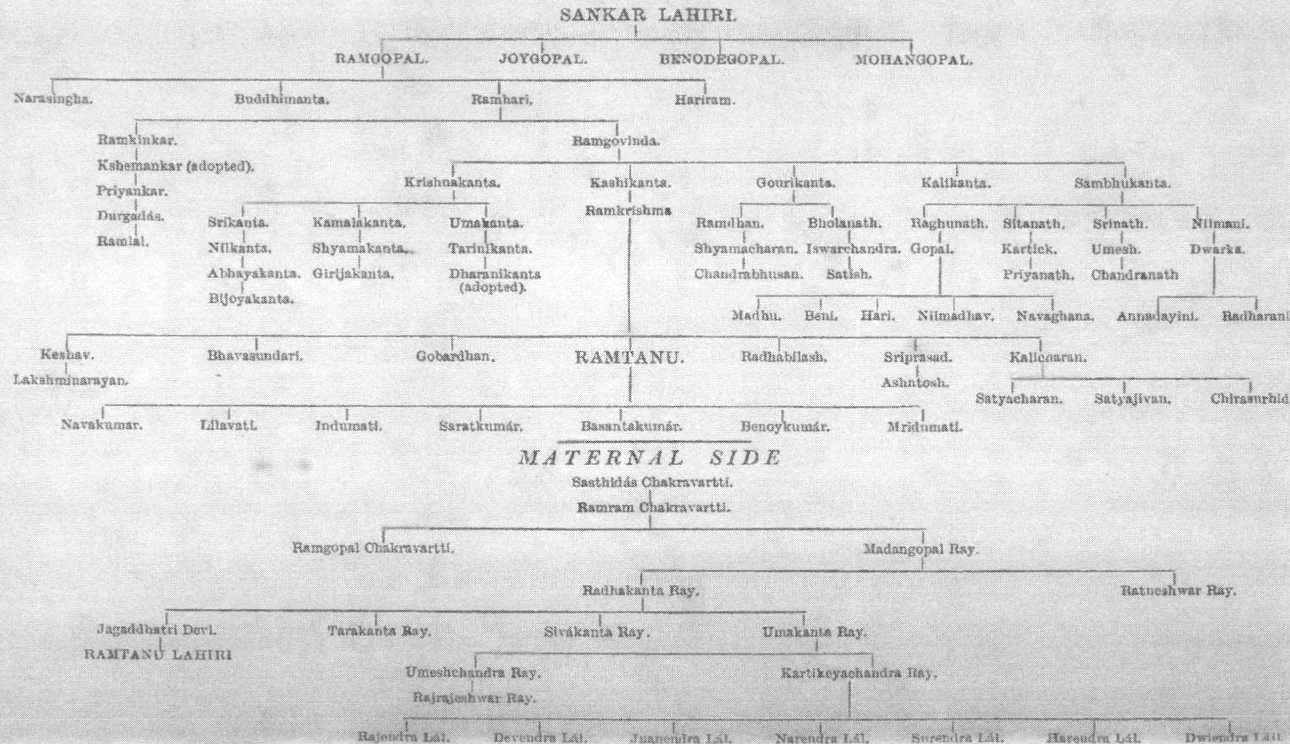

AN OLD MAN'S STORY.

Being an Auto-Biographical Sketch by Guru Charan Bose!

I Was born at Bagbazar, in the northern division of Calcutta on the 1st of January 1826. My revered father (peace be to his memory) represented the ancient and well known Bose family of Bagbazar, the founder of which settled in Calcutta during the Mahomedan period, when the Maharatta Cavalry, composed of males and females, undertook plundering expeditions against Bengal and its principal towns, and committed depredations upon their cattle, flocks and crops.

According to the time honored custom of the higher grade of Kaesto families, as soon as I was six years old my father placed me under a Guru mohasae to get an elementary education in Bengali. Under his tuition, I learnt to read and write my mother tongue and to cast accounts.

I continued under him for four years, making pretty fair progress in the rudiments of the Bengali language; and then, when I completed my tenth year, I was transferred to an Anglo-Vernacular school, commonly called the Hare school, because the late D. Hare, whose name is a "household word" among the people of Bengal, was the founder and the superintendent of it. I studied English as well as Bengali in this institution for a period of five years. I was a rigid Hindu up to the fourteenth year of my age; my faith in idolatry, and the rites and ceremonies which popular Hinduism prescribes, was very firm. I had an imperfect knowledge of Christianity. But this period, under divine grace became a crisis in my life. The English education which I received in the Hare school opened the eyes of my understanding, and I preceived the folly of image worship. My faith in Hinduism was shaken; it failed to satisfy my spiritual cravings. I felt myself a great sinner; my sinful propensities were very powerful; they got the better of reason and conscience, I had no control over them. I stood in absolute need of power from God to effect the purification of my heart, the government of my passions, and the union and communion of my soul with Him. But this was not to be found in Hinduism, or in any other non-Christian religion of the world. All of them insist upon the doctrine of good works. I found that I had not the power of performing good works. "When I would do good, evil was present with me." So I gave up the open worship of idols, and joined a debating club, the members of which professed themselves to be theists, and who in their meetings freely discussed theological subjects. Like the Brahmos of the present day they believed in one God, but ignored a written revelation. Their teaching aimed at the moral, social, and intellectual improvement of Hindu society; but they were bitterly opposed to the Bible and the Christian religion, of which they had vague and hazy ideas. They cared very little about the invisible realities of the unseen world which the Bible reveals. There were sometimes very warm discussions in the club, but in nine cases out of ten the members hopelessly differed from each other, and seldom was there any thing like rational conclusion on the points under debate. They believed in the existence of God, but maintained, like the Agnostics of modern Europe, that He was "unknown and unknowables." As they were unbelievers in a revelation they could not point out any reasonable atonement for the sin-sick soul, anxious to be purified from its natural corruption, perversion, and pollution. My mind was at this time in a very unsettled state so far as religion was concerned. I had very little of that peace of mind which I afterwards enjoyed when I became a Christian. I believed in a personal God, that He was a hearer and answerer of our prayers, therefore I prayed to Him day and night to lead me to the truth. And gradually I was led to it. I commenced to read the Bible and the evidences which proved its genuineness and authenticity. I cultivated the acquaintance of educated native converts, and European missionaries, by whose assistance I made considerable progress in my enquiries after truth. For three years I continued my enquiries, so that when I was eighteen years old I was fully convinced of the divine origin of Christianity. The Lord in answer to my prayers opened my mental eyes, and all doubt and unbelief were by degrees removed from my mind. I found out that Christianity was the only religion which suited my condition as a helpless sinner; its wonderful plan of salvation through a crucified Saviour, who by His precious death on the cross satisfied Divine mercy and justice, made a great impression on my mind. The study of the Mosaic dispensation, as revealed in the Old Testament, convinced me that the religion of Christ was not a new religion, "a cunningly devised fable," as many half-educated and well educated Hindus now-a-days believe, but founded on historical facts; that it was the perfect development and fulfilment of that ancient religion which was revealed in the Law of Moses; that it was as old as the creation, older than all the religious systems palmed upon the world by philosophers.

The Christian religion is built upon the promise made to the first man and woman immediately after their fall from a state of original righteousness: "And I will put enmity between thee and the woman, and between thy seed and her seed; it shall bruise thy head, and thou shalt bruise his heel" (Genesis iii, 15.) It teaches that Jesus the son of Mary, of the family of David, was born in Bethlehem. In Him believers beheld the glory of the promised Messiah. That He was the "Word of God, the Word was with God, and the Word was God, and the Word was made flesh, and dwelt among us." And though this *logos* theory has been a stumbling block to the unbelieving world on account of its myst ry, yet humble minded men, enlightened by the Holy Spirit, have believed in it. "The Divinity of Jesus Christ is the science of sciences".

I was now in the eighteenth year of my life. I fully believed in the inspiration of the Bible. The doctrine of vicarious atonement made by Jesus Christ produced a deep impression on my mind. I openly declared my faith in Him, and resolved to embrace the Christian religion by public baptism. This resolution of mine alarmed my relatives and friends beyond measure. They persecuted me day and night. Sometimes they would try to dissuade me from my purpose, but failed to do so. I was narrowly watched by them, they snatched away my Bible and every religious work I had in my possession, and consigned them to the flames. I was strictly forbidden to visit Missionaries and native Christians on pain of incurring their displeasure.

My faith in Jesus gradually increased. I made up my mind to leave home and take shelter wherever I could find it. I consulted my Christian friends, and they sent me to the old Bishop's College at Sheebpore; this was in September 1842.

I was then a married man; I had a child-wife when I left home; I spoke to her about the step which I was going to take and advised her to follow me; but she was too young and ignorant to appreciate my motives; so she absolutely refused to comply with my request.

I believed I should be quite safe in Bishop's College from the persecuting attempts of my relatives and friends. But it was far otherwise; I encountered there heavy trials.

One afternoon when I was reading the Bible in a quiet room upstairs, my youngest brother stepped into the room, and informed me that my mother and some other relatives had come from Calcutta in a budgerow and wanted to have an interview with me. Without any suspicions in my mind, and moved by filial respect, I hastened to the College ghat, got into the budgerow, and took my seat. My mother and other relatives hemmed me on all sides and then raised a howling cry, holding me fast, and persuading me to give up the idea of becoming a Christian and to return home. My situation in the boat was most trying. I was alone there, entirely in the power of heathen relatives, whose sole object in coming to Bishop's College was to take me back home by brute force if persuasions failed. My fears and suspicions were confirmed when I found out that a number of open boats filled with latials (bludgeon men) surrounded our budgerow. The flood tide had just set in with great force. A cousin, who was naturally of a violent disposition, caught hold of my clothes. The females kept on their lamentations. My poor mother overpowered by grief struck her head on the floor of the cabin, beseeching me to change my mind. All of a sudden, at the command of my cousin, the budgerow was under weigh, and the open boats, filled with *latials*, more than one hundred men in number, surrounded it. They rowed towards Calcutta. My situation was the most critical that could be imagined. I was placed upon the horns of a dilemma. Natural affection on one side, and the salvation of my immortal soul on the other, struggled in my mind for mastery. I had learnt to pray, and faith in Jesus got the victory. "Who is he that overcometh the world, but he that believeth that Jesus is the Son of God?" (1st John v, 5) I said, 'Blessed Jesus uphold me by Thy Spirit, and deliver me from my troubles.' The Lord heard my prayers, and saved me from death and heathenism.

The College authorities having learnt that my heathen relatives by a combination of lies and subterfuges had enticed me into their boat and were dragging me home against my will and inclination, lost no time in chasing them and coming to my rescue, The late Revd. A. Street, the then Professor of the Bishop's College, with the assistance of the College students and servants, stepped into a boat belonging to the College, and rowed straight towards the *latials*, whose prisoner I was. The river in front of Garden Reach became the scene of a naval engagement on a small scale. The fighting on both sides was very earnest. Several persons were seriously wounded. The *latials*, being skilful swimmers jumped overboard and took to the shore. My heathen relatives were left in the lurch. When they found that their mercenary protectors had deserted them they were at their wits' end. Their anger knew no bounds, and they vented all their fury on me, as I was the author of all their troubles. They threatened to kill me; they command me again and again to change my mind and to deny the faith. But I turned a deaf ear to their threats. Although the event happened nearly half a century ago, and is "a thing of the past," yet it is fresh in my mind. It was a season of fiery trial to me.

When my cousin found that I would not yield to his wishes, he caught hold of me bodily, brought me out on the deck of the boat, and after beating me "black and blue" with a cudgel, pitched me right into the middle of the stream. Being the time of the full moon, the tide was very strong, and it carried me away to a good distance. I fancied that I was going to have a watery grave. Suddenly the back of my head struck against the rudder of another budgerow riding at anchor not far from the shore, I caught hold of the rudderbands with both arms and clung to them.

Professor Street and his followers came to my rescue. They picked me up in their boat, and carried me back to the College premises. I suffered most grievously from the effects of the beating for a few days. As soon as I felt better I was anxious to undergo the rite of baptism, so I came back to Calcutta. I was introduced to the late Bishop Dealtry, who was then the Archdeacon of Calcutta and Secretary to the C. M. Society. He baptised me in Christ Church, Cornwallis Square, in the presence of a large number of Calcutta people, who were drawn to the Church more out of curiosity then any thing else, as conversions in those days from the higher classes were 'few and far between.' I now found rest from the persecuting attempts of my Hindu relatives, whose conduct towards me was as kind after my baptism as before it was cruel. Before my baptism I was employed as a teacher in the Hare School, but I was now obliged to resign the appointment, as I was strictly forbidden by the rules of the school to teach and preach to the boys my newly adopted sentiments.

When thus thrown out of employment, I became homeless, penniless and friendless. But the Lord raised a number of Christian friends and sympathizers to assist me with money and good advice. They kindly offered to help me to secular employment, under Government, or in private firms. But as I expressed a desire of being employed in Mission work, in November 1842 the Calcutta Corresponding Committee of the C. M. Society appointed me as a Missionary labourer in the Agurparah Mission with the late Revd. F. J. DeRozario, whom the Lord has recently called to the home above.

In this Mission I laboured with head and heart for a long time. In fact I spent the best part of my life here, teaching in the large Anglo-vernacular school, preaching in the villages round about, and helping in the church services.

I have mentioned before that I was a married man. I had left a child wife at home. Her parents, after my conversion, narrowly watched her. They adopted every measure in their power to prevent her from joining, or rather rejoining me. Thus, for a period of full nine years I was separated from her.

During this interval I did not forget my Christian duty towards her. I prayed to the Lord often to restore her to me and made several desperate attempts to rescue her from heathenism and its concomitant evils. But I met with defeat and disappointment because the Lord's time had not come. At last in 1851, the Lord heard my prayers. All obstacles were removed. My father-in-law, who had hitherto opposed "tooth and nail" my wife's coming to me, departed this life. My wife became of age to think for herself. Believing that the Lord's time had arrived I renewed my attempts with redoubled zeal. I made her restoration to me a matter of earnest prayer. I was allowed access to her late father's house. I ascertained from every source that was open to me that my wife, in her heart, was quite willing to join me though, on account of the false modesty and timidity common in Hindu females, she could not say so. I was advised to have recourse to law. With the kind assistance of the late Revd. Mr. Cuthbert, one of our former secretaries,, Mr. M. Wylie, the then head of the Calcutta Police, and a few sympathizing friends I adopted legal measures against my wife's guardians. My efforts at last were crowned with success. With the full and free consent of her heathen relatives, my wife joined me. I stayed in Calcutta for a short time and then took her to the Agurparah Mission. After carefully instructing her in the principles of Christianity, she was baptized on the 15th of August 1852, by the late Revd. T. Sandys, our veteran Missionary, in Christ Church, Agarparah.

I continued to work in the Mission happily; my long connection with it was prosperous; there were many interesting conversions from the English school. The Lord also blessed me with a large family and "supplied all my need." My income was limited, and I lived as the phrase is "from hand to mouth," yet I managed "to make two ends meet." I was never in actual want. I fully realised in my life the meaning of the aphorism. "The blessing of the Lord it maketh us rich." "Having food and raiment I was content therewith." My Bible taught me that wealth in this sinful world could not augment my happiness. The rich man in the parable who was clothed in purple and fine linen and fared sumptuously every day died, and lifted up his eyes *in hell.* But poor Lazarus was carried by ministering angels into Abraham's bosom. In 1878 my health entirely gave way. Malarious fever broke out at Agurparah and in the adjoining villages like wild fire, people died like ants and flies. With my large family I suffered most grievously from malaria. I became quite unfit for active service, the hard work of the English school and the malarious fever told severely on my constitution. I was then in the fifty-fourth year of my life. In this hour of distress, I cried unto the Lord and he delivered me from my troubles. "Call upon me in the time of trouble: so will I hear thee, and thou shalt praise me." (Psalm l, 15). My sons were at school at the time, and too young to help me in supporting the family. I applied through the Secretary to the Calcutta Corresponding Committee of the C. M. Society. The Commitee (I will never forget their kindness) allowed me to quit Agurparah, and to reside in Calcutta, sanctioning for my support the allowance which I now draw.

I have been residing in Calcutta for the last ten years. I am now in the evening of life, an invalid, in the neighbourhood of seventy, the scriptural period of human existence; but though I have lost considerably the buoyancy and energy of youth and manhood, yet thank God I am not quite bed ridden.

I try to promote His glory so far as health permits, realizing in my life his gracious promise "They shall bring forth fruits in old age." (Psalm xcii, 4). "And even to your old age I am he; and even to hoar hairs will I carry you" (Isaiah, xlvi. 4).

When I take a retrospective view of my chequered life, I find my trials, temptations, shortcomings, imperfections, and frailties have been very many, that I am an "improfitable servant," "the vilest of vile" and 'my righteousnesses are as filthy rags." My hope is on the Cross. "The blood of Jesus Christ hath cleansed me from all my iniquities."

Nearly half a century ago, when I left home for Christ, I was alone; I had none to share with me my joys and sorrows; I was persecuted right and left; I was thrown by my cruel relatives to the mercy of the waves to meet with a watery grave. And yet when I cried, like Jonah of old, the Lord, heard me, "out of the depths He delivered me." I am now gray headed and gray bearded, blessed with a Christian family, all the members of which, except one, have been, by the grace of God, settled in life. There is nothing to disturb my Christian peace. If it be admitted that old age to a Christian is the childhood of immortality, I realize it to a great extent. I can therefore take up the Psalmist's words and say, "What shall I render unto the Lord for all His benefits to me? I will walk before the Lord in the land of the living, I will take the cup of salvation and call upon the name of the Lord." (cxvi Psalm.)

The best preparation for death and higher life is to be "steadfast in faith." "to watch and pray." I thank God through Jesus Christ our Lord that He has always led me by His spirit to contemplate death and the invisible realities of Heaven. I am therefore ready to depart this life. The Blood of Jesus has cleansed me from my past sins and created in me a sure and certain hope of life eternal. But should it please the Lord to spare my life longer (I dare not ask to live for His will be done on earth as in heaven) I will consecrate it to His service: "For me to live is Christ and to die is gain."

TRUE SAYINGS.

The Bible is an infallible guide, which tells us how to become right with God.

Look at these true sayings:

"How then can man be justified with God, or how can he be clean that is born of a woman?"—Job xxv. 4.

"Who can say, I have made my heart clean, I am pure from my sin?"—Prov. xx.9.

"For there is not a just man upon earth, that doeth good and sinneth not"—Eccles. vii. 20.

"There is none righteous; no, not one."—Rom. iii 10.

"They are all gone out of the way, they are together become unprofitable, there is none that doeth good, no, not one."—Rom. iii. 12.

Does your conscience echo these words, and constrain you to admit, "I have sinned"? Then look again—

"While we were yet sinners Christ died for us."—Rom. v. 8.

Jesus Christ "His own self bare our sins in His own body on the tree."—I Pet. ii. 24.

Hear His own gracious words—

"If any man thirst let him come unto Me and drink."—John vii. 37.

"Him that cometh to me, I will in no wise cast out."—John vi. 37.

"He that heareth My word and believeth in Him that sent Me hath everlasting life, and shall not come in to condemnation, but is passed from death into life."—John v. 24.

CHISTIAN TRACT AND BOOK SOCIETY,

2nd Edition. 23, CHOWRINGHEE. *Feb. 1902.*

THE "OLIVE ELECTRICAL PRINTING WORKS,"

1,